S0-FKA-748

AUDITING IN THE ELECTRONIC ENVIRONMENT:

THEORY, PRACTICE AND LITERATURE

Delroy L. Cornick

Lomond Books
Mt. Airy, Maryland
1981

Library of Congress Catalog Number: 80-81813

ISBN: 0-912338-23-7 (Clothbound)
0-912338-24-5 (Microfiche)

Printed in the United States of America.

Composition by Barbara McGiffin.
Printing by BookCrafters, Inc.

Published by
Lomond Publications, Inc.
P.O. Box 88
Mt. Airy, Maryland 21771 U.S.A.

PERMISSIONS

The author appreciates permission to reprint or draw from copyrighted works as follows:

Systems Auditability and Control Study by Stanford Research Institute. Copyright 1977 by the Institute of Internal Auditors, Inc., 249 Maitland Avenue, Altamonte Springs, FL 32701.

"Impact of Computers on Society as Illustrated by Government Files," *U.S. News & World Report*, February 22, 1971. Copyright 1971 by U.S. News & World Report, Inc., Washington, DC.

Modern Computer Concepts: The IBM 360 Series by Edward J. Laurie. Copyright 1970 by South-Western Publishing Company, Cincinnati, OH.

Computers in Action: How Computers Work by Donald D. Spencer. Copyright 1974 by Hayden Book Company, Inc., Rochelle Park, NJ.

Design of Real-Time Computer Systems by James Martin. Copyright 1967 by Prentice-Hall, Inc., Englewood Cliffs, NJ.

"EDP Documentation: Ten Ways," *Administrative Management*, June 1969. Copyright 1969 by Geyer-McAllister Publications, Inc., New York, NY.

Computer Control Guidelines and *Computer Audit Guidelines*. Copyright 1970 and 1975 by Canadian Institute of Chartered Accountants, Toronto, Canada.

The People Side of Systems: The Human Aspects of Computer Systems by Keith R. London. Copyright 1976 by McGraw-Hill Book Co. (U.K.) Limited, Maidenhead, Berkshire, England.

"Computer Abuse: A Practical Use of the AICPA Guide," *EDPACS*, February 1978. Copyright 1978 by Automation Training Center, Inc., Reston, VA.

EDPACS, passim. Copyright by Automation Training Center, Inc., Reston, VA.

Datamation Magazine, passim. Copyright by Technical Publishing Co., New York, NY.

Data Processing Digest, passim. Copyright by Data Processing Digest, Inc., Los Angeles, CA.

ABI/INFORM, passim. Copyright by Data Courier, Inc., Louisville, KY.

Internal Controls for Computerized Systems by Jerry Fitzgerald. Copyright 1978 by Jerry Fitzgerald & Associates, Inc., Redwood City, CA.

"SAS No. 3 and the Evaluation of Internal Control," *The Journal of Accountancy*, March 1977, by E.G. Jancura and F.L. Lilly. Copyright 1977 by American Institute of Certified Public Accountants.

To Janet, Karen, Susan, Lisa, Delroy Jr.
and my mother, Leola.

FOREWORD

During the 1970s, many business and government executives—jolted by the Equity Funding scandal early in the decade and by increasing occurrences of computer crimes—developed a better awareness of the difficulties the auditing profession faces in trying to keep pace with the electronic environment. The auditing profession itself, through the American Institute of Certified Public Accountants, Institute of Internal Auditors, and groups such as the U.S. General Accounting Office, has also recognized and sought to alleviate the gap in the knowledge and experience level of auditors. Yet despite general recognition of the need to better equip auditors to work within the electronic environment, few books that are both scholarly and readable have been published on the subject. This resource can help alter that situation.

As the author describes, in the past 15 years there has been a quantum jump in the number of computers that process a wide range of financial and other vital information which business and government managers use in decisionmaking. Also, the pace of change in computer technology in recent years has been staggering, creating complex internal control questions. Like it or not, professional auditors live in a new and greatly more electronic world and they cannot afford to be asleep at the switch!

How worried are executives about the possible lack of adequate internal controls over the electronic system which produce so much information upon which key decisions are made? In a recent research project underwritten by the Financial Executives Research Foundation which studied internal controls in the business world, the researchers found that heavy dependency on computers—and how that dependence affects internal controls—was clearly the most troubling issue. Within government few internal auditors have equipped themsleves for the electronic environment, but those few have pointed out numerous internal control weaknesses in the electronic environment that could cause government executives to lose sleep.

So, both the executives and managers who rely on electronic systems for information—and the auditors who must check for controls in those systems—have a growing uneasiness about their level of knowledge about the electronic environment and whether controls are adequate to assure that reliable information is produced. As in all areas of life, that uneasiness can be allayed only by first understanding the problem better and then taking action to solve the problem. This study can make a major contribution toward that end.

The author is to be commended on the thoughtful organization and readability of this book. It permits readers to approach the subject in digestible segments, to go only as far as his interests dictate, and to initiate further research beyond this book as needed.

Arthur L. Litke
U.S. General Accounting Office

PREFACE

My purpose in writing this book is to provide a ready reference to the theoretical issues in EDP auditing and a guide to the conceptual and practice-oriented literature for internal and external accounting and auditing practitioners, managers, trainers in both the private and public sector, and faculty and students.

The book is divided into two parts: Part I—Theory and Practice, and Part II: Annotated Bibliography and Additional References.

Several important issues are examined in Part I. For example, the issues of computer security and abuse, the auditor's independence in systems design and development, meeting the computer "head-on" (i.e., auditing with and through the computer rather than "around" the computer) and the adequacy and effectiveness of controls and computer assisted auditing techniques in meeting this obligation.

Finally, as we have become an information-rich society more and more people have become "literate" in computers and our lives have become more and more circumscribed by the computer. Therefore, societal and legal controls of the computer environment are becoming of greater concern to auditors as evidenced by the Foreign Corrupt Practices Act and the Privacy Acts enacted by the U.S. Congress in the decade just ended.

In Part II, I have attempted to present certain of the literature which deals with these issues, such as the impact of computers on auditing standards, internal control, evidential matters, training and development of auditing competence and information security.

Most of the literature is taken from the last two decades. This literature review adds to that provided by Frielink (1961) who provides a survey of 71 articles and reports covering the period from 1952 to 1960 and Jancuro and Berger (1973) whose compilation of articles covered the late 1960s and the early 1970s.

The book contains 166 annotated references arranged by topics and in chronological sequence numbered from the earlier citations. This will give the reader a sense of the dynamics of the profession, including those areas where little different has been written over the years. In addition, there are 161 additional references.

The book is by no means exhaustive or inclusive. In this era of information explosion any book of this sort will be out of date by the time it is published.

Some of the annotations are considerably longer than is customary in conventional bibliographies, particularly in those instances where the complexity, significance, and thoroughness of the original material warrants such treatment. Hence, some entries have been extended to almost review length.

The annotations do not necessarily describe the entire work but rather only those portions of the original material that deal with the issues, techniques and theories that are the subject of this literature search. Manufacturer, trade association and vendor materials were kept to a minimum.

It became evident to me in doing the research for this book that much of the material that impacts upon practice includes unpublished dissertations, staff documents, memoranda, discussion drafts, minutes from workshops and meetings of professional societies, and in government, business and industry files and desk drawers.

My special thanks are to Dr. Lowell Hattery, for guiding my academic career, and for the faith and support in publishing this book; to Mr. Arthur Litke, formerly of the U.S. Federal Power Commission for whom I developed a staff document on this subject over a dozen years ago, and to my research assistant on this project, Mr. Gerald Turner, a computer science specialist in both government and industry and currently Assistant Professor in Business Administration at Morgan State University, Baltimore, Md., particularly for the section on computer technology and the area of computer security.

My thanks and apologies to the many people involved in this effort: Mrs. Carol Montgomery and Mrs. Roylene Sims, who typed the several drafts, for their patience, understanding and dedication in seeing me through this project and my good friend, Tom Noorani for the charts and diagrams.

My apologies to the several certified public accountants to whom I turned for criticism and technical assistance: Ms. Christi M. Kasler, Howard L. Carter, and Irving Hoffman of Fox & Company; Mrs. Yovonda D. Brooks of Lucas, Tucker & Co.; James S. Schaefer of the Chessie System and Professor William L. Campfield, Florida A&M, and Edward McFadden, Systems Analysis, U.S. Social Security Administration. I wish also to acknowledge the cooperation in granting me permission to quote from their many publications: Ms. Sylvia M. Geller, Production Editor, EDPACS; William E. Perry, EDP Auditors Foundation; Lee Hansen, Institute of Internal Auditors; Ms. Margaret Milligan, Data Processing Digest Inc.; and Ms. Loene Trubkin, Data Courier, Inc.

Delroy L. Cornick

CONTENTS

LIST OF FIGURES

LIST OF TABLES

PART I
THEORY AND PRACTICE

CHAPTER I
INTRODUCTION

The electronic environment in which today's auditor operates is a turbulent environment. It is characterized by rapid advancements in computer technology, the ubiquity of computer applications, the increasing concern for such issues as privacy, fraud, waste and computer abuse and security.

Fortunately, perhaps, societal pressures are on the auditor's side in the form of requirements of the Privacy Act, the Foreign Corrupt Practices Act of 1977, the Inspector General Act of 1978 and other statutes that require management to institute controls sufficient to provide reasonable assurances of data integrity, confidentiality, and completeness.

There is also tension among vendors, users, and data processing staff on the one hand and management and auditors on the other over the extent of trading off between the need for audit trails and controls and the need for low cost hardware and software and getting the system "on the air" with the least cost and in the shortest time.

The role of the auditor is influenced by these forces as evidenced by his increasing involvement in program efficiency and effectiveness, compliance and standards—both federal and non-federal auditors require that the auditor meet the computer "head-on" and appear to be reducing around-the-computer options in more and more situations.

The auditing paradigm remains essentially unchanged as data processing technology expands. Auditing theory rests upon objectives and these objectives relate to identifying and evaluating internal control and the existence of audit trails which, parenthetically, are two of the major concerns articulated in the various federal laws cited above.

However, the surrounding conditions or environmental forces that act upon the auditor will ultimately determine the direction that auditing practices take and raise the question of the auditor's survival in an electronic environment.

The challenge to the auditor is to close the gap between EDP audit capability and rapidly advancing data processing technology.

In his report to Congress in 1977, the Comptroller General of the United States pointed out that the record of auditing in the federal agencies is spotty at best: "In some agencies, little audit attention has been paid to automatic data processing despite its importance to agency programs."[1] He wrote:

> Responses by auditors to the challenge of computer auditing have been uneven. Some organizations in and out of the government have done excellent work; others have avoided contact with computers whenever possible. Such audit work does not meet recognized audit standards.[2]

There is sufficient evidence to indicate that the Comptroller General's comments are relevant outside the federal government as well.

The Comptroller General's report indicated that in the Department of Defense, with over 4,400 computers and 2,264 professional audit staff members, "only 234 auditors (about 10%) were considered to have extensive ADP training and experience."[3] The report states:

> When the magnitude of automated systems and their far-reaching impact on agency operations, programs, and resources are considered, the adequacy of coverage by internal audit staff is questionable and, in our view, a much greater ADP audit capability is needed in many of the agencies.[4]

The Stanford Research Institute (SRI) in a recent report states:

> . . . Inadequate attention is being given to the importance of internal controls in developing computer-based information systems and in establishing data processing operations. This conclusion applies not only to individual organizations, *but to the data processing industry in general.* [Emphasis added.] The reason is that each state in the evolution of EDP systems brings new control problems which require new solutions.[5]

The report concluded that an important need exists for EDP audit staff development because few internal audit staffs have enough data processing knowledge and experience to audit effectively in the data processing environment.[6]

However, the accounting profession as a *learning system* has met the challenges of machine accounting (EAM) and one can conclude that it shows the same promise of meeting the challenge of the computer and artificial intelligence.

This conclusion is based upon advances in computer assisted audit techniques, the legal environment which places management square on the side of controls and audit trails, the EDP auditor training and professional development support by standard setting bodies, universities and colleges, and the accounting industry itself.

What this discussion suggests, however, is that while the learning mechanisms are in place, the auditing community has not responded as quickly as the challenges to it have come.

THE TECHNOLOGICAL CHALLENGE

In 1950, there were between 10 and 15 digital computer installations in the United States compared with more than 70,000 in 1975. One writer indicated that by the early 1980s there will be over one million minicomputers alone![7]

In addition to computers installed, the growth in the number of terminals connecting users with the various computer installations has grown from 250,000 in 1970 to over a million in 1975 and was estimated to reach *three million* by 1980.[8]

Computer systems are an interactive process in which direct access, real time online processing is achieved. Data are maintained on an up to date basis or current operating status. Transactions and inquiries are processed as they occur. Also low cost computers are placed at various points of data entry and linked with a central computer via distributed communication network of terminals and other remote data entry processes. The development of operating system software, integrative systems and data base management systems pose new challenges to the auditor.

The behavior implications cannot be ignored. Job displacement anxieties as computer employment expands, concentration of EDP knowledge and skills in the hands of comparatively few, and finally the computer present either a challenge, a system to beat, or a threat to privacy and societal wellbeing, hence a target for abuse.

Not only has the number of computer installations increased sharply in the past two decades but the number, variety and magnitude of computer applications have grown: payroll, benefit payments, Social Security benefit system, contracts, grants, revenue sharing. The computer plays a significant role in our $1.4 trillion economy.

Two challenges have arisen alongside the technology development: 1) computer abuse and security and 2) the impact on internal control and audit trails.

Computer Abuse and Security

News of some incident of computer fraud or abuse is almost a daily occurrence. In early 1980, a Social Security Administration programmer (at Woodlawn, Maryland outside of Baltimore) reportedly diverted $500,000 in payments to her own use; a crime is committed by a person on release pending trial because the computer was down which would have supplied the judge with the data suggesting the person was dangerous and should be kept in pre-trial detention.[9]

The Stanford Research Institute in its study on computer abuse found that in 65 reported cases of computer abuse from 1964 to 1973, losses averaged about $1 million per year.[10]

The following six cases represent a few of those cited in the Stanford Research Institute study on computer abuse:

6421–***Hancock vs. Texas***, **Texas–Program Theft.** A programmer stole $5 million worth of programs he was maintaining for his employer and attempted to sell them to a customer of his employer. He was convicted of grand theft and lost two appeals based on programs not being property as defined by theft laws. He served five years in prison.

6431–***MICR Deposit Slips Fraud***, **New York City–Fraud.** A depositor put a large sum of money in his account and asked for 1000 MICR-coded deposit slips. He placed them on counters in the bank and accumulated money in his account from other depositors.

6831–***Mansfield Embezzlement***, **California–Embezzlement.** A chief accountant embezzled $1 million from his employer over six years. He used a computer for financial modeling of his company to gauge appropriate changes in accounts receivable and payable to remain undetected. He was convicted and given a ten-year prison term.

6834–***Youth Corps Payroll Fraud***, **New York–Embezzlement.** A data center employee printed Youth Corps payroll checks for nine months at 100 checks per month for a total loss of $2,750,000.

6924–***Commercial Time-Sharing Staff***, **Fraud.** A systems programmer gained legitimate LOGON to his employer's competitor's service and tested possible privileged system commands. He discovered enough weaknesses to penetrate privileged mode where he could obtain confidential data.

7016–***Pharmaceutical Company***, **New Jersey–Vandalism.** An employee destroyed online data files after being given notice of termination.

In addition to fraud, there have been widespread instances in which the computer was the victim, i.e., breaking and entering computer facilities and destroying hardware, software and data.

Unionization of data processing personnel is an important issue in data processing today.[11] What effect will labor-management disputes among data processing people have on computer abuse and security?

During the legislative hearings on the Inspector General Act of 1978 (PL95-452) it was revealed that:

- $440 million in the food stamp program were spent erroneously
- between $6.3 and $7.4 billion of HEW funds were misspent annually as a result of fraud, abuse, and waste.

Most of the examples provided during the testimony involved fraud.

Waste and mismanagement, while a serious problem, is less easy to identify and quantify through auditing. Although program management may be at fault, the problem of identification of inefficiency is often computer related.

Finally, there is the issue of confidentiality of information and data security. Social Security information, credit card data, medical and life insurance data are only a few of the files existing on 200 million Americans covering birth to death (see Figure 1.1), which call for secure data systems.

EDP Impact on Internal Control and Audit Trails

The computer impacts on two fundamentals of auditing, namely, the existence of audit trails and internal control (especially the importance of division of duties as a measure of internal control).

Audit trails are those sign posts that provide the capability to follow an accounting action from any point in a system with absolute certainty in either direction, i.e., to either its origination or its ultimate destination.[12]

Audit trails exist in an automated system but in a different form than in manual systems. The existence of audit trails in an EDP environment is brought about by three conditions:

1. Computers do not think for themselves. They must be programmed. These programs must be developed by human effort and translated into machine language; therefore at the point of man-machine interface there is or should be some auditable record.

2. The internal accuracy and reliability of the computer itself reduce to negligible proportions the occurrence of machine error, and printouts can generally be assumed to be accurate representation of inputs and programmed processing.

3. When an operation is programmed into the machine it will perform the operation the same way unless altered by a set of instructions to do it differently. Hence, the use of test data and controls over unauthorized changes of the instructions serve to provide internal control.

FIGURE 1.1 IMPACT OF COMPUTERS ON SOCIETY AS ILLUSTRATED BY GOVERNMENT FILES

Social Security Administration – In these files are earnings records on 9 out of 10 jobholders in the U.S. Also: information on 26.2 million receiving Social Security benefits and 20 million older people under medicare.

•

Internal Revenue Service–Tapes store details from tax returns of 75 million citizens. These tapes are available at cost to States and the District of Columbia.

•

U.S. Secret Service–Its computer tapes hold names of "about 50,000 persons" who might attempt to harm or embarrass the President or other high Government officials.

•

Federal Bureau of Investigation–Now in the process of computerizing fingerprint files on more than 86 million people, including 19 million who have been arrested on criminal charges.

•

Department of Agriculture–Keeps data on 500,000 borrowers and 50,000 investors in programs of Farmers Home Administration, as well as records of 300,000 farmers buying federal crop insurance.

•

Department of Transportation–Keeps on tap names of 2.6 million citizens who have been denied driver's licenses or whose permits have been suspended or revoked.

Pentagon–Has files on some 7 million military personnel and civilians who have been subjected to "security, loyalty, criminal and other type investigations."

•

Veterans Administration – Preserves files on 13.5 million veterans and dependents who are now receiving benefits or have received them.

•

Department of Labor–Has files on some 2 million persons in federally financed work and training programs, coded by Social Security numbers.

•

Department of Justice–"Data bank" has names of more than 13,200 individuals who have been involved in riots and civil disorders since mid-1968.

•

Department of Housing and Urban Development–Maintains records on 4.5 million Americans who bought homes with loans guaranteed by the Federal Housing Administration. Also planned for computerization: an "adverse information" file on more than 300,000 builders and other businessmen.

THUS: Information on just about every American is stored away in one agency or other. And with the federal computer network spreading, there is virtually no limit to the volume of information that can be filed for quick retrieval.

SOURCE: Reprinted from *U.S. News & World Report*, February 22, 1971.

In the combination of these three basic concepts, it can be seen that the procedures or instructions which the machines must follow actually constitute an audit trail through the mechanized portions of the data processing system.

The second area of concern is the division of duties and responsibilities in an EDP environment.

There are two concurrent phenomena in the EDP environment. One is *decentralization* of "users" by remote terminals, microcomputers, etc., and the other is *centralization* through Data Base Management Systems (Supervisory Software Systems) and centralization of EDP controls and processing into the hands of the EDP specialist—the systems analyst, the programmer, the operator, librarian, etc.

In manual systems, the processing is generally done by accounting-oriented persons, i.e., the accounts payable clerk, the accounts receivable clerk, the voucher clerk, the payroll clerk. Secondly, the data is moved through the system manually and under "visible" control. That is, the checks and adding machine tapes are handed to a bookkeeping staff member who checks the tape, follows another processing step and passes it on to another operator who checks the previous processing, processes it further and passes it on.

In the data processing system, the accounting is not only machine-processed—in machine sensible format—but also involves non-accounting personnel, i.e., the computer personnel and users.

However, the auditor must bear in mind that computers do not operate themselves. The data that emerges from the computer starts somewhere and the results or outputs end up somewhere. As long as controls are established at critical points along this route, the auditor can rely on the system.

Finally, internal control measures and audit trails will exist because of "management's" need to exercise its accountability and stewardship function.

Management's Role in EDP Auditing

Management is responsible for establishing adequate and effective accounting procedures and internal control measures which, when properly followed in the processing of accounting transactions, will produce financial reporting that fairly presents the financial position and results of operation. Management needs detailed information and the ability to trace various transactions back to their source in order to operate the business effectively and to answer questions arising inter nally as well as externally from customers, vendors, government, etc. As one writer once put it, "It is difficult to imagine an accounts receivable system in which it would be impossible to readily determine the nature of each charge to a customer's account and the specific items making up the account balance."[13] Or consider a situation in which the inventory accounting was programmed on a moving average method rather than a first in-first out (FIFO) method without the knowledge or prior authorization of management. The many instances of computer abuse, fraud and defalcation, and the theft of company assets without the knowledge of management highlight management's responsibility and interest in controls over the EDP function.

The legislative history of auditing is in effect a documentation of management's responsibility, both public and private.

For example, the Budget and Accounting Procedures Act of 1950 provided that the head of each executive agency should establish and maintain systems of accounting and internal control designed to provide effective control over and accountability for all funds, property, and other assets for which the agency is responsible, including appropriate internal audit. The Second Hoover Commission, in 1955, called for improvement in internal audit in each agency for the purpose of ascertaining the extent of compliance with financial policies and procedures set by management.[14]

In 1961, the annual report of the Joint Financial Management Improvement Program for the first time included a special section on internal auditing and stated in part that "as a counterpart of this accounting responsibility basic legislation rests in the head of an executive agency responsibility for an adequate system of internal control, including appropriate internal audit."[15]

The Foreign Corrupt Practices Act of 1977 provides that every issuer which has a class of securities registered pursuant to section 781 of this title and every issuer which is required to file reports pursuant to section 780(d) of this title shall:

- Make and keep books, records, and accounts, which, in reasonable detail, accurately and fairly reflect the transactions and dispositions of the assets of the issuer; and

- devise and maintain a system of internal accounting controls sufficient to provide reasonable assurances that
  1) transactions are executed in accordance with management's general or specific authorization;
  2) transactions are recorded as necessary to permit preparation of financial statements in conformity with generally accepted accounting principles or any other criteria applicable

to such statements, and to maintain accountability for assets;
3) access to assets is permitted only in accordance with management's general or specific authorization; and
4) the recorded accountability for assets is compared with the existing assets at reasonable intervals and appropriate action is taken with respect to any differences.[16]

Of course there are Internal Revenue requirements, SEC releases, the privacy laws, etc., that impact upon management in the area of data processing and information systems.

The U.S. General Accounting Office's Supplemental Standards (effective January 1, 1980) note that both auditors and management officials have an interest in assuring that systems design, development and overall operations achieve the objectives of adequate internal control and effective auditability—that is, the capability to trace a transaction from its initiation, through all the intermediate processing steps, to the resulting financial statements and, similarly, information in the financial statements can be traceable to its origination. Furthermore, the GAO standard calls for systems applications which faithfully carry out the policies *management* has prescribed for the system (emphasis added).[17]

The Role of the Auditor in An EDP Environment

The role of the auditor has expanded beyond financial auditing to include compliance, program and performance auditing. Therefore the term "audit" includes not only the work done by accountants in examining financial reports but also work done in reviewing compliance with applicable laws and regulations; efficiency and economy of operations; and effectiveness in achieving program results.[18]

Much has been written concerning financial auditing, but the subject of performance auditing is and will be increasingly important.

Performance Auditing

The General Accounting Office's audit standards, in addition to the financial and compliance component, include standards for auditing economy and efficiency and program results. These standards extend to all auditing activities where federal monies are involved and in effect become a mandate to the auditing profession—governmental, internal, and public accountants are to become involved in performance auditing.

Performance auditing is defined variously. Examples are:

- *Public Accountants.* A performance audit or operational audit is: a formal and systematic review by qualified individuals to determine the extent to which an organization, or a unit or function within an organization, is achieving the goals prescribed for it by management and to identify conditions in need of improvement. The forms that reviews take may include any or all of the following: analysis, evaluation and description.[19]
- *Federal General Accounting Office.* To assist agency management in attaining its goals by furnishing information, analysis, appraisals, and recommendations pertinent to management's duties and objectives.[20]

The terms, performance auditing or operational auditing, are usually used to establish a distinction between auditing of accounting and related records for the purpose of expressing professional opinions on financial statements, and auditing which examines the operating, managerial or administrative performance of selected aspects of an activity or organization beyond that required for the audit of the accounts. The purpose of such expanded auditing is primarily to identify opportunities for greater efficiency and economy or for improving effectiveness in carrying out procedures or operations. The objective is improvement in relation to the goals of the organization.

Unfortunately, such labels as performance auditing, operational auditing and financial auditing can cause confusion. The boundaries between them even on a conceptual basis, are not sharp and clear. As versatile as our English language is, we have not been able to sharpen our terminology in many areas of accounting and auditing. Financial auditing requires the auditor to concern himself with aspects of management or administrative performance and control. He cannot confine his attention to accounting records. The auditor of financial statements, if he is doing the job properly, will find himself on much the same ground as the so-called operational auditor.[21]

In carrying out this concern with efficiency and effectiveness the auditor will become concerned increasingly with issues such as organization, records management, personnel management, information systems, and program evaluation (i.e., elements which determine the extent to which programs are achieving their intended objectives). As program evaluators, auditors should have a basic knowledge of research methodology, organization theory and design, systems analysis in addition to data processing systems.

As government and industry become concerned increasingly with waste, fraud and abuse, program auditing will increase. In conducting these audits the auditor will become involved with electronic data processing as more and more non-financial activities are computerized. Examples are the increasing use of computers in manpower planning, use of interactive data base for manpower management particularly in matrix management systems; social services delivery systems such as worker caseloads, demographic data, and service planning, law enforcement purposes, and management planning and decision making.

The concerns of internal control, data accuracy, and authorization are of equal importance in the *non*-financial and compliance component of auditing.

The Auditing Paradigm

The auditing paradigm[22] appears to be grounded in two areas, namely, evidence and internal control. A review of the literature on the impact of electronic data processing on the auditor's objectives supports the notion that they are unaffected by the technology of data processing. The objectives remain the same, i.e., to examine, evaluate, report upon, and advise management with respect to the financial and operational aspects of the agency. The auditor is to secure sufficient competent evidential matter through extended audit procedures—inspection, observation, inquiries, confirmation, and the existence of audit trails to afford a reasonable basis for his opinion regarding the financial statements, operations, program effectiveness or whatever are the purposes for the examination.

The second area concerns the separation of duties so that no one person has complete control of both the custodial and reporting functions.

It is in these two areas that the greatest challenge from the computer has come as pointed out earlier. However, advances in *EDP auditing technology*, including the auditor's involvement in the design and pre-installation phase of data processing systems or applications provide a response to this challenge.

ADVANCES IN EDP AUDITING TECHNOLOGY

There are advances in computer technology which allow the auditor to audit "through" the computer. Audit software development has provided the auditor with the capability of using the computer to:

1. perform statistical analysis, i.e., random sampling of specified records according to precision and confidence level requirements;

2. perform regression analysis;
3. select summarize, and report data;
4. review records for calculations and the algorithic procedures by which balances and extensions were arrived at;
5. check fields for errors, omissions, valid conditions, etc.; and
6. test data generators used to define specificities for generating transactions that will be used to create files of test data.

The Institute of Internal Auditors study by Stanford Research Institute lists 28 computer assisted tools and techniques.

Computer programs may be developed by the auditor for the particular engagement. They may be developed by the client, or they may be generalized packages available from accounting firms, software developers, or manufacturers.

The use of the computer provides the auditor with the opportunity to perform a more selective and effective audit of activities and procedures. This is particularly true in cases where large volumes of data are involved.

The computer can assist the auditor with the employment of the "auditing-by-exception" concept by permitting coverage of a greater area of business activity, and utilizing human resources in the more judgmental areas of the analysis and in the evaluation of the problem areas so highlighted.

It is obvious that the use of the computer for accounting purposes will continue to require the auditor to modify his audit techniques and his thinking relative to the extent of testing required in his audit examination, since the computer can process large volumes of data in much less time than can be done by using manual means. He may become more involved in an operational-type audit, in addition to auditing the financial and accounting activities. The development of data-based systems provides the auditor with operational information which previously was not integrated with the financial data and was not useful in conducting the audit.

The auditor must be careful not to abdicate his responsibility to EDP specialists in this changed audit environment. The extent of his involvement in the EDP area must be sufficient to satisfy himself that his opinion with respect to the financial statements is accurate, on the basis of the work performed. EDP specialists can assist in the technical aspects of developing and using test data and computer programs, but the auditor must assume the role of determining the test data requirements and the nature of the output to be obtained.[23] To fulfill this role it is important that the auditor develop the necessary competence to function responsibly in an EDP environment.

DEVELOPING THE EDP AUDIT CAPABILITY

Finally, there is the matter of training and developing EDP audit capability pursuant to professional standards.

The auditor in an EDP environment needs to understand the entire system sufficiently to enable him to identify and evaluate the system's essential accounting control features. Furthermore, the standards of professional practice both in and out of government require that in an EDP environment the audit staff must include persons having the appropriate computer skills—either staff members or consultants to the staff.

Adequate technical training and proficiency as an auditor in an EDP environment should as a minimum include:

1. A basic understanding of computer systems, including equipment components and their general capabilities.
2. A basic understanding of widely installed computer operating systems and software.
3. A general familiarity with the file processing techniques and data structures.
4. Sufficient working knowledge of computer audit software to use existing standardized audit packages.
5. The ability to review and interpret system documentation including flowcharts and record definitions.
6. Sufficient working knowledge of basic EDP controls to
   a. Identify and evaluate the controls in effect in the client's installation.
   b. Determine the extent to which such controls should be tested and to evaluate the results of such tests (although not necessarily to execute such tests).
7. Sufficient knowledge of EDP systems to develop the audit plan and supervise its execution.
8. A general familiarity with the dynamics involved in developing and modifying programs and processing systems.

While the general auditor's EDP knowledge may not extend beyond the very basic level, someone on the audit staff, either a staff member or consultant to the staff, must have the appropriate computer knowledge and skills.

There are a number of sources available for the auditor to develop EDP competencies.

Courses by Computer Manufacturers. Computer manufacturers are the major source of computer training today. They usually offer general orientation courses as well as courses in programming and operating particular machines. In general, the content of the courses and the quality of instruction have been very good.

Courses by Colleges and Universities. The colleges and universities have responded slowly to the need for training in electronic data processing. Since 1965, however, the number of courses offered has increased, and it is expected to more fully satisfy the needs of the business and government community. Many colleges and universities have equipment available (at least on a limited basis) for use in connection with the courses; many offer evening courses in adult education programs.

Courses at Local Technical Schools. Courses are offered in most metropolitan areas by both private and public technical schools. At least one computer manufacturer has established technical institutes for the purpose of providing local computer training.

Self-Instruction and Programmed Learning. The general principles of electronic data processing and many elements of programming can be learned through self-instruction, and there are a number of programmed self-study courses available. Several manufacturers use the programmed learning method extensively. Home-study computer courses are offered by several home-study institutions.

On-the-Job Training. Most qualified business data processing personnel have been trained on the job. Most have completed manufacturer courses and/or introductory courses at colleges and universities, but the major part of their expertise has been achieved through on-the-job experience. This method is economical for the practicing CPA only under certain circumstances. Staff members, for example, may be trained on the job by arrangement with a local installation. Some CPAs have benefited from the cooperation of a client moving into a new EDP installation.

Professional Development Courses. The Professional Development Division of the American Institute of Certified Public Accountants offers courses in Computer Concepts—featuring "hands on" experience on the computer, the "Control and Audit of EDP Systems." In addition, more specialized courses such as "System Flowcharting,"

"Program Flowcharting and Decision Tables," "Selection of an EDP Service Center," and Evaluation, Selection and Installation of EDP Systems and Generalized Retrieval Languages are also offered. Plans for additional EDP oriented courses are constantly under development.

Seminar and Training Programs. Many organizations such as the American Management Association offer seminars on computer data processing topics. The Association for Computing Machinery (ACM) offers a number of seminars on advanced topics. Several excellent seminars are offered through the EDP Auditors' Association and its many local chapters.

In addition, there are the Interagency Auditor Training Center, Washington, D.C.; Office of Personnel Management, ADP Management Training Center, Washington, D.C.; Department of Defense Computer Institute, Washington, D.C.; Canadian Institute of Chartered Accountants, Toronto, Canada; Institute of Internal Auditors, Altamonte Springs, Florida; and American Institute of Certified Public Accountants, New York, New York.

Literature, Books, Reports, etc.. Special studies and reports such as those published on computer science and technology by the National Bureau of Standards, the Institute of Internal Auditor's Systems Auditability and Control Study, the Computer Audit Guidelines and Computer Control Guidelines by the Canadian Institute of Chartered Accountants and many others, together with hundreds of textbooks, journals, etc., many of which are cited in Part II of this book, are available for self study and more formal training arrangements.

CONCLUSIONS

From this discussion, there appear to be certain major themes which serve as a framework for viewing auditing theory and practice in an electronic environment. These themes are listed here and dealt with in more detail in the subsequent chapters.

The framework for discussion then is: What are the changes in computer technology? (Chapter II); What is the impact of these changes on the auditing paradigm? (Chapter III); What is the state of the art with respect to internal control in an EDP environment? (Chapter IV); What are the developments in computer assisted audit tools and techniques? (Chapter V); and, finally, What is the state of the art with respect to training, organizing, and developing EDP auditing competence? (Chapter VI).

A review of the literature in Part II, which by no means exhausts the subject, provides further data on the state of the art with respect to theory and practice.

FOOTNOTES

[1]U.S. General Accounting Office, *Computer Auditing in the Executive Departments: Not Enough Is Being Done*, report to the Congress by the Comptroller General of the United States (Washington, DC: U.S. General Accounting Office, 1977), p. i.

[2]*Ibid.*

[3]*Ibid.*, p. 18.

[4]U.S. General Accounting Office.

[5]Stanford Research Institute, *Systems Auditability and Control Study: Executive Report*, research prepared for the Institute of Internal Auditors, Inc. (Altamonte Springs, FL: The Institute of Internal Auditors, Inc., 1977), p. 10.

[6]*Ibid.*, p. 6.

[7]"Even the smallest machine will have its own 'brain'." *Business Week*, 14 September 1974, p. 171.

[8]Stanford Research Institute, *op. cit.*, p. 4.

[9]*Washington Post*, February 15, 1980, pp. A1, A2.

[10]Stanford Research Institute, *Computer Abuse*. Prepared for National Science Foundation, Springfield, VA: National Technical Information Services, U.S. Department of Commerce, 1973.

[11]It is estimated that by 1980 over 3.5 million people or over 4% of the work force will be working directly with computers. This fact suggests that the opportunity for computer crime, fraud, etc. will increase.

[12]*Guide for Auditing Automatic Data Processing Systems*, 1 July 1966, p. 5-1.

[13]John R. Spellman, "Auditing the EDP System," *Arthur Andersen and Company Chronicle*, April 1962, pp. 54-67.

[14]U.S. Commission on Organization of the Executive Branch of the Government, *Budget and Accounting, A Report to the Congress* (Washington, DC: U.S. Government Printing Office, 1955), pp. 59-60.

[15]United States Senate, *Financial Management in the Federal Government*, staff of the Committee on Government Operations, U.S. Senate 1st Session, 87th Congress, Document 11, February 13, 1961 (Washington, DC: U.S. Government Printing Office), p. 39.

[16]*United States Code, Supplement I*, containing the General and Permanent Laws of the United States, enacted during the 95th Congress, 1st Session, January 4, 1977 to January 18, 1978 (Washington, DC: U.S. Government Printing Office, 1979, p. 269).

[17]U.S. General Accounting Office, *Auditing Computer-Based Systems: Additional GAO Audit Standards*, Washington, DC: U.S. Government Printing Office, 1979, pp. 5-6.

[18]U.S. General Accounting Office, *Standards for Audit of Governmental Organizations, Programs, Activities and Functions*, Washington, DC: U.S. Government Printing Office, 1972 (reprinted 1974), pp. 2-3.

[19]For example, see Thomas Eifler, "Performing the Operations Audit," *Management Education Portfolio*, NY: AICPA, 1974.

[20]U.S. General Accounting Office, *Internal Auditing in Federal Agencies*, Washington, DC: U.S. Government Printing Office, 1974, p.1.

[21]Ellsworth Morse, "Performance and Operational Auditing," *Journal of Accounting*, June 1971, p. 41.

[22]A theory suggests statements which discover, explain, and predict a phenomenon, and is more appropriate to the natural sciences than the idea of socially constructed reality of which accounting is a part. The term "paradigm" is more appropriately used in the sense that Kuhn uses it, that is, the constellation of beliefs, values, techniques, and so on shared by the members of a given community since the paradigm is more successful in solving problems as they arise than alternatives. "A paradigm governs not a subject matter but rather a group of practitioners." Thomas S. Kuhn, *The Structure of Scientific Revolutions* 2nd edition, enlarged, Chicago: University of Chicago Press, 1970, pp. 175, 180.

[23]Stanford Research Institute, *Systems Audit. . ., op. cit.*

CHAPTER II
OVERVIEW OF THE ELECTRONIC ENVIRONMENT

TECHNOLOGY AND TERMINOLOGY

The auditor is required by the standards which govern audits of computer-based systems to review hardware controls, operating systems (O/S) controls, and other input/output control systems.[1]

In meeting this requirement the auditor is confronted by a semantic jungle of terms such as BASIC, FORTRAN, PASCAL, ROM, RAM, DOS, VS, OS, DPBS, CPU, CPM, TTY, MODEM, Floppy Disks, Bytes, and Bits. To do a thorough job of explaining these and other terms would be beyond the scope of this volume. Therefore, our purpose is to provide some trail through this underbrush.

The reader is provided some fundamental notions of computer hardware; software, including languages, flowcharting, operating systems, and data base management systems; peopleware; computer service centers; documentation standards; and control features. This chapter should be read in conjunction with the chapters on Internal Control (Chapter 4) and Auditing Tools and Techniques (Chapter 5) . Collectively, these chapters and the annotated readings in Part II provide a *modest* foundation on which to build an understanding of the electronic environment in which the auditor functions.

A SYSTEMS APPROACH TO THE ELECTRONIC ENVIRONMENT

The system in which the auditor functions is a complex whole comprised of various subsystems (Figure 2.1): the management subsystem—planning, control and authorizing; the technical subsystem—the hardware, software, peopleware; and the user subsystem (which may or may not be within the management system, e.g., bank customers)—data transportation networks.

The social, political and legal environments have been discussed in Chapter 1.

FIGURE 2.1 A SYSTEMS APPROACH TO THE STUDY AND EVALUATION OF THE ELECTRONIC ENVIRONMENT

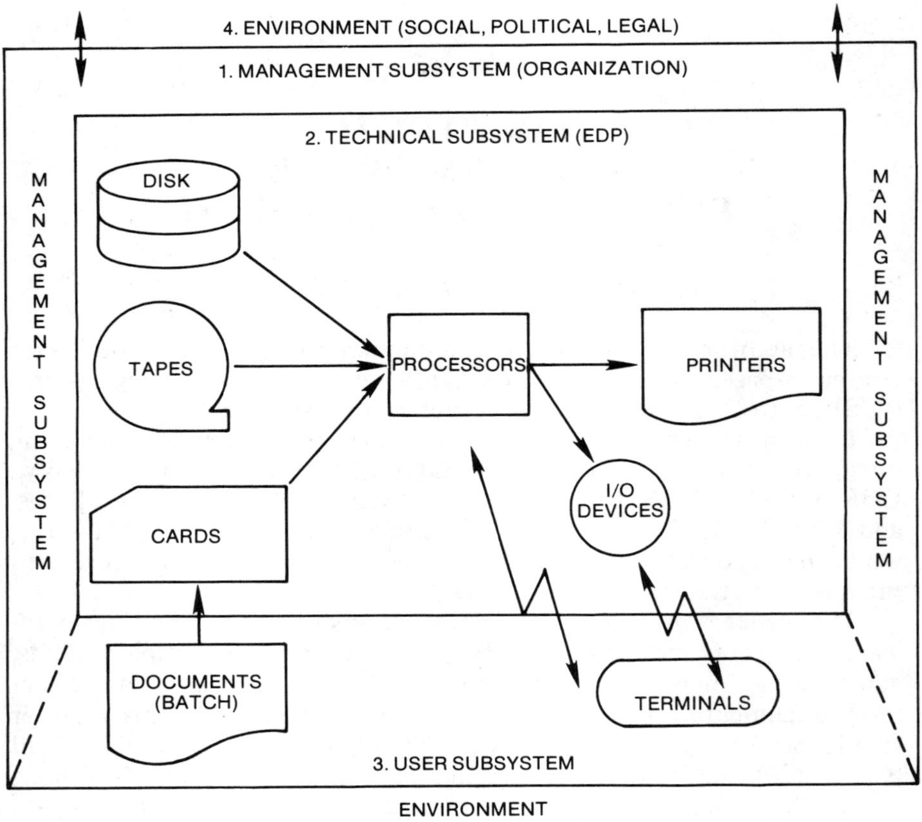

In this chapter, the technical, i.e., the electronic data processing subsystem together with the user subsystem is discussed.

COMPUTER HARDWARE

Basically, the computer system consists of a central processing unit (CPU) and peripheral equipment, i.e., input/output devices (I/O) and auxiliary memories or storage devices (Figure 2.1).

Modern equipment technology today permits data to be transmitted via voice grade phone lines from remote geographical areas to a computer, processed, and displayed visually on a cathode ray tube (CRT) with both alphanumeric and graphic displays, not unlike the home television set. Other examples of input/output (I/O) devices are:

Page Readers. These devices can read all letters of the alphabet, numbers 0 through 9, standard punctuations, and special symbols used in programmed functions. This input device permits processing directly.

Microfilmer. A microfilmer decodes data from magnetic tapes, displays it on the face of a cathode ray tube (CRT) and photographs the image onto 16 millimeter role microfilm.

Optical Character Recognition (OCR). Optical character recognition equipment can be connected online to a computer system or used offline. Machine or hand printed characters such as pencil-marked documents and symbols can be read and data entered directly into the system or to a magnetic tape unit or card or paper punch.

Communication Systems (Voice Input). Audio response system equipment is used to facilitate handling customer checking accounts, speed up deposits and withdrawal information in banks.

Shared Processors. These are keyboard to disc systems in which keyboards are controlled by a minicomputer that places keyed data temporarily onto discs prior to transmission to a computer-compatible tape.

The variety and sophistication of the computer hardware is illustrated by the advancement in microprocessor technology and distributed intelligence, i.e., data communication systems.

Microprocessors

In addition to development of various hardware components, there is the advance in miniaturization and "micronization," which has increased the use of computers, particularly at points of transactions, i.e., decentralization of computer capability. For example, the *entire* computer configuration in Figure 2.1 can fit into a small office, desk-top arrangement (minicomputer).

Distinction is also made between a micro and a minicomputer. A minicomputer is defined variously—by bit word length, by weight, by size of memory ranging from 4K-32K words and other physical and qualitative characteristics.

The microprocessor is comprised of a micronized processor (CPU), usually a very small silicon chip or silicon card. A silicon chip may contain 5,400 transitors in an integrated circuit approximately 2/10 of an inch square (.210 x .217 inches or .04 square inches).

A microprocessor performs the arithmetic and controls function of a computer. Typically, it has a read-only memory (ROM) to store the computer program or instructions and a random-access memory (RAM) to store applications or programmed data and I/O capability which interfaces with peripheral equipment (printer, teletype, terminal, CRT).

The use of microprocessors and remote access hardware has given rise to *distributed* systems. A distributed system is one in which certain systems functions are performed in locations other than the central data processing facility. For example, all the sales, accounts receivable and inventory activities can be processed in the regional office (using a mini or microprocessor) and the results of operations would then be sent to the central data processing facility for updating and feedback to the region for the next day's activities. This allows the regional office to operate online but ties into the central computer facility on an offline basis, perhaps during the night after business hours.The system provides accounting or operational capability at the point of use. However, the programs and data to support the system may require mass storage in the central computer. The online minicomputer can "call in" what it needs and perform whatever processing is required or cited (i.e., a minicomputer network tied to a "maxi" or host computer). The use of distributed systems creates control needs over access, authorization, etc. Various hardware and software controls, such as passwords, catalogs of eligible users, and restricted or scrambled fields, are used to protect the system from unauthorized or illegal entry, errors, etc. These are discussed later in this chapter under Control Features.

Data Communication

In Figure 2.1, it is shown that the user subsystem interacts with the computer through either a batch system or through online data communication network. The data communication network (distributed intelligence) is a network of terminals, often described as distributed intelligence, and microprocessors or minicomputers when used as input/output devices or as control portions of the data communication network.

These components are defined as:

1. **Terminals/Distributed Intelligence**—Any or all of the input or output devices used to interconnect with the online data communication network. This resource would specifically include, without excluding other devices, teleprinter terminals, video terminals, remote job entry terminals, transaction terminals, intelligent terminals, and any

other devices used with distributed data communication networks. These may include microprocessors or minicomputers when they are input/output devices or if they are used to control portions of the data communication network.

2. **Multiplexer, Concentrator, Switch**—Devices that enable the data communication network to operate in the most efficient manner. The multiplexer is a device that combines, in one data stream, several simultaneous data signals from independent stations. The concentrator performs the same functions as a multiplexer except it is intelligent and therefore can perform some of the functions of a front-end communication processor. A switch is a device that allows the interconnection between any two circuits (lines) connected to the switch. There might be two distinct types of switch: a switch that performs message switching between stations (terminals) might be located within the data communication network facilities that are owned and operated by the organization; a circuit or line switch that interconnects various circuits might be located at (and owned by) the telephone company central office. Typically, organizations perform message switching and the telephone company performs circuit switching.

3. **Modems**—A hardware device used for the conversion of data signals from terminals (digital signal) to an electrical form (analog signal) which is acceptable for transmission over the communication circuits that are owned and maintained by the telephone company or other common carrier. MOdulator/DEModulator.

4. **Transmission Channels**—The common carrier facilities used as links (a link is the interconnection of any two stations/terminals) to interconnect the organization's stations/terminals. These communication circuits include, not to the exclusion of others, satellite facilities, public switched dial-up facilities, point-to-point private lines, multiplexed lines, multipoint or loop-configured private lines, WATS service, and many others.

5. **Front-End Communication Processor**—A device that interconnects all the data communication circuits (lines) to the central computer or distributed computers and performs a subset of the following functions: code and speed conversion, protocol, error detection and correction, format checking, authentication, data validation, statistical data gathering, polling/addressing, insertion/deletion of line control codes, and the like.

Software

Software in its simplest definition is the non-machine interface; it is the set of commands under which the computer operates. Software is discussed in terms of languages, flowcharting and logic designs, operating or supervisory systems and data base management systems.

Languages

Languages refer to the set of instructions which the machine performs. Essentially, there are five language levels (Figure 2.3). However, the auditor should be familiar with the terms *machine* language, *assembler* language, or *compiler* or programming language.

FIGURE 2.2 COMPUTER LANGUAGES

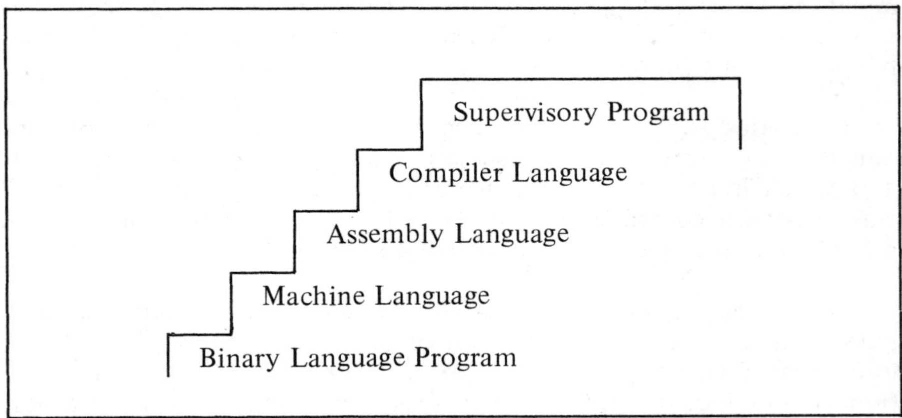

SOURCE: Edward J. Laurie, "Hierarchy of Programming Language Operation (Figure 5-20)," *Modern Computer Concepts: The IBM 360 Series.* Cincinnati: South-Western Publishing Company, 1970, p. 158.

Machine Language. Inside the computer, all instructions are executed by means of electronic pulse in either on or off position (1 or 0 in binary). Therefore, machine language is the set of instructions written in binary notation which can be executed by the machine on a one-to-one basis.

Assembler Language. A symbolic language program that prepares a machine language program by substituting absolute operation codes for symbolic operation codes and absolute or relocatable addresses for symbolic addresses. Generally, the symbolic instruction (for example, TOTPAY, the addition of an employee's regular pay and overtime) would be translated into a specific machine address or location.

Compiler Language. Compiler language or problem-oriented language is a language independent of the hardware and relates more closely to the procedures being coded. A single statement may cause several machine language instructions to be generated.

The sequence then is for the programmer to program in *compiler* language which is then *assembled* or compiled by the computer into *machine* language which is then stored on cards, tape or disk and available for use by the programmer (the former data referred to as the source program, the latter as the object program).

Several compiler languages commonly used are:

1. **Algebraic Languages:**
   - FORTRAN – **For**mula **Tran**slation
   - BASIC – **B**eginners **A**ll-purpose **S**ymbolic **I**nstruction **C**ode
   - APL – **A** **P**rogramming **L**anguage (Inverson's Language)
   - ALGOL – **Algo**rithmic **L**anguage
2. **Business Languages:**
   - COBOL – **Co**mmon **B**usiness **O**riented **L**anguage
   - RPG – **R**eport **P**rogram **G**enerator
   - PL/1 – **P**rogramming **L**anguage One (**1**)
   - PASCAL – Blaise Pascal, French Mathematician, 1642.

These languages represent the level of man-machine interface. Programmers code from the flowchart which the computer assembles or compiles into machine language as discussed above.

Flowcharting

A flowchart is a pictorial diagram of a sequence of steps required to solve a problem (the problem-solving logic), usually drawn with conventional symbols representing different types of events and their interconnectedness at each stage. The level of detail must be sufficient for unambiguous coding of the program, i.e., writing of instructions for a sequence of computer flowcharts, program flowcharts, process flowcharts, or document flowcharts.

Systems Flowchart	Sequence of major activities comprising a complete operation or system, including manual operations.
Program Flowchart	Detailed instructions from which the program is coded.
Process Flowchart	Work simplification technique which shows the flow of tasks or activities by function or individual.
Document Flowchart	The flow of documents or reports from person to person or function to function.

Often the flowcharts will show control points which are those critical points which require some type of comparison, edit or validation to insure accuracy, validity, or completeness of the data.

The symbols used generally conform to the International Organization for Standardization (ISO) International Standard 1028—"information processing"—and American National Standard, Flowchart Symbols and Their Usage in Information Processing, ANSI X3.5-1970. IBM usages beyond the above standards are three symbols: off-page connector, transmittal tape, and keying, which are identified IBM.

Symbols are in three groups: (1) basic symbols; (2) processing and sequencing symbols related to programming; (3) input/output, communication link, and processing symbols related to systems.

The following illustrates the use of flowcharting and programming in a simple accounting problem.[2]

> The Widget Manufacturing Company wishes to use BASIC to solve a simple accounting problem. A welding machine worth $9,000 is to be depreciated over 20 years by the use of a double declining-balance depreciation. The following program was written by one of their accountants from the flowchart shown:

Step 1. Flowcharting.

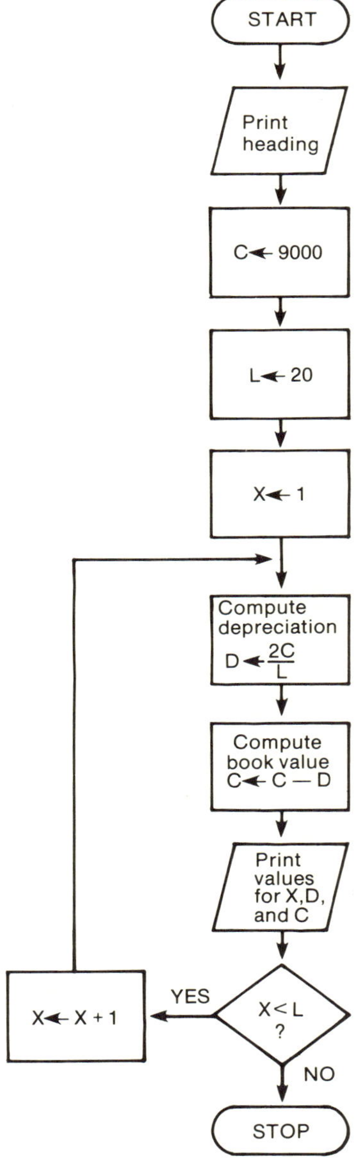

Flowchart for accounting program

Step 2. Coding

```
100  REM ACCOUNTING PROBLEM
120  PRINT "YEAR," "DEPRECIATION," "BOOK VALUE"
140  LET C = 9000
160  LET L = 20
180  FOX X = 1 to L
200        REM COMPUTE DEPRECIATION
220        LET D = 2*C/L
240        REM COMPUTE BOOK VALUE
260        LET C = C-D
280        REM PRINT X, D, AND C
300        PRINT X, D, C
320  NEXT X
340  END
```

Statement 120 causes three headings to be printed by the teletypewriter. Statements 140 and 160 cause the variables C and L to be set to 9000 and 20, respectively. The variable C represents the original value of the machine, and L represents the number of years over which its value is to be depreciated. Statements 180 through 320 determine the depreciated and book value for each year, printing the values as they are calculated. Statements 100, 200, 240, and 280 are placed in the program to supply supplementary comments (or REM's).

Step 3. Processing

This program produced the following output.

YEAR	DEPRECIATION	BOOK VALUE
1	900.00	8100.00
2	810.00	7290.00
3	729.00	6561.00
4	656.10	5904.90
5	590.49	5314.41
6	531.441	4782.97
7	478.297	4304.67
8	430.467	3874.20
9	387.42	3486.78
10	348.678	3138.11
11	313.811	2824.30
12	282.43	2541.87
13	254.187	2287.68
14	228.768	2058.91

15	205.891	1853.02
16	185.302	1667.72
17	166.772	1500.95
18	150.095	1350.85
19	135.085	1215.77
20	121.577	1094.19

The flowchart provides the auditor with a useful tool for determining the sequence and logic the program is programmed to follow, including the program's use of subroutine (utility) routines. These routines are operations which are required frequently and are therefore written once and are available on an as-required basis. They include mathematical computations (e.g., square root, percent values or decision functions), linear programming (e.g., decision tables), or network control functions (PERT, etc.).

Operating Systems

Operating systems are software which handle the relationship between programs which perform the input/output work and the programmer-coded routines which perform various accounting applications—selection of applications to be performed, the I/O devices to be used, file checking, interruption if queried from remote terminals, etc.[3]

The functions that are likely to be performed by the operating system of a complex multiprogrammed system are listed below:[4]

1. **Input/output control.** Scheduling the operations on input/output units and channels, checking for correct functioning, and so on.

2. **Communication line control.** Reading bits or characters from the line-control equipment and assembling them into messages. Controlling the terminals, and scanning them to detect whether they have something to send. Feeding messages bit by bit or character by character to the communication equipment. Error checking, and so on.

3. **Message setup services.** Giving an edited, checked-out message to the main programs and setting up a message-reference block in the required format.

4. **Handling displays.** For example, light-panel displays or cathode ray tube displays which need repetitive scanning.

5. **Communicating with the operator.** Notifying the operator, possibly on the machine console, of error or exception conditions, requirements for tape changing, and so on. Permitting the operator to give instructions to the system.

6. **Scheduling the message processing.** Deciding which message to work on next, on a basis of priorities, response-time requirements, and other factors.

7. **Scheduling the machine functions.** Deciding which machine function is to be done when these conflict.

8. **Queue control.** Building queues of items or of requests for input/output operations. Working off the queues in the best sequence.

9. **Core storage allocation.** Assigning core to various functions as required.

10. **Allocation of other equipment.** As well as assigning core, it may be necessary to assign other components of the system to various functions as required.

11. **Communication between separate computers.** Transmitting data to, or receiving data from, another on a multicomputer system.

12. **Control of an offline computer**, where this is a standby function as well as offline processing and will take over when a failure occurs in the online machine.

13. **Linkage between programs and subroutines**, when these may be fixed in core or relocatable.

14. **Handling interrupts.** Analyzing the cause of the interrupt. Transferring control to the appropriate priority routine. Storing registers, switches, or data from the interrupted program to ensure that a logically correct return can be made.

15. **Selecting and calling in the required programs.** Deciding whether these are already in core or whether they must be read in. Deciding which used programs can be overwritten when core is needed.

16. **Retaining working data, registers**, and so on, when control switches from one program to another without an interrupt.

17. **Controlling time-initiated actions.** Initiating a given action at a predetermined clock time or after a given elapsed period.

18. **File security.** Ensuring, as far as possible, that file records are not overwritten incorrectly by testing programs or by errors in operational programs.

19. **Fault indication and reliability checks.** Taking appropriate action when errors of all the various types are detected.

20. **Diagnostics.** Operating online diagnostics for dealing with error for increasing confidence in the system, and for assistance to the equipment engineers.

21. **Switchover.** Organizing switchover to a standby computer when a failure occurs.

22. **Fallback.** Organizing a degraded mode of operation when a component of the system fails, for example, a file or a communication buffer. Switching to the twin in a duplexed file system. Organizing recovery from fallback, for example, returning a file to the system and updating records that would otherwise have been updated during its down period.

23. **Handling overloads.** Taking emergency action on a system which can be jammed by an overload.

24. **System testing aids.** Temporary routines to aid in real-time program debugging and the testing of the operational system.

25. **Performance monitoring.** Temporary routines to gather statistics on system performance.

When the supervisor is in control of the computer system, the system is said to be in the supervisory state. When the supervisor has turned control over to the particular program, the system is said to be in the problem state.

During the supervisory state, the supervisor—by calling in various utility programs from disk storage—can take care of any error detection and the recovery from such errors, program loading, the handling of the input and output devices, and any required communication between the operator and the program. It is important for the auditor to understand functions and uses of operating systems in assessing the adequacy of controls. Certain of the control functions will be built into the application programs while others will be built into the operating system.

The supervisor will take control from a problem program or any of the processing programs used by the supervisor whenever an interrupt signal is received. There are five kinds of interrupts recognized by the system:

1. **Supervisor Call.** This is a request for the supervisor to intervene on the part of the problem program. That is, the programmer can include an instruction in his program which calls for the supervisor to take over. Typically the programmer might call for input or output, and since this is handled by the supervisor it constitutes a programmed interrupt.

2. **Input/Output Interruption.** When an input or output device has finished the particular job assigned to it, a signal is sent and the supervisor takes over. The supervisor will then assign further chores to the I/O device and return control to the program working at the time. This is one of the ways that the supervisor "buys" time to allow it to shuttle back and forth around the system taking care of its own chores.

3. **External Interruption.** For now, it will be sufficient for us to note that there is an *interrupt key* on the computer console and the computer operator can use this key to have the supervisor take over from a problem program.

4. **Program Check.** Certain types of errors can occur in a program, such as trying to divide by zero—an undefined mathematical operation. In earlier computer days the programmer would have to be certain to include, before each divide, some kind of test to be sure that this condition could not occur. Or, if it did occur, he had to have included in his program a method of taking care of the adjustment for such an error. In the IBM 360 systems, the supervisor intervenes when such an error occurs. It will either put one of the programmer's remedial choices into action or it will cause the job to terminate and will dump out information regarding the state of the programmer's job at the time the interruption occurred.

5. Machine Check. If there is a machine malfunction, the operating system goes into what is called a *wait state* and any other types of interruptions are blocked (*masked*). Recovery from a machine malfunction can get complex, so most operating systems provide a basic set of recovery subroutines to help restore the situation.[5]

Data Base Management Systems

Another software package is the data base management system (DBMS). A data base management system is a fairly complex software system to store, retrieve and update data in the direct access computer files. Also, the DBMS interfaces with any other programs (operating system or application programs) that are utilized in the overall data processing system and that relate to the data base itself.

Certain files, for example, sales, sales return, inventory and accounts receivable may have several common data elements. Formerly, the sales program, inventory accounting and customer accounts would have been maintained separately. The data base approach provides for the creation of a central dictionary or index of all data elements to be stored or processed and the organization of data so that it can be used both for routine production runs and for inquiries.

Certain of the various arguments *for* data base systems are of concern to the auditor. For example, data base systems allow a non-programmer to interface with the data base and provide for *centralized* control of the data. From an auditor's view not only does the data base system offer a challenge but also the advent of the position of the data base administrator (DBA) responsible for the overall control of the data base system.

The importance of the DBA's role can be seen from noting some of his/her duties. For example, deciding the information content, determining access strategies, defining authorization checks, monitoring the system, and defining a strategy for back-up and recovery.[6] This last point means that the data base administrator is charged with the security of the system against unauthorized entry through the assignment and control of passwords, control of the programs that access the data base, control over user access to the system, i.e., the use of the data, and designation of "restricted" data and memory areas. Hence, the data base administrator is the human element or the point at which man-machine interfaces, who defines rules for access to the data base and determines how the data will be stored.

What we have, therefore, is a system whereby all the data needed for various applications are commonly stored, i.e., *integrated*, accessed by a variety of users—non-computer personnel, i.e., *shared*—under the

FIGURE 2.3 ILLUSTRATION OF A DATA MANAGEMENT SYSTEM

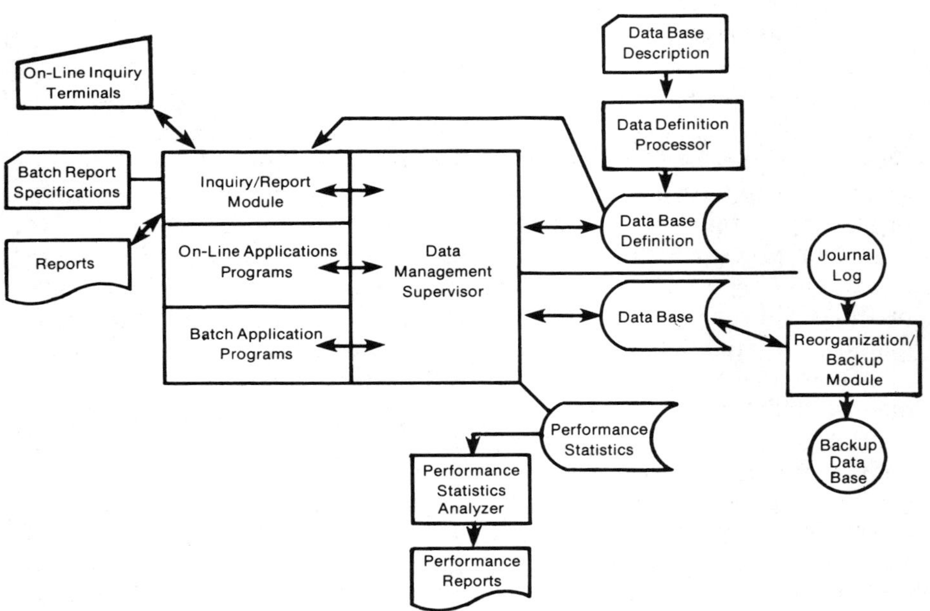

control of a single individual or function. Hence, it is a system which minimizes the audit trail, reduces man-machine interface and impacts upon the describable practice of separating and segregating duties.

Finally, an important element in DBMS is the *data dictionary*. The dictionary is a data file about the data stored in the data base. The data dictionary includes among other things which data are used by which programs and which departments require which data.

The auditor must review, test and evaluate data base system controls, processing and the surrounding environment. For example, a major concern is security or control over access to the data base and data base elements–controls must be established so that a user online for inventory data cannot access employee salary and wage data.

PEOPLEWARE

Minicomputers and remote terminals have added to the complexity of the EDP auditing problem by involving "users," "non-accountants," and "non-computer people" in the process. There are also involved EDP personnel including systems analysts, programmers, computer operators, data base administrators, librarians, key punch operators, TTY operators, control clerks, EDP managers, etc. (Figure 2.4).

FIGURE 2.4 TYPICAL ORGANIZATION OF AN EDP DEPARTMENT

- Directory of information processing
  - Manager of programming
    - Project leaders
      - Programmers
    - Documentation librarian
      - Documentation clerks
  - Manager of systems and procedures
    - Project leaders
      - Systems analysts
      - Data communications specialists
  - Manager of data processing operations
    - Keypunch supervisor
      - Keypunch leaders
        - Keypunch operators
    - Processing control group
    - Equipment operations supervisor
      - Shift supervisors
        - Unit record equipment operators
        - Computer operators
    - Tape librarian
      - Assistant tape librarians

These people together with the hardware and software perform the functions formerly done by the bookkeepers, accounts payable clerks, accounts receivable clerks, payroll clerks, etc. This shift is significant in several ways. Among them are:

1. There are reduced checks and balances provided by the manual transfer of data and records from one person to another. Sometimes this involved detailed verification between the parties or "eyeballing" by experienced accounting personnel.

2. There arises often a lack of communication among auditors and systems people and conflicts over value. While both represent management, the former are concerned with control and audit features that the latter may find costly and time consuming. The systems people are concerned with accomplishing design, debugging and operations.

3. There is increased opportunity for computer fraud and abuse by increasing the number of people who have access to a computer, data files and programs, and the number of people with system knowledge.

4. The computer tends to reduce the extent of activities that can be separated since many are under the control of the equipment itself and fewer workers are involved.

5. The auditor may approach the task of auditing in an EDP environment with less rigor than with manual systems recognizing his own limited knowledge of computer systems; hence, as is true in most cases of implementation of new technology, there is a redistribution of power—in this case "expert" power vis-a-vis the computer professional.

COMPUTER SERVICE CENTERS

Advances in computer technology and the reliance on computers have resulted in widespread use of computer service centers. Many auditors, whose clients use these facilities, are involved in third-party reviews (i.e., review and evaluation of the audit reports prepared by service center's independent auditors) to assess the risk to the client using the service center.

In many instances where an organization uses a service center, its own EDP function is concentrated in a small group. For example, an EDP coordinator may be the only link between the client and the center. The coordinator may transmit the data, check the error and invalid transaction report, resubmit the corrected data, receive the hard reports and outputs from the service center, and, as importantly, assign the passwords to all the terminal operations.

DOCUMENTATION STANDARDS

While technically documentation could be discussed under the topic of software, it is sufficiently important to auditors to merit separate consideration.

Documentation consists of those records which describe the system and procedures for performing data processing tasks.

Often, EDP installations will have a documentation library, staffed, and under security arrangements.

Documentation generally consists of problem statements, flowcharts, file layouts, grid charts (data items by programs), decision tables, run write-ups, operating instructions, coding sheets, test data and user manuals (Figure 2.5).

F. Stuart Magie, Jr. offers ten points on developing effective documentation.[7]

> 1. Each processing system should have a *system flow diagram*: a complete diagram of the system from data control clerk through each computer operation and back to the data control clerk. This flow chart, in order to be meaningful to the particular installation, should be created in a standard manner that is adopted by that particular installation.
>
> 2. A *general narrative* of the complete data processing system should be created and should include a "picture" of the total system from the user through the data control clerk and computer operations back to the user. It should include such things as input/output schedules, number of computer operations, methods for balancing and clerical procedures, etc.
>
> 3. A *detailed program abstract* should be found in the form of a narrative or program abstract written for each computer operation. The abstract should describe in detail that particular operation. A standard method for writing abstracts should be established for the installation in order to simplify the efforts of analysts and programmers to read abstracts and thereby know what is to be found within the program. It has been my experience that the abstract should start by defining the name and number of the system, followed by the name and number of the particular program within the system. Next should be a short description of the objective (or the problem solved by) this particular program step. After the objective there is a description of all input files. The next section of the abstract will contain a description of all output files. This section also refers to any output reports produced by this

particular computer step. After the output files have been fully described, the last section of the abstract should indicate the problems that must be solved by the computer program. This description, whether done with matrix tables or in narrative fashion should communicate enough detail for the programmer to create and construct the proper logic to build the necessary program.

4. There should be a *detailed program logic narrative*, which can be best systematized by requiring all programmers to write a narrative describing their program, after it is implemented into production. In order to enforce this rule, a program is not accepted without the logic narrative.

5. A *current program listing* of the present production program must be retained as documentation for the program. This listing will be produced by the final assembly and filed with the other documentation.

6. In order for the programmer to positively assure that the program functions are as per specifications, *test data* must be created. Usually "static" test data are created by the programmer and "systems" test data supplied by the user or by the analyst. The test data that most thoroughly "checks" the program should be maintained on file. This includes not only card decks, but a listing of the test data and the results. Whenever a change is made to the program, the test data can be rerun and thereby prove if the new version of the program is correct.

7. The *record layout* of all files must be included either with the abstract or filed by themselves with each program within a system. Also, samples of the printed output and input should be filed. In this section of the file, one other piece of documentation must be kept and that is keypunch operator punch instructions.

8. Clear *computer operator instructions* must be created for the operator to follow when running each program. Two copies are usually made: one filed in the documentation book and the other is forwarded to the computer operations department with the program.

9. Any other documentation should be kept as *miscellaneous documentation* and filed. These may be memos and letters from and to the user or customer of this particular system.

10. *Clerical instructions* may be written if the system requires any manual handling prior to keypunching, or requires clerical handling after computer operation.

The auditor is concerned with the various control features to assure data integrity as represented in the documentation.

FIGURE 2.5 ILLUSTRATION OF RUN MANUAL AND SYSTEMS DOCUMENTATION

SECTION	DESCRIPTION OF CONTENTS	EXHIBITS
Problem definition	A description of the reason why the program was prepared.	Problem statement, reasons for the system.
System description	A general outline of the system in which the program operates. The section also contains layouts for inputs, outputs, and files related to the program.	Systems flow chart, logic file, card layouts, output printer layouts.
Program description	The documentation of the logic and coding. Contains the program flowcharts, decision tables, program listing, and other descriptions which document the content of the program.	Decision tables, program flowchart coding, assembly printouts.
Operating instructions	The instructions required to run the program on the computer. This is the same as the computer operator instruction provided to the equipment operator which will be described later in the chapter.	Operators and users manual, library instruction.
Program controls	Summarizes the controls built into the program to deter errors.	Run manual, edit routines, control unit instructions.
Acceptance record	Contains a documentation of the test plan and test data used to test the program before acceptance, the program change record, and record of approvals.	Test deck, key punch sheet, memory dump, results of testing.

CONTROL FEATURES

Control features are those devices built into the hardware or programmed into the software by vendors and application programmers in an attempt to assure that the system performs properly and that corrective measures can be taken in case of error conditions.

Control features include parity checks, limit controls, code validity checks, transmission tests for blank or zero filled data fields, input entry logs, passwords, cryptography,[8] the transformation of data to make it unreadable without a key, hash totals, file label checks, and file reducing.[9]

The hardware and vendor's software specifications generally describe the various built-in control features. Programmable checks are described in the system documentation. These checks are discussed in the chapter on Internal Control.[10]

FOOTNOTES

[1]Discussion of the standards for audit review of general controls in computer-based systems in U.S. General Accounting Office, *Auditing Computer-Based Systems*, Washington, DC: U.S. General Accounting Office, 1979, pp. 10-12.

[2]Donald D. Spencer, *Computers in Action*, NY: Hayden Book Company, Inc., 1974, pp. 135-137.

[3]Edward J. Laurie, *Modern Computer Concepts: The IBM 360 Series*. Cincinnati: South-Western Publishing Company, 1970, Chapters 6 and 7, pp. 189-257. Although discussed specifically in relation to the IBM 360, it is a good introduction for the auditor to the concept of supervisory programs.

[4]James Martin, *Design of Real-Time Computer Systems*, Englewood Cliffs, NJ: Prentice-Hall, Inc., 1967, pp. 140-141.

[5]Date, C.J. *An Introduction to Data Base Systems*. 3rd ed. Reading, MA: Addison-Wesley Publishing Company, 1981, pp. 25-27.

[6]Laurie, *op. cit.*, p. 245-246.

[7]F. Stuart Magie, Jr., "EDP Documentation: Ten Ways," *Administrative Management*, June 1969, pp. 62-64, reprinted by permission of the publisher.

[8]Various terms are used for the cryptographic procedure–data encryption, enciphering, scrambling and privacy transformation.

[9]In addition to manufacturers and vendors, hardware and software specifications, discussion of various controls are contained in several references used in EDP auditor training. Among them are: James Martin, *Security, Accuracy and Privacy in Computer Systems*, Englewood Cliffs, NJ: Prentice-Hall, Inc., 1973; U.S. General Accounting Office, *Guide for Reliability Assessment of Controls in Computerized Systems: Financial Statement Audits*, Washington, DC: U.S. General Accounting Office, 1976; Robert L. Patrick and Robert P. Blanc, *Computer Science and Technology: Performance Assurance and Data Integrity Practices*, Washington, DC: U.S. Department of Commerce, National Bureau of Standards, 1978; and Gordon B. Davis, *Auditing and EDP*, New York, NY: AICPA, 1968, especially Chapters 4 and 5.

[10]See also Part II–Annotated Bibliography for definitions and additional discussion of various control features.

CHAPTER III
THE AUDITOR'S TASK IN AN EDP ENVIRONMENT

Not only have the technological advances in computers impacted upon the role of the auditor but also the ubiquitous use of the computer in every aspect of our living. James Martin (*Security, Accuracy, and Privacy in Computer Systems*) points out a myriad of applications. For example, a large city uses a computer to control its police operations, and there are nearly 2,000 types of U.S. Government files holding personal information about individuals.[1] Computers are used in medical diagnoses, satellite communications, student records, employee information, manpower needs analysis and planning, inventory controls, and production operations.

Therefore the computer impacts upon the auditing function whether it be financial or management auditing. Regardless of the objective of the audit or the technological environment in which it takes place, the auditor's task is to render a professional opinion based upon "evidence" appropriate to the objectives and nature of the audit. For example, consider management auditing. Management auditing consists of an informed and constructive analysis, evaluation, and recommendations regarding the broad spectrum of plans, processes, people and problems of an economic entity. The evidence obtained in such an audit would permit the auditor to render an opinion with respect to: (1) the optimum arrangements that management has established for running an entity; (2) the effectiveness of systems in accomplishing established goals and objectives; and (3) the profit inhibitors, e.g., inadequate communications, poor organization structuring and responsibility assignments.[2]

THE AUDITOR'S TASK

Although the auditor may be involved in any one of the four basic types of audits described in Chapter 1 (Financial, Compliance, Performance, or Program) and although the system under review may be manual or automated, the fundamental task of the auditor remains the same, namely, to render an opinion, arrive at conclusions, make informed judgments and recommendations relative to the "fairness of the financial statements," "compliance with existing regulations," "the cost-effective manner in which a program is conducted," or the "degree to which a given program is operated in accordance with the goals and objectives of management."

The conclusions, opinions, judgments, recommendations are to be based upon sufficient, competent and relevant evidence.[3]

EVIDENCE AND THE AUDITOR

Evidence implies the existence of external signs, easy to see or perceive. Evidence is a matter of fact, it is either in itself a fact or it is the reproduction of facts as in the case of the photograph and the testimony of witnesses. Evidence is information. Conclusions and inferences may be based or reached upon this information. As one author stated, "Reasonable investigation that uncovers no reason to doubt the proposition effectively supports it."[4]

The ultimate objective of the auditor's usual examination of financial statements is to enable him to express a professional opinion to the effect that such statements present fairly the financial position and results of operations of his client in conformity with generally accepted accounting principles applied on a basis consistent with that of the preceding year. This means that what is reported is a "fair" representation, the real business world of the client.[5] By "fair," is meant a reasonable degree of assurance, arrived at by professional and competent efforts.

Thus, in financial auditing, every assertion in the financial statements, although not a matter of dispute, must be considered subject to question, and any factual information brought to the mind of the auditor to enable him to decide the truth or falsity of financial statement assertions is evidential matter.[6] Thus, financial statements may be viewed as a whole series of propositions to be proved, and audit evidence includes all facts which the auditor uses in proving or disproving these propositions. For example, the auditor indicates that he "examined" the accounting records which may mean he inspected them carefully with a view to discovering their real character.

In program auditing, evidence often rests not so much upon traditional auditing techniques as upon social science research techniques. These techniques relate to the choices of sampling procedures, including the size and selection; data collection instruments; selection of the proper statistical techniques, and the proper design of the conditions for the collection and analysis of data in a manner that serves to provide evidence tending to prove or disprove the matters at issue.[7]

The amount and kind of evidence should be in sufficient quantity that the findings and conclusions reached are not merely guesswork or determined by chance. The legal fraternity gives some clues or guidelines which may be of value to auditors—the evidence offered must be such that a reasonable man could draw from it the inference of the existence of the particular fact to be proved.

The amount and kinds of evidential matter required to support an informed opinion are matters for the auditor to determine in the exercise of his professional judgment after a careful study of the circumstances in this particular case. In many cases the auditor finds it necessary to rely on evidence that is persuasive rather than convincing. It is not sufficient that the evidence is such that he has no reason to doubt the representations contained in the financial statements but he must have sufficient competent evidential matter to remove any substantial doubt. This raises the problem of types of evidence and the broad question of the relative weight to be given to classes of evidence.

A Typology of Evidence

Auditing evidence may be divided into three classifications: (1) least convincing, (2) more convincing, and (3) most convincing.

Auditing evidence which is least convincing is that which has been prepared by, or in the possession of, an employee who is under audit. Most of the bookkeeping and accounting records represent evidence of this first type. The representations may be inaccurate, incomplete, or false. The second type of evidence, more convincing, usually consists of original documents or other accounting documents prepared in departments other than the accounting department. The third type of evidence consists of documents, papers, and records kept by outsiders and certificates furnished by them. In addition, it includes evidence arising from the auditor's own personal inspection.

These three classes of evidence are stated somewhat differently by Mautz[8] and the auditor's opinion indicates that evidence can be classified in three ways: (1) absolutely convincing, (2) possibly persuasive, and (3) neutrally persuasive, i.e., not leading to doubt.

Mautz further classifies evidence into natural evidence, created evidence, and rational argumentation. He also submits the following in audit work sequence classification of evidence in terms of availability and variety or reliability:

1. Systems of Internal Control
2. Accounting Records
3. Physical Items
4. Documents
   a. Third party documents to the auditor
   b. Client to the third party to the auditor
   c. Client to third party to the client to the auditor
   d. Third party to the client to the auditor
   e. Client to the auditor
5. Mathematical Computations by the Auditor
6. Representations by the Client.

Mautz concludes that competent evidential matter includes:

1. Real evidence—actual examination by the auditor of the thing in question.
2. Testimonial evidence—oral or written statements by people.
3. Indirect evidence—documents, books and records, actions and events, and any other fact that the auditor uses in forming an opinion on financial statements.

Further, he maintains that if the auditor can utilize the advantages of classification, he will surely have a clearer understanding of availability, variety, and reliability of audit evidence. Several authors have presented various typologies of evidence which are summarized in Figure 3.1.

It is the subject of evidence which has been of most concern in the EDP era.

Evidence and EDP

The use of computers has an impact upon the availability of evidence. Integrated systems, real-time, online systems may produce output with little intermediate input, or the output may not be directly traceable to the input, particularly when the transformation process is complex or sophisticated, and may be set into motion by very little input. For example, in an integrated data processing system, the determination by the computer that the inventory level of a particular item has fallen below a certain point may set into motion a series of automated events such as purchase requisition and re-order procedures.

Another example is that the ledgers, subsidiary journals, and other data may be in machine sensible form, i.e., on punched cards, reels of

FIGURE 3.1 CLASSIFICATION OF AUDIT EVIDENCE

Benjamin Newman	Sidney W. Peloubet	Mautz and Shapaf
1. Accounting records.	1. Individual business planning process, patterns, etc.	1. Physical examination by the auditor of the thing represented in the accounts.
2. Primary documents, sales slips, invoices, deposit slips, etc.	2. Individual accounting systems, personnel, methods, etc.	2. Statements by independent third parties, (a) written, (b) oral.
3. Substanitating documentary evidence sales order, purchase orders, customer remittances, etc.	3. Records and papers of the company.	3. Authoritative documents (a) prepared outside client, (b) prepared internally.
4. External (observation and inquiries).	4. Physical identification established by observation or count.	4. Statement by officers, and employees of the company, (a) formal, (b) informal.
5. Working papers, reconciliations, etc.	5. Records and papers of others (public documents, deeds, etc.)	5. Calculations performed by the auditor.
6. Company policies and procedures.	6. Independent calculations of balances and flows.	6. Satisfactory internal procedures.
7. Relationships or accounts, i.e., sales to receivable, inventory to purchases, etc.		7. Subsequent actions by the company.
8. Overall evaluation.		8. Subsidiary or detail records with no significant indications of irregularities.
9. Client's written representations.		9. Interrelationships with other data.

SOURCE: Benjamin Newman, *Auditing–ACPA Review Manual*, NY: John Wiley & Sons, Inc., 1958, pp. 10-12; Sidney W. Peloubet and Herbert Heston, *Integrated Auditing*, NY: The Ronald Press, 1958; R.K. Mautz and Hussein A. Shoraf, *The Philosophy of Auditing*, American Accounting Associates, 1961. Compiled by the author.

magnetic tape, discs, etc. Decoding the data generally involves the use of experienced computer personnel, time, and, often, special computer programs. The benefit or need for the data must be worth the cost of securing the data. If the auditor imposes upon the system certain data needs, printouts—audit trail requirements—because of his lack of adjustment and innovation in auditing EDP, the system may well become "audit bound."

Traditionally the auditor has relied on audit trails, i.e., a system of providing a means for tracing items of data from processing step to step, particularly from a machine produced report or other machine output back to the original source data. However, the computer era has ushered in the era of vanishing audit trails, particularly of the printed or hard copy variety.

There are certain characteristics of evidence which are affected in an EDP environment. EDP affects the quantity and quality of evidence (as set forth in Figure 3.2).

FIGURE 3.2 CHARACTERISTICS OF EVIDENCE

QUANTITY	QUALITY
1. Availability	1. Reliability
2. Sufficiency	2. Relevancy
	3. Accuracy

Availability. When the introductory media are prepared automatically at the time a transaction occurs, the problem of availability of audit trail is further complicated. For example, a time clock with an attachment that prepares input media when the clock is punched means there is no other documentary evidence of the transaction for the auditor's inspection. The auditor may view this as a threat to traditional auditing techniques.

The loss of interim hard copy will have its principal effect in the verification of account balances at interim points. In some cases individual transactions are merged and posted collectively to single accounts or distributed among several accounts as the result of a single integrated machine program.

Although it is apparent that the audit trail can be eliminated in an integrated system, i.e., updating all related files from a single data input, the needs of customers, government agencies, auditors, and management will require the system to include audit trails. Some audit trail is necessary to provide the detailed business information for the period of time that will satisfy legal, accounting and practical requirements. An organization with an integrated computer system cannot afford to loose control by establishing a system without adequate provisions for a management trail. The auditor might do well to view *audit* trails as *management* trails.

The special importance of the financial statements and other records as evidence in legal matters such as bond transactions, grants, etc. place a great responsibility upon management to provide the type of evidence an auditor needs in rendering his opinion about the "fairness" of the financial statements, compliance, program effectiveness, etc.

Sufficiency. The auditor is required to express his professional opinion rather than a statement of fact that the financial statements present "fairly" the financial position of the organization. Also, the term "fairly" indicates that the statements may not be completely accurate in all details. What is indicated, however, is that the auditor obtained a reasonable degree of assurance that the accounting data presented do not include a material amount of error.

The problem of sufficiency of data may be met by scientific statistical sampling. In fact, auditing is more systems-testing than transactions-tracing. For example, by utilizing a generalized computer program, a statistically valid sample of computer records can be produced for the auditor to examine. If the auditor examines 100 vouchers from a universe of over 2,000 vouchers and finds only two errors, he can be 94 percent certain that the error rate in the universe would not exceed 5 percent.

Other statistical sampling techniques would allow the auditor, within a predetermined confidence level, to state that the real value of the accounts receivables, for example, is between plus or minus X dollars of the value stated on the client's books.

Reliability. Reliability is the measure of the repeatability of the systems to produce the same output from the same input. If internal controls are established over the program, i.e., steps taken to insure that the program is not altered or manipulated during processing (as through switches or through the console typewriters), then the program should process data the same way. For instance, payroll data should be processed the same way by the same payroll program. Reliability may also be defined in terms of high confidence that the system will perform satisfactorily.

Relevance. Data are valid if they measure or pertain to what they purport to mean or measure. That is, one can have confidence in a statement only to the degree to which the data or statements measure that which they are supposed to measure or represent.

Accuracy. Accuracy is a measure of the difference between the data and the actual or true value of whatever the data represents. Barring mistakes or systematic errors, the accuracy of data can be improved by refining the instruments or improving the methods by which the data are gathered and processed.

There are various audit procedures, briefly described in Figure 3.3 (described in greater detail in Chapters IV and V). Each of these techniques produces evidence, although a particular characteristic of the evidence may be stressed in certain techniques and not in others.

The degree to which EDP-generated data reflect the financial position and results of operations is affected by various "threats to validity."[9] In an EDP environment, these threats include, but are not limited to, threats to data integrity, data confidentiality and ADP availability. These terms are defined as:

1. **Data Integrity**—the state that exists when automated data is the same as that in the source document, or has been correctly computed from source data, and has not been exposed to accidental alteration or destruction.[10]

2. **Data Confidentiality**—the state that exists when data is held in strict confidence and is protected from unauthorized disclosure. Misuse of data by those authorized to use it for limited purposes only is also considered to be a violation of data confidentiality.

3. **EDP Availability**—the state that exists when required EDP services can be performed within an acceptable time period even under adverse circumstances.

As indicated, the auditor in an EDP environment is still concerned with obtaining the necessary quantity and quality of evidence to form an opinion; that is, while the objectives are the same, the tools and techniques available to an EDP auditor must keep pace with the rapid change in computer systems technology.

FIGURE 3.3 AUDIT PROCEDURES IN SECURING EVIDENCE RELATING TO INTERNAL CONTROL AND "FAIRNESS" OF FINANCIAL STATEMENTS

QUANTITY/QUALITY	AUDIT PROCEDURES
Availability of evidence	Examine the controls that management has instituted because of the constraints imposed upon the system by government, customers, various levels of management, etc.
Sufficiency of evidence	Apply modern sampling techniques to determine the levels of vouching, testing that the auditor needs to do.
Reliability of evidence	Test the systems to determine if the system produces what it is supposed to do, determine the controls over documentation, manipulation of machine through consoles, switches, etc., and changes in programs. Does the system run and produce according to the flow charts and program writeups?
Relevance of evidence	Determine that the system checks valid codes and transactions, and that the proper type of transactions go to the proper accounting summaries.
Accuracy of evidence	Determine what electro-mechanical checks are built into the system, as well as controls built into the programs.

APPROACHES TO AUDITING IN THE EDP ENVIRONMENT

While the objectives of auditing remain the same, i.e., to seek evidence with regard to the output of the system, the auditor generally has two approaches, namely auditing-around-the-computer and auditing-through-the-computer (Figure 3.4).

The concept underlying the "around the computer" approach is simply that if the original data are correct and these data are eventually posted correctly to the final accounts, it can be assumed that the intermediate stage, namely, the processing of the transactions, has been done properly. The concept underlying the "through the computer" approach is that if the processing is done accurately and completely—and the input data are correct—the end product is accurate and complete. Hence, the emphasis is on the processing system being tested and proved out satisfactorily.

FIGURE 3.4 ILLUSTRATION OF AUDITING TECHNIQUES "AROUND" AND "THROUGH" THE COMPUTER

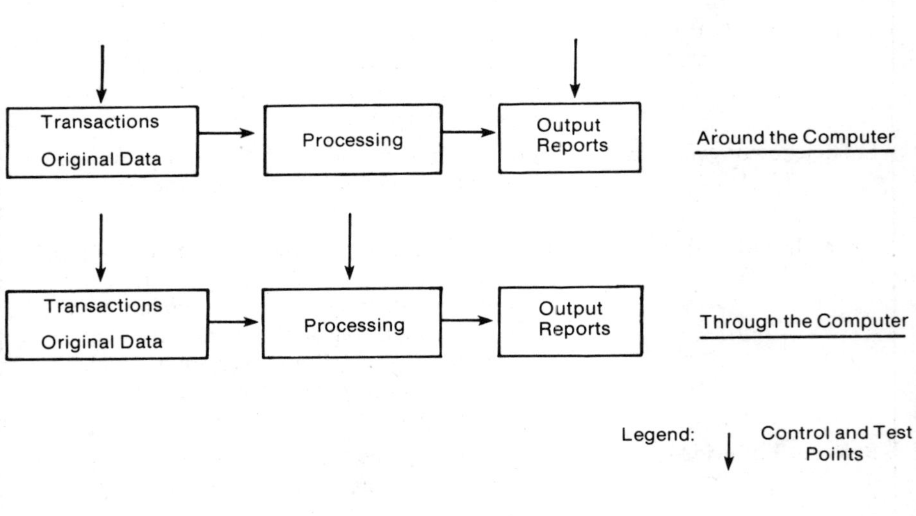

Although the thrust of the AICPA Standards for Auditing Computer Systems (S.A.S. no. 3) and the U.S. General Accounting Office Supplemental Standards is to require auditors to rely less on auditing around the computer and more on auditing through the computer, there remain enough circumstances in which the former approach is appropriate that it warrants discussion.

Auditing Around the Computer

Various techniques are emphasized when auditing around the computer (Figure 3.4). Among them are:

1. **Auditing by Exception.** Auditing by exception is another

variation of auditing without using the computer. The auditor in receiving hard copy can check, for example, the following:

- Detailed costs accounts which show no charges recorded for some time.
- Payroll checks which exceed the normal limits on the amount of pay authorized.
- Employee time cards for which there were no master records or payments.
- Employees subject to FICA holdings for whom withholdings were not taken.

2. **Extended Audit Procedure.** The auditor will place increased emphasis on observations, confirmations, inquiries and inspections.

3. **Evaluation of Internal Control.** The auditor will place heavy emphasis on the evaluation of internal control, particularly processing control–I/O verification, edit function, hardware and programmed controls.

4. **Use of the Computer in Auditing.** The auditor may use the computer to total selected fields, to merge and sort various input tapes, and to compare data from two or more sets of records.

Because of the widespread use of computerized sampling techniques they are discussed further.

Computerized Sampling Techniques

There are several auditing software packages which perform statistical sampling of various files. The programs will select a statistically valid random sample and create an output tape and listing of the selected records. The number of records depends upon the total number of records in the file (the population) and the confidence and precision levels selected by the auditor. Confidence is the degree of sample reliability expressed as a percentage required by the auditor under the circumstances; for example, "95 percent certain that . . . ."

Precision is a measure of materiality expressed in numbers or amounts. To illustrate, the auditor wishes to be 95 percent certain that based upon the *number* of errors found in the sample of a particular size in relation to the population, the maximum number of errors in the population does not exceed a certain limit or the auditor may state: "If I can be 95 percent certain that the inventory value is within $50,000 of the client's stated value, I will accept the client's value."

FIGURE 3.5 AN APPROACH TO AUDITING WITHOUT USING THE COMPUTER

AUDIT APPROACH	IMPLEMENTATION
Review of System	Interviews with personnel in data processing. Use of questionnaire; examination of general systems description, flowcharts, run writeups, etc.
	General review of major controls, error listing and procedures for resubmitting corrections.
	Review of controls for each application vital to the audit.
Tests of Systems	Examination of evidence for controls (error listings, batch control records, authorizations, etc.).
	Use of printouts to trace items in output to source documents, source documents to reports, reports totals to controls, etc.
	Checking of transactions sample for correct processing.
Evaluation of Records	Tests to check correctness of summary accounts (foot, crossfoot, etc.).
	Tests of samples of detail items by confirmations, reasonableness tests, etc.

Auditing Through the Computer

The concept which underlies the "through" the computer approach is that if the processing is done accurately and completely and the input or organization data are correct, then the end product is accurate and complete.

Therefore, in this approach the emphasis is on the *processing* system. Hence, it is important that the processing system being tested is proved out satisfactorily.

There are several tools and techniques that have been developed to assist the auditor in testing and proving out the processing system.

Eleven techniques are discussed in Chapter V.

FIGURE 3.6 ILLUSTRATION OF THE APPLICATION OF THE AUDITAPE SYSTEM TO SAMPLING A&G RECORDS

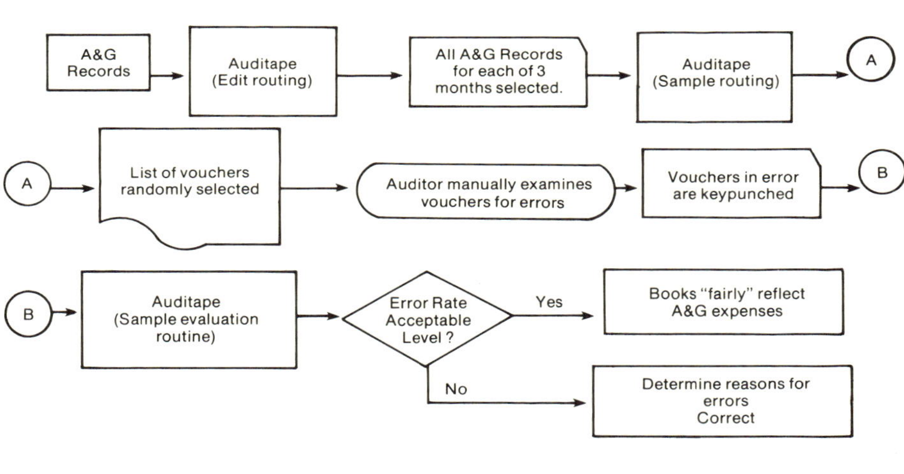

Importance of Internal Control

Regardless of which approach is used the auditor continues to place emphasis upon the quality control standards under which the data flow through the system from input to output, from initial transactions to final reports or data storage.

Identifying and evaluating the effectiveness of such standards are the subject of the discussion in the next chapter on Internal Control.

FOOTNOTES

[1]James Martin, *Security, Accuracy, and Privacy in Computer Systems*, Englewood Cliffs, NJ: Prentice-Hall, Inc., 1973, pp. 3-4.

[2]William L. Campfield, "Trends in Auditing Management Plans and Operations," *The Journal of Accountancy*, July 1967, p. 42.

[3]U.S. General Accounting Office, *Standards for the Audit of Governmental Organizations, Programs, Activities and Functions*, Washington, DC: U.S. Government Printing Office, 1972; reprint ed., 1974.

[4]R.K. Mautz, "Evidence, Judgement, and the Auditor's Opinion," *Journal of Accountancy*, April 1959, p. 43.

[5]I think of the accounting system and reports as a symbolic representation of the various transactions including management choices and decisions which result in changes with respect to things owned (assets) and things owed (liabilities and equity) and/or on goals, objectives, and activities of the organization. Accounting in a sense is modeling, that is, placing of symbols according to certain rules to form a structure which corresponds to a real world under study. The accounting system is both an analogue and schematic model. In the former, dollars are used to represent the values and in the latter the accounting equation depicts the relationship between management decisions and activities on the goals and objectives of the organization (profits, effectiveness, etc.). See Gordon L. Lippitt, *Visualizing Change: Model Building and the Change Process*, Fairfax, VA: NTL Learning Resources Corporation, Inc., 1973.

[6]For example, the financial statements may contain a representation that cash in bank is $100,000. The auditor must satisfy himself first that the statement really refers to cash in bank and secondly, that the amount is actually $100,000. In this case, the auditor would secure bank statements as to the amount shown on the books. The auditor is then in a position to give his opinion that the statement "cash in the bank of $100,000 'fairly' represents the position of the company."

[7]Various tests and references on the application of social science research to program evaluation and policy analysis are available. Among them are: D.L. Cornick, "Towards an Action/Contingency Theory of Budgeting," Ph.D. dissertation, University of Southern California, 1979; David Fox, *The Research Process in Education*, New York: Holt, Rinehart and Winston, Inc., 1969; Harry P. Hatry, *et al.*, *Practical Program Evaluation for State and Local Government Officials*, Washington, DC: The Urban Institute, 1973, especially the bibliography, pp. 127-134; Peter H. Rossi and Walter Williams, *Evaluating Social Programs: Theory, Practice and Politics*, NY: Seminar Press, 1972; and Claire Selltiz, *et al.*, *Research Methods in Social Relations*, 3rd ed., New York: Holt, Rinehart and Winston, Inc., 1976.

[8]Mautz, *op. cit.*, p. 43.

[9]Threats to validity are analogous to threats to validity in research findings in which confounding variables such as fatigue on the part of the research subjects, interview bias, etc., may account for the results rather than the experimental variables. Donald T. Campbell and Julian C. Stanley, *Experimental and Quasi-Experimental Designs for Research*, Chicago: Rand McNally College Publishing Company, 1963, pp. 5-6. In financial auditing, the auditor seeks evidence that the financial reports and the financial status of the firm have been energized by

bona fide (i.e., authentic, made in good faith, free from error or conforming exactly to truth or to a standard) transactions and management decisions.

[10]U.S. Department of Commerce, *Guidelines for Automatic Data Processing Risk Analysis*, Washington, DC: National Bureau of Standards, Federal Information Processing Standards Publication No. 65, 1979.

CHAPTER IV
THE ROLE OF INTERNAL CONTROL IN EDP AUDITING

It was pointed out in Chapter I that the auditing paradigm remains essentially the same as the computer environment expands, namely, to obtain competent evidential matter (audit trails) and to make a proper study and evaluation of the existing internal control. Much of the literature from the earliest days of the use of electric accounting machines (EAM) to the present era of minicomputers and telecommunications supports the single paradigm theory.

There are innumerable "how to" books, guides, reports, manuals on the subject of internal control, some of which are presented in Part II—Annotated Bibliography. Several are reviewed in this chapter to illustrate not only the variety of sources on the subject but also to illustrate the similarity of the various approaches, to underscore the importance of internal control in the EDP environment, and to highlight certain issues.

For example, while much of the literature emphasizes the technical aspect of control systems there is growing attention to the "behavioral" implications of control. Especially with the rise of unionism,[1] job displacement anxieties that sometime accompany the initial stages of EDP growth,[2] and the motivations of would-be perpetrators, including the challenge of "beating the system," or cheating a large corporation.[3]

THE OBJECTIVES OF INTERNAL CONTROL

Standards of audit practice require that there be "a proper study and evaluation of the existing Internal Control as a basis for reliance thereon and for the determination of the resultant extent of the tests to which auditing procedures are to be restricted."[4]

Internal control comprises the plan of organization and all the coordinate methods and measures adopted by an organization to:

- Safeguard its assets.
- Assure the accuracy and reliability of financial information.
- Assure compliance with laws, regulations, executive orders and other imposed requirements.
- Promote economy, efficiency, and effectiveness in operations.

More specifically, the basic elements of an internal control system include:

1. A plan of *organization* that provides segregation of duties appropriate for proper safeguarding of the entity's resources.
2. A system of *authorization and record* procedures adequate to provide effective accounting control over assets, liabilities, revenues, and expenses.
3. An established *system of practices* to be followed in performance of duties and functions of each of the organizational departments.
4. Personnel of a quality commensurate with their responsibilities.
5. An effective system of *internal review.*

The responsibility for internal control, as discussed in Chapter I, rests with management in exercising its stewardship over the agency or organization.[5]

The auditor's responsibility is the proper study and evaluation of the existing internal control, that is, to determine the extent to which the system can be relied upon to insure accurate information, to insure compliance with laws and regulations, and to insure efficient and effective operations. This concept of study and evaluation is expanded in the EDP environment to include the auditor's participation in reviewing the design and development of new data processing systems, both hardware and software, or applications, and significant modifications.[6]

The concept of "evaluation" presupposes the existence of objectives by which actual performance is to be measured. Therefore the study of internal control must take place in the context of objectives.

EVALUATING INTERNAL CONTROLS

Many of the internal control questionnaires used by auditors are written in terms of objectives. The Canadian Institute of Chartered

Accountants in its study of computer controls provides a number of objectives (and related verification techniques), several of which are presented in Figure 4.1.[7] Once the control techniques have been documented, the auditor must then begin the evaluation process by judging whether or not the techniques provide reasonable assurance that the objective is achieved, only partially achieved or not achieved (Figure 4.2). If the judgment is that the objective is achieved it means that there is reasonable assurance that the material errors or irregularities associated with the objective will be prevented or detected by the stated control techniques. A judgment to the contrary means that reasonable assurance is lacking and that errors or irregularities could occur and not be detected and corrected through routine execution of the stated processing and control techniques.

The auditor must then make a judgment based upon the internal control study whether or not the need for additional audit tests are unlikely, likely or virtually certain unless another information source can be used or the auditor is satisfied that the risk is acceptable.[8]

Judgment is difficult to define but is generally based upon experience and/or various techniques for decisionmaking under uncertainty. Measures of "acceptability" may include the concept of *materiality* or *expected value*.

As used here, materiality is the notion of whether or not a reasonable person, manager, auditor, investor, client, would have assigned significance to the item or facts in making his decision. That is, would the decisionmaker have arrived at a different conclusion or taken a different course of action.

The expected value concept involves an assessment of the risk (dollar value of a loss, for instance) weighed by the probability or likelihood of the risk occurring (one chance in 50, for instance).

Both concepts involve judgment which is discussed in more detail in Chapter VI.

The SAS No. 3 Review

Many CPA audit firms and internal audit functions have established an "SAS No. 3 review" capability. "SAS No. 3" refers to the statement on auditing standards (AICPA) which calls for an assessment of the internal control in an EDP environment. The capability generally consists of a general auditor with some experience with EDP including proficiency in at least one programming language. This person (or persons) may be teamed with an EDP computer specialist.

FIGURE 4.1 SELECTED AUDIT AND CONTROL OBJECTIVES AND ASSOCIATED VERIFICATION TECHNIQUES

OBJECTIVES	VERIFICATION TECHNIQUES
• To provide effective organizational control over the concentration of functions in the EDP Department.	Establish through review and analysis of the input phase of the processing cycle, that the EDP Department is *not* involved in the initiation of transactions.
• To insure that management exercises effective control over deployment of computer resources.	Determine through review of approval procedures, standards, manuals and related documentation, that management participates in the establishment of standards.
. . . .	
• To prevent or detect accidental errors occurring during processing by the EDP Department.	Ascertain through examination of control logs and other documentation, that the control group scrutinizes all input and re-entry documents for completeness.
	Trace a few rejected items to the related documentation to verify that they do in fact violate the edit controls and that they have been subsequently corrected and re-entered.
• To prevent or detect fraudulent manipulation of data during processing by the EDP Department and to prevent misuse of classified information.	Establish through discussion and observation, that computer operators, programmers and systems designers do not have access to related assets or to unused critical documents.
• To provide security against accidental destruction of records and to insure continuous operation.	Determine, through review of operating instructions and library procedures that the maintenance of back files is provided for.
• To ensure the completeness of data processed by the computer.	Determine through discussion and observation, the existence, terms of reference and independence of the control group.
• To ensure the accuracy of data processed by the computer.	Determine the existence of manual editing procedures. Trace out-of-balance conditions from control logs to evidence of subsequent correction and re-entry.
	Determine, through observation, that self-checking digets are being used or key codes not otherwise controlled.
	(Cont'd)

FIGURE 4.1–Cont'd.

OBJECTIVES	VERIFICATION TECHNIQUES
• To ensure that all data processed by the computer is authorized.	Determine that the authorization function is separate from the responsibilities for processing transactions and for custody of assets.
• To ensure the adequacy of management audit trails.	Determine, through discussion, observation, and examination of documents and printouts of machine sensible files, that each item can be identified and subsequently retrieved.
• To ensure that adequate documentation exists and is effectively controlled.	Determine, through observation and inspection, the existence of documentation standards and that these specifically include standards relating to each of the following: systems documentation, programming documentation, operating documentation, library or file control documentation, keypunching and/or other data conversion documentation, and input and output control documentation.

SOURCE: Objectives are based on types of controls in *Computer Control Guidelines* (1970), especially Chapters II through VI; verification techniques are based on those in *Computer Audit Guidelines* (1975), compiled by the author with permission from the publisher, the Canadian Institute of Chartered Accountants, Toronto, Canada.

Essentially, the auditor determines the "materiality" or impact of EDP on the company or agency's accounting system. For example, in an agency which is labor intensive, salaries and wages may account for over 70 percent of its expenditures. Then a computerized payroll system and other computerized human resources control systems such as manpower planning utilization would be material. The second step is to determine the adequacy of the general controls over the EDP function within the organization. This is done by a review of the general control procedures based upon representations by the client. If the auditor is satisfied with the adequacy of the general controls, he then reviews the controls over the various applications (i.e., payroll, inventory, etc.). If the auditor is satisfied that the system *as presented by the client* is adequate, then he proceeds to *test* both the general controls and the application controls. If the auditor is not satisfied with the results of

FIGURE 4.2 STUDY AND EVALUATION OF EDP-BASED SYSTEMS

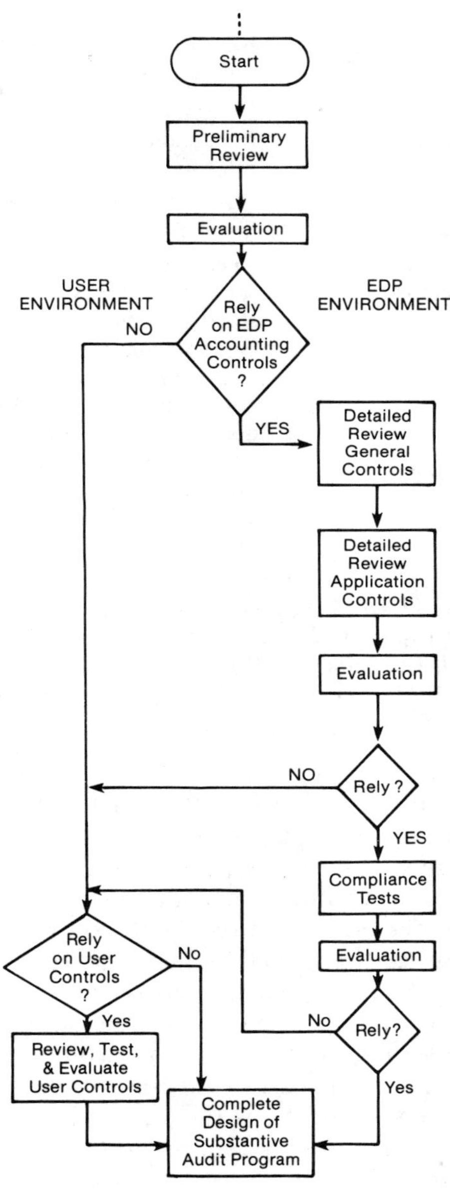

the client's representations or the test results he will then audit "around" the computer and increase the reliance on extended audit procedures—confirmations, observations, larger samples, third party evidence, etc. On the other hand, if the auditor is satisfied with the adequacy of controls he will audit through the computer, using various computer assisted auditing techniques (see Chapter V). Where the client uses a computer service, the auditor will evaluate the internal control at the service center and/or conduct a *third party review* to assess the risks to the client based upon an evaluation of the service center's independent auditor's report. This third party review is discussed later in this chapter. The SAS No. 3 review addresses both the managerial controls and the EDP department controls.

The systems approach concept discussed in Chapter III (see Figure 3.1)—that is, the managerial subsystem, the technical subsystem and the user subsystem—provides a framework for the discussion of managerial controls, EDP general controls and application controls.

MANAGERIAL CONTROL

Managerial control refers to the system of separation of duties, a network of authorizations and approvals, a system for safeguarding assets, and provision to insure that the organization operates as prescribed by management.

Two areas of concern in meeting these objectives are (1) those controls to provide security and reduce the threat of computer abuse and (2) the auditor's role in systems development. Auditors are becoming increasingly concerned with management's efficient and effective use of EDP as evidenced by the growing emphasis placed on EDP management auditing and the use of the system's development life cycle (SDLC) approach discussed below.[9]

The Auditor's Role in Systems Development

Both auditors and management officials have an interest in assuring that system design, development, and overall operations achieve the objectives of adequate internal control and effective auditability. For systems already in existence when audits are made, the auditor should determine whether the objectives of the systems are being achieved.

As capabilities of computer-based information systems have grown, the systems and applications have grown more complex and interrelated. Initially, there were separate automated applications for personnel, payroll, and labor cost accounting. Each application or system would be processed independently of the others, and their input material would be generated from separate and distinct sources and be processed against separate data files.

With the integration of application systems now being encountered, the payroll, personnel, and labor-cost-accounting applications can be interrelated subsystems of a far larger online system, and the outputs of one subsystem can now be the inputs for another without any human review. Thus, a control weakness in one segment of the system may have completely unanticipated effects causing catastrophic results. Such mistakes, waste, and general confusion may even adversely affect the viability of the organization.

Furthermore, because of the difficulty in effecting changes after an EDP system has been implemented, the auditor may want to become familiar with the design and testing of new EDP systems at an early stage in the development process in order to anticipate possible problems in future audits of these systems.[10]

The U.S. General Accounting Office Standards provide six objectives and related tests of requiring auditor participation in system design, development, and modification.[11] These objectives are:

> **Objective 1**: To assure that systems/applications faithfully carry out the policies *management* has prescribed for the system.
>
> Policies setting forth what is expected of ADP systems should be established by management, and the auditor should determine whether these policies are being carried out in the design. The auditor should ascertain that an appropriate approval process is being followed, both in the development of new systems and in the making of modifications to existing systems. The auditor should consider the need for approval of the system's design by data processing management, user groups, and other groups whose data and reports may be affected. Also, the auditor should review the provisions for security that are required by management to protect data for programs against unauthorized access and modification.
>
> If management's requirements are not being met, the auditor has the responsibility to report such shortcomings to the appropriate officials who can effect corrective action. Frequently in the past, efforts to bring new systems/applications on the air by scheduled dates have resulted in some management-desired elements or controls being set aside by system designers, for later consideration. The auditor, in retaining his independence during the system design and development cycle, should report such actions to top management for appropriate resolution.

Objective 2: To provide assurance that systems/applications provide the controls and *audit trails* needed for management, auditor, and operational review.

In financial applications, it is considered a basic tenet that there be a capability to trace a transaction from its initiation, through all the intermediate processing steps, to the resulting financial statements. Similarly, information in the financial statements must be traceable to its origination. Such capability is referred to by a variety of terms—audit trail, management trail, transaction trail, etc.—and is also highly essential in nonfinancial systems/applications. A proper assessment of the reliability of the output can be made only when each step can be isolated and the controls over it (both manual and automated) can be evaluated.

Audit review of the system design and development process can help assure management that this capability is in fact being engineered into the system/application.

Objective 3: To provide assurance to management that systems/applications include the *controls* necessary to protect against loss or serious error.

The system design and development processes include (1) definition of the processing to be carried out by a computer, (2) design of the processing steps to be followed, (3) determination of the data input and files that will be required, and (4) specification of each individual program's input data and output. Each of these areas must be properly controlled, in consonance with good management practices, and the auditor's review of these matters must provide management assurance that the system/application, once placed in operation, will meet this objective.

(It is possible for properly designed systems, with excellent control mechanisms built in, to have these controls bypassed or overridden. This area is addressed under supplemental standards 2 and 3.)

Note that almost every system has manual aspects (e.g., input origination, output disposition) and these should be covered for adequacy by the auditor reviewing systems controls.

Objective 4: To provide assurance that systems/applications will be efficient and economical in operation.

Determining whether an organization is managing and utilizing its resources (personnel, property, space, etc.) in an efficient and economical manner, and reporting on the causes of inefficiencies or uneconomical pratices, including inadequacies in management information systems, administrative procedures, or organizational structures, are set forth in the basic standards booklet as a basic characteristic of audit work in reviewing Government programs. With the development of complex systems/applications, the internal auditor's review should also demonstrate that operations will produce desired results at minimum cost. For example, early in the system's development stage, the auditor should review the adequacy of the (1) statement of mission needs and system objectives, (2) feasibility study and evaluation of alternative designs to meet those needs and objectives, and (3) cost-benefit analysis which attributes specific benefits and costs to system alternatives.

Objective 5: To assure that systems/applications conform with applicable *legal* requirements.

Legal requirements applicable to systems/applications may originate from a variety of sources. One such requirement is compliance with privacy statutes enacted at State and Federal levels, in which certain types of information about individuals are restricted as to collection and use. Appropriate safeguards are obviously necessary in such systems. Conversely, those organizations subject to the Freedom of Information Act should have systems/applications designed so that appropriate and timely response can be made to legitimate requests under the statute. The applicability of the Federal Information Processing Standards program to the system involved should also be checked by the auditor. If such standards apply, they should be included in the auditors' review.

Once again, auditor participation in the design and development process will serve to assure management that these requirements have been considered and satisfied.

Objective 6: To provide assurance that systems/applications are *documented* in a manner that will provide the understanding of the system required for appropriate maintainance and auditing.

The auditor should determine whether the design/modification process produces documentation sufficient to define (1) the processing that must be performed by programs in the system, (2) the data files to be processed, (3) the reports to be prepared for users, (4) the operating instructions for use by computer operators, and (5) the user group instructions for preparation and control of data. The auditor should also ascertain whether management policy provides for evaluation of documentation and adequate test of the system before it is made operational. These steps are to assure that reliance can be placed in the system and its controls.

The methods of achieving these objectives will be determined by the circumstances attending the specific situation. Generally, such audit work will cover reviewing adequacy of management policies, examining approvals, documentation, test results, and cost studies and other data to determine whether management policies and legal requirements are being followed; and determining whether the system possesses the necessary control features and trails.

> The auditor should not become part of the system design/development team to perform work under this supplemental standard. His involvement should be limited to reviewing what is being done by the team and reporting to management his objective evaluation of the effort.
>
> At the completion of the design and development phases, and during final system testing phases, the auditor should verify that the implemented system conforms with these six objectives.

One technique that holds promise in meeting the above objectives is the Systems Development Life Cycle (SDLC).

Systems Development Life Cycle (SDLC)[1 2]

As discussed earlier in this chapter, there are imperatives that auditors, both internal and external, become involved in the systems development process, i.e., the design and testing prior to going "online." By carefully controlling the system development process, one can achieve higher levels of accuracy and reliability in the computer application systems developed and satisfy the goals of achieving quality application systems within cost and on schedule. The System Development Life Cycle is a technique used to divide the system development process into a small number of distinct phases with formal management control points placed between and during each phase.

The objectives in using an SDLC technique are twofold: to provide a more structured management scheme for controlling costs and schedules, and to ensure proper and responsive communications channels among users, EDP auditors, hardware planning personnel, top management, and the data processing personnel responsible for developing the application systems. While there are various definitions and techniques, SDLC may be viewed in terms of seven phases:

- **Project definition**—that phase whose primary purpose is to define the user requirements and uses for the system.

- **System analysis and design**—that phase in which an overall description of the system is prepared.

- **Detailed design and programming**—that phase that focuses on the internal components of the system and the development of computer programs needed to form the system.

- **System test**—that phase in which the system is exercised to determine the correctness and completeness of implementation to the user requirements as manifest in the design documents.

- **Conversion**—that phase in which the tested system and operational procedures are initiated to move the system into a full operational mode.
- **Operational**—that phase concerned with ongoing operation, program changes, and maintenance, and
- **Post-implementation**—that phase concerned with whether the system performs as intended by the user, with focus on methods to improve the development process.

There are controls established throughout these phases. The requirements of each must be satisfied before the particular phase or the next phase can be continued. The controls are divided in terms of general management (the point of interface between the managerial and the technical subsystems) and controls within the technical subsystem.

The six managerial controls discussed in the *SAC* study are:

- **Control Point 1**—The EDP auditor, user, and the project leader review the project organization, the arrangements with the user for communications, and the plans and work program for the design. This central point helps the project leader to establish a good working relationship with the user to ensure that the system reflects user requirements.
- **Control Point 2**—The user, EDP auditor, and project leader review the analysis and planned cost for completeness and accuracy. In addition, the project control and communications plan is discussed and changed if necessary. The user plays a major role at this control point in assuring himself that proper analysis has taken place.
- **Control Point 3**—The user, EDP auditor, and project leader review the conceptual design documentation for accuracy, completeness, and any changes that may have occurred. A revised cost-benefit plan is developed, and the EDP auditor presents the findings to top management.
- **Control Point 4**—The user, EDP auditor, and project leader review the project organization resulting from the first phase, the communication links established between team members, users, and EDP auditors, schedules and work plans, and other items germane to the specific project.
- **Control Point 5**—The user, EDP auditor, computer operation personnel, and the project leader review the conversion plan for

completeness of detail and personnel involved. Plans for communicating the production schedule to top management are discussed as well as other miscellaneous considerations germane to the specific project.

- **Control Point 6**—The user, EDP auditor, and project leader review all problems not yet resolved, adequacy of documentation, and any incomplete activities identified. Final reports on the project status can then be written by the EDP auditor.

Nine (9) computer processing controls are discussed in the SAC study:

- **Control Point 1**—The EDP auditor, user, project leader, and design analysts review the detailed design output reports for completeness and clarity. The EDP auditor attempts to ensure that sufficient design documentation exists to allow for a clear understanding by the test team and the EDP audit staff.

- **Control Point 2**—The user, EDP auditor, project leader, and design analysts review the file requirement specifications and the input requirements associated with them. The user attempts to ensure that the file requirements do not implicitly or explicitly change the original system specifications.

- **Control Point 3**—The user, project leader, EDP auditor and other data processing personnel responsible for hardware planning review the equipment requirements to meet the requirements of the designed systems. Completeness of the equipment requirement is important to avoid unanticipated equipment costs at a later date.

- **Control Point 4**—The EDP auditor, user, and project leader review the design from cost, data processing standards, and general management points of view. The project leader is interested in ensuring that all loose ends from the past two phases are in place before moving into the detailed design phase.

- **Control Point 5**—The EDP auditor, project leader, user, and data processing personnel make a final review of plans, equipment, costs, project organization, and communications channels to ensure that all participants have agreed upon the status and direction of the project. The project leader is primarily concerned with assuring top management that sufficient systems analysis and design have taken place before the detailed design phase.

- **Control Point 6**—The EDP auditor, user, and project leader review the documentation scheme and documents available describing the file systems, interface data handler programs, and program run documents for compliance to standards, completeness, accuracy, and clarity. The project leader is primarily concerned with ensuring that the project team is providing adequate documentation to meet data processing and user documentation standards.

- **Control Point 7**—The EDP auditor, the project team members, testers, and user review the detailed system design to ensure that it follows from the general system design and still meets the user's requirements. In addition, the test plan is reviewed for completeness, timing, and cost. The conversion plan and associated paperwork are reviewed for reasonableness, completeness, and clarity. As this is the last checkpoint before the test phase, the project leader takes special care to ensure that the original design requirements are still intact or that a traceable trail exists that explains to top management and users why the system has changed.

- **Control Point 8**—The EDP auditor, testers, user, and project leader review the test team organization to ensure that the proper people are present and that the project test plan is complete and consistent. The project leader is primarily concerned with assuring himself that the test plan will completely test the system and in particular will test the internal controls designed in the system.

- **Control Point 9**—The EDP auditor, user, and testers develop test data, build masterfiles, review test results and monitor the test plan progress to ensure that it is adhered to throughout the test phase.

These are controls over system quality. The SDLC techniques do provide an opportunity for users and auditors to participate in all stages of application development and, hopefully, provide a means to develop more reliable and higher quality systems that can provide a high degree of data integrity[13] including the general and application controls governing the EDP function.

Security Controls and Computer Abuse

It is axiomatic that the various objectives of internal control—safeguarding assets, accuracy and reliability of financial information, economy efficiency, and effectiveness of operations—require that management establish adequate controls in areas of physical facilities, personnel and security.

The subject of computer abuse provides a useful framework for discussion of internal control as it relates to physical facilities, personnel and security controls. One definition of computer abuse is: "all types of acts distinctly associated with computers and data communication in which victims involuntarily suffer or could have suffered losses, injuries or damages, or in which perpetrators receive or could have received gain.[14]

The Stanford Research Institute study on computer abuse concluded that the computer plays the four basic roles of object, environment, tool and symbol (Figure 4.3). This model may be of use to auditors in assessing internal control as it relates to computer abuse.

The SRI study report observed that computer technology has introduced new factors concerning types of perpetrators, the forms of assets threatened, and embezzlement methods. The study concluded that:

- Programmers, system analysts, and computer and keypunch operators, either alone or in collusion with bank employees traditionally associated with embezzlement, represent new occupations in positions of trust and temptation. Asset data electronically and magnetically stored within computer systems are becoming popular targets, along with the negotiable instrument forms of assets.

- Computer-related embezzlement methods include old elements of kiting, lapping, creating fictitious float, and manipulating checks, cash, and inactive accounts; but they now are perpetrated in EDP environments requiring modification or at least detailed knowledge of the computer programs and data file structures. Computer programs represent more exact and predetermined processes compared with the work procedures assigned to people in the previous manual systems, presenting a different environment for the embezzler.

- The characteristics of the average bank embezzler have not changed much in the past 35 years. According to the FBI he is about 32 to 36 years old, he is married, and he has two children. However, one significant embezzlement feature has changed: the average bank embezzlement now continues for more than three years before discovery, a year longer than the period shown in 1935 statistics. According to the FBI, most embezzlers are not motivated by living beyond their means.

- Of the cases examined in one study, 41 percent involved the unauthorized extension of credit to a customer and resulted in no personal benefit to the embezzler. In 22 percent of the cases,

FIGURE 4.3 THE FOUR ROLES OF THE COMPUTER IN COMPUTER ABUSE AS OBJECT, ENVIRONMENT, TOOL AND SYMBOL

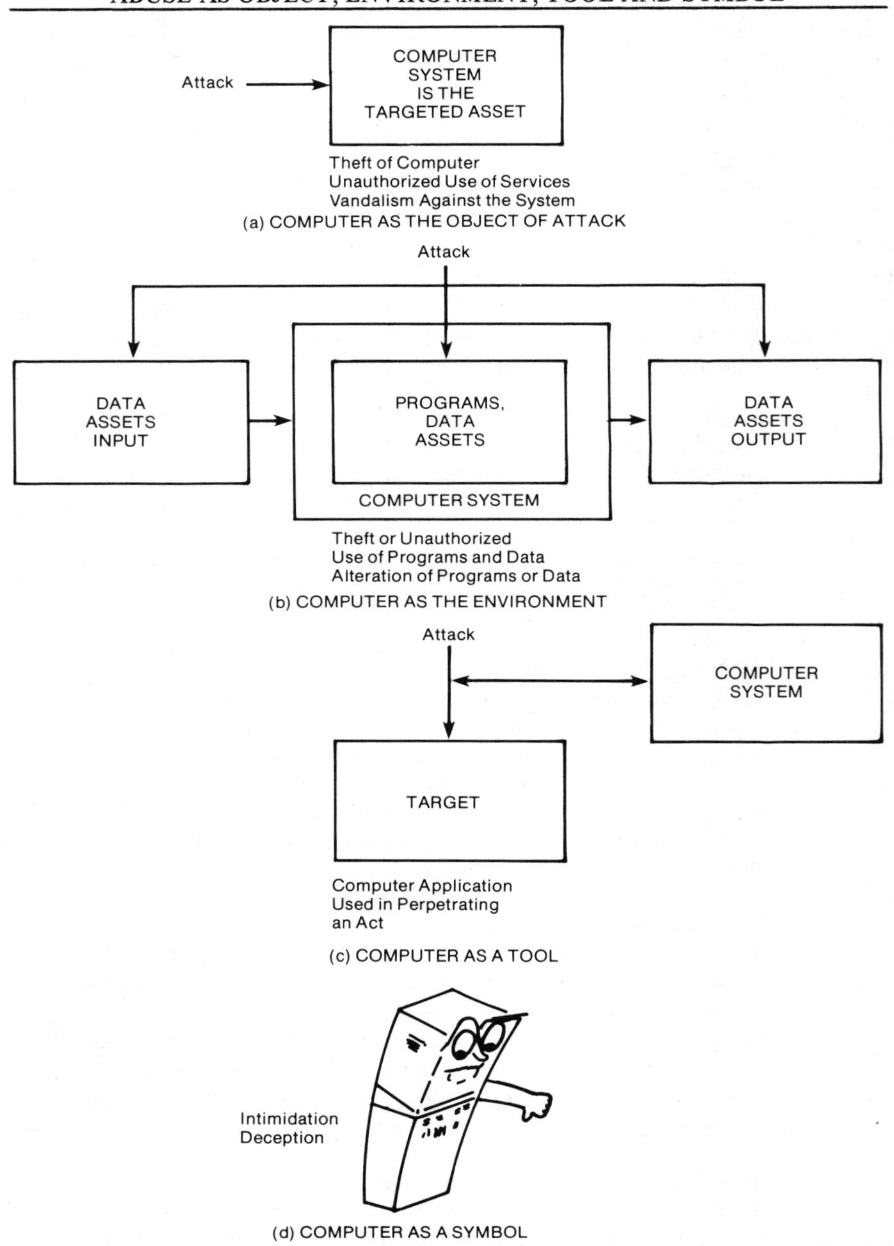

SOURCE: Stanford Research Institute, *op. cit.*, p. 31.

the perpetrator used stolen funds to engage in other business. Only 19 percent of the perpetrators were living beyond their means or were gambling.

- Two kinds of simple embezzlement (without collusion) are associated with computer systems. External embezzlement is performed outside the computer system but requires the manipulation of input and output based on a knowledge of the computer application. Internal embezzlement originates from within the computer system staff. It requires the following:

  (1) Access to a computer
  (2) Access to data files
  (3) Access to computer programs
  (4) System knowledge
  (5) Means of converting fraudulent activity to personal gain.

  Embezzlement can consist of both internal and external fraud when perpetrated by several people in collusion.[15]

In an EDP environment there is the problem of separation between the data processing function and other functional areas of the organization and the problem of separation of various duties *within* the data processing function.

EDP has exacerbated this problem in several ways. It has resulted in: (1) reduction in the amount of human intervention; (2) centralized processing or integration of the various functions into a single or few computer programs; (3) transmitting data from one computer program to another—in many cases with little display of intermediate data in non-machine sensible form; (4) controls no longer visible; and (5) exposing the system to manipulation and fraud by the small number of people and the high degree of mechanization. An EDP system often places a single person, who has both operational knowledge and easy access to procedures and programs at all levels, in a position to both perpetrate and conceal errors or irregularities in the normal course of his or her duties.

Who are these perpetrators? The Stanford Research Institute reported that they are:

1. White-collar amateurs rather than emotional or professional criminals.

2. Seldom women.

3. Between the ages of 18 and 30.

4. Knowledgeable of the computer and the system to be penetrated.

5. Motivated by diverse objectives such as the challenge of penetrating the system and the "Robin Hood" syndrome, i.e., to get even with the victim company which the perpetrator believes does great harm to society.

Figure 4.4 provides a schema of a computer abuse incident which is a useful guide to auditors in assessing the potential for computer abuse incidents.

The importance of the various internal controls to reduce the risks of computer abuse may be emphasized by relating cases of fraud to the effectiveness of various controls. Consider the following illustrations:[16]

1. An EDP employee embezzled $190,500 by inflating payroll totals in order to make use of blank checks produced at the beginning and end of the payroll printer runs. He filled in the blank checks and forged the endorsements. The absence or ineffectiveness of various controls were deemed significant in the above situation. For example:

   a. a deficiency in the requirement that there be separation of functions within the EDP department and between the EDP department and users.

   b. a control function should be responsible for receiving all data to be processed, insuring that all data are recorded, following up on errors detected during processing to see that they are corrected and resubmitted by the proper party, and verifying the proper distribution of output.

   c. control totals should be produced and reconciled with input control controls.

2. A computer operator printed copies of unemployment checks and deleted the copied record from the file. An auditor discovered the $10,000 fraud in a computer audit run. Again, an examination of internal controls revealed the ineffectiveness of various controls, for example, a deficiency in the requirement that:

FIGURE 4.4 SEQUENTIAL FLOW DIAGRAM OF COMPUTER ABUSE INDICENT

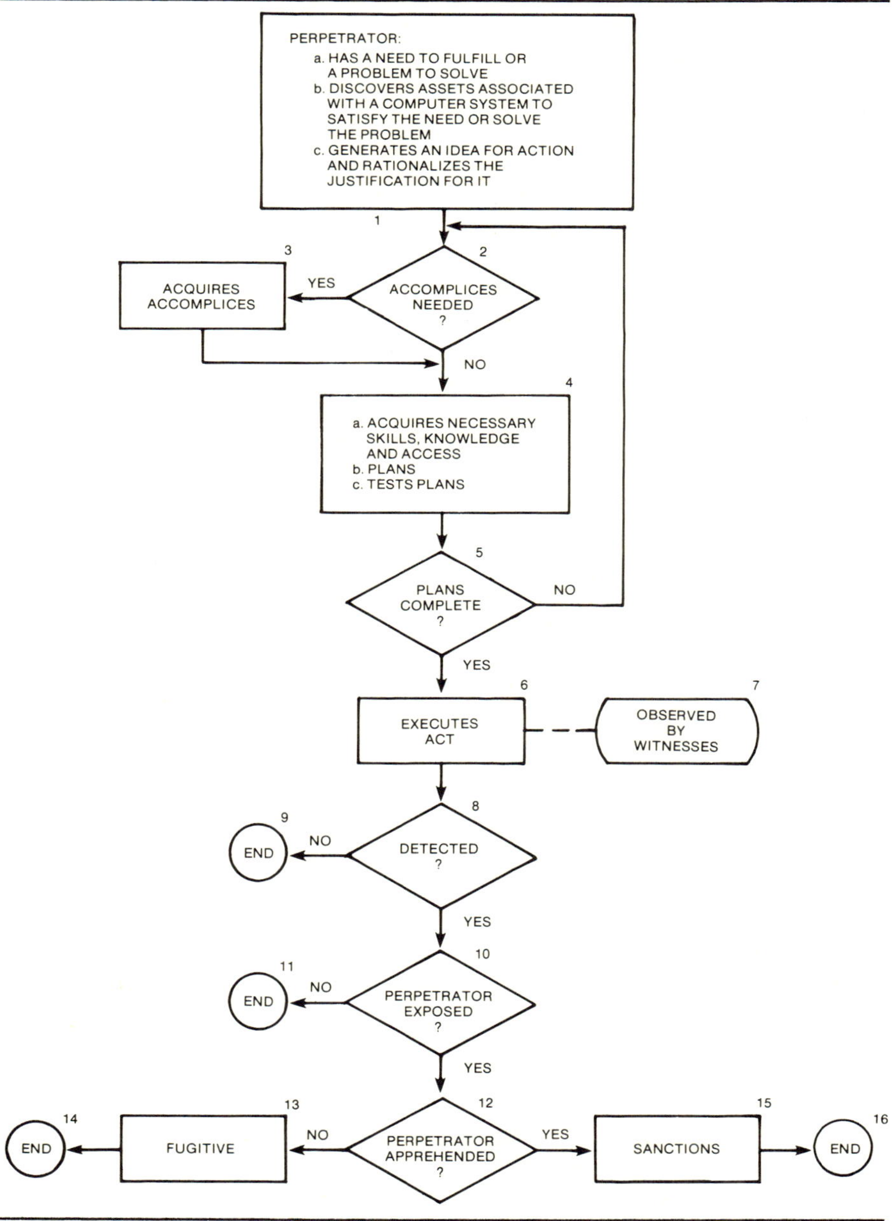

SOURCE: Stanford Research Institute, *op. cit.*, p. 37.

a. the internal auditors or some other independent group within an organization should review and test computer processing activities on a continuing basis.

b. run-to-run controls should be verified at appropriate points in the processing cycle.

Personnel management—including supervision, motivation, and professional development of personnel—is not only integral to the successful management of the EDP function but is also a security factor. Related to personnel management and security is the emerging significance of unionism in data processing. The potential for strikes, restrictions over separation of duties, and risk to data integrity may be enhanced by the negotiating process and/or the ensuing agreements.[17]

As pointed out earlier, the auditor is required to assess motivation and human behavior as part of his assessment of internal control.

Behavior may range from deliberate sabotage to enthusiastic support for the organization and the system (Figure 4.5),[18] *goal* directed, i.e., motivated. The behavior may result from normal resistance to change, from the shift in the distribution of power which generally accompanies technological change, or from a variety of needs.

Internal Control and Motivation

The effectiveness of internal control systems depend upon people, their motivations and their acceptance of the system of controls. Designers of control systems are still apparently far more concerned with the technical excellence and sophistication of their systems and procedures than with their implications for human behavior. The behavioralist theory maintains that control is in reality the individual member of an organization who exercises control, who accepts or rejects the standards, who does or does not exercise care in the performance of his or her duty, or who responds to pressures other than the pressure to conform to the standards or controls.[19]

The acceptance or rejection or response to other pressures may be due to a variety of needs or goals towards which individual behavior is directed, i.e. the individual's motivation. Almost a half-century ago Chester Barnard wrote that the behavior of individuals are the results of psychological factors and social factors which have determined the history and the present state of the individual in relation to his present environment.[20]

FIGURE 4.5 HUMAN BEHAVIOR IN AN EDP SYSTEM ENVIRONMENT

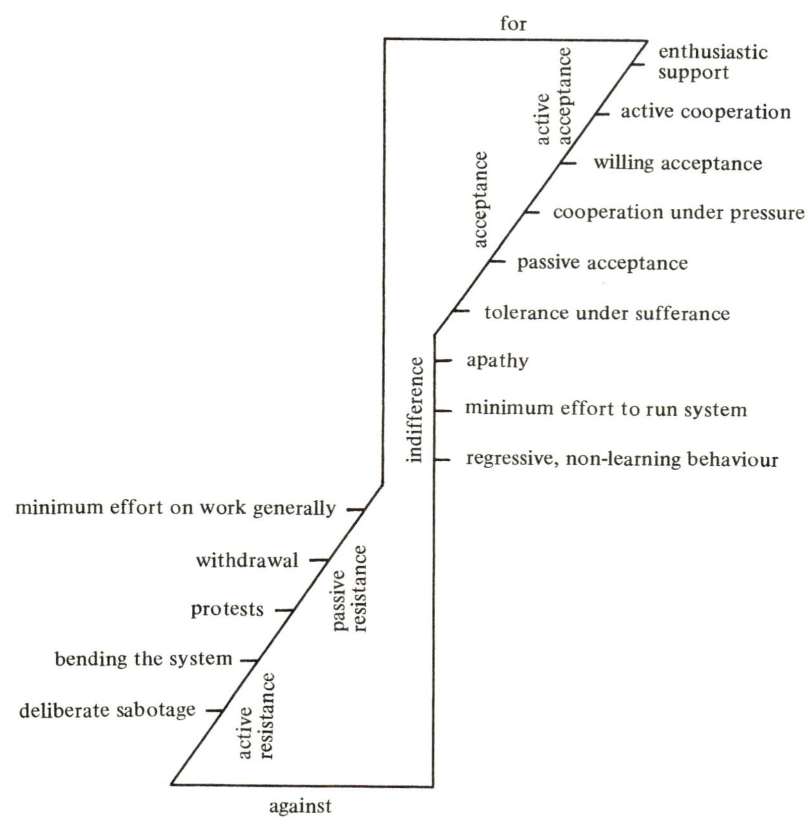

SOURCE: Keith R. London, "Figure 4.5: The System Acceptance/Rejection Spectrum," *The People Side of Systems: The Human Aspects of Computer Systems*, McGraw-Hill Book Co. (U.K.) Limited.

Related to this notion are the findings which stem from the research of Elton Mayo, Roethlisberger, and Whitehead at the Hawthorne Plant of the Western Electric Company in the early 1930s. It was found that psychological factors and sociological factors had a bearing on worker motivation. Among these findings were:

1. Objects, persons, and events are carriers of social meanings. They become related to employee satisfaction or dissatisfaction only as the employee comes to view them from his personal situation;

2. The personal situation of the worker is a configuration of relationships composed of a personal reference involving sentiments, desires, and interests of that person and a social reference constituting the person's social past and his present interpersonal relations;

3. The position or status of the worker in the company is a reference from which the worker assigns meaning and value to the events, objects, and features of his environment, such as hours of work, wages, etc.;

4. The social organization of the company presents a system of values from which the worker derives satisfactions or dissatisfactions according to his conception of this social status and the expected social rewards;

5. The social demands of the worker are influenced by social experiences in groups both inside and outside the work plant;

6. And a complaint is not necessarily an objective recital of facts. It is a symptom of personal disturbances the cause of which may be deep seated.[21]

Each of the above factors may have significance in directing behavior away from compliance with the control systems towards opposition or indifference (Figure 4.5). The relevance of each of the above six findings to computer abuse is seen in the following discussion.

The notion that objects, persons and events are carriers of social meaning is significant when one considers that either the company and/or the computer may be seen as "evils." The computer may be putting people out of work or the company may be a multinational firm which is doing business with a nation currently in disfavor. Hence, the company's computer system may be the object of attack (see Figure 4.3).

The personal situation of the worker may be a factor in computer abuse. The causative factors for employee fraud are illustrated in a study by U.S. Fidelity and Guaranty Company as summarized in Krauss and MacGahan (see page 37) where living beyond one's means, gambling, alcoholism-related extravagance of spouse or children ranked highest among the various causes of fraud.

The position or status of the worker in relation to hours worked or wages can trigger revenge or "getting even" as a motive for computer abuse and fraud—situations in which a lack of fair play is perceived, such as inadequate compensation.

The social organization of the company can be interpreted as the position which the company, its policies and activities fit into the social values and norms of the employee, e.g., doing business with a country currently in disfavor.

The social demands of the worker are influenced by social experiences both within and outside the organization. Finally, complaints may be evidence of deep seated resentment and active resistance (bending the system or deliberate sabotage) to the company and to the EDP system in particular.

Therefore, in assessing the effectiveness of the internal control system the "people side" must always be considered. For example, a degree of quality of personnel commensurate with responsibilities is one of the essential elements of effective internal control. Elements of an effective personnel system should include:

1. an employee selection policy which stresses competence and honesty

2. a continuing training program

3. the proper screening of prospective employees

4. management's recognition of its moral obligation to employees to help them keep honest:

    a. undue temptation should not be placed before them

    b. genuine concern should be shown the employees' feelings and problems

    c. danger signals should be recognized

5. employee responsibility for accomplishing reasonably defined duties and tasks and secondary or non-priority tasks assignments for periods of main workload hiatus.[22]

Finally, as Leonard Krauss and Aileen MacGahan in their book on computer fraud pointed out, the probability of a company being a computer fraud victim is a function of three variables: the dishonesty of the would-be perpetrator; the opportunity the company provides the potential perpetrator through having inadequate controls, preventive measures, and deterrents; and the would-be perpetrator's underlying motive for committing fraud.[23]

TECHNICAL SUBSYSTEM CONTROLS

Technical subsystem controls refer to those controls within the EDP system which are classified as either *general* controls or *application* controls. General controls comprise: (a) the plan of organization and operation of the EDP activity; (b) the procedures for documenting, reviewing, testing and approving systems or programs and changes thereto; (c) controls built into the equipment by the manufacturer, i.e., hardware controls; (d) controls over access to equipment and data files; and (e) other data and procedural controls affecting overall EDP operations.

Application controls comprise those controls which relate to specific tasks of recording, processing and reporting of data. Application controls often are classified as "input controls," "processing controls" and "output controls."[24]

General Controls

More specifically, general controls are those controls that relate to all EDP activities and include:

1. Provision for the segregation of functions between the EDP Department and users, and among various activities *within* the EDP Department.

2. Provision for general authorization over the execution of transactions, for example, prohibiting the EDP Department from initiating or authorizing transactions.

3. Provision for security including controls over access of the computer programs, data files, data transmission, input and output material, and personnel.

4. Provision for documenting, review, testing and approval of new systems; control over program changes, and documentation procedures.

Eugene A. Blish has identified 19 general EDP controls (Table 4.1).

TABLE 4.1 GENERAL EDP CONTROLS

CONTROL NUMBER	TYPE	DESCRIPTION
1	Organization and operation	Segregation of functions between the EDP department and users.
2		Provision for general authorization over the execution of transactions.
3		Segregation of functions within the EDP department.
4	Systems development and documentation	The procedures for systems design, including the acquisition of software packages, should require active participation by representatives of the users and, as appropriate, the accounting department and internal auditors.
5		Each system should have written specifications which are reviewed and approved by an appropriate level of management and applicable user departments.
6		System testing should be a joint effort of users and EDP personnel and should include both the manual and computerized phases of the system.
7		Final approval should be obtained prior to placing a new system into operation.
8		All master file and transaction file conversions should be controlled to prevent unauthorized changes and to insure accurate and complete results.
9		After a new system has been placed in operation, all program changes should be approved before implementation to determine whether they have been authorized, tested, and documented.
10		Management should require various levels of documentation and establish formal procedures to define the system at appropriate levels of detail.
11	Hardware and systems software	The control features inherent in the computer hardware, operating system, and other supporting software should be utilized to the maximum possible extent to provide control over operations and to detect and report hardware malfunctions.

(cont'd)

TABLE 4.1–Cont'd.

CONTROL NUMBER	TYPE	DESCRIPTION
12		Systems software should be subjected to the same control procedures as those applied to installation of and changes to application programs.
13	Access	Access to program documentation should be limited to those persons who require it in the performance of their duties.
14		Access to data files and programs should be limited to those individuals authorized to process or maintain particular systems.
15		Access to computer hardware should be limited to authorized individuals.
16	Data and procedural	A control function should be responsible for receiving all data to be processed, insuring that all data are recorded, following up on errors detected during processing to see that they are corrected and resubmitted by the proper party, and verifying the proper distribution of output.
17		A written manual of systems and procedures should be prepared for all computer operations and should provide for management's general or specific authorization to process transactions.
18		Internal auditors or some other independent group within an organization should review and evaluate proposed systems at critical stages of development.
19		On a continuing basis, internal auditors or some other independent group within an organization should review and test computer processing activities.

SOURCE: Eugene A. Blish, "Computer Abuse: A Practical Use of the AICPA Guide," February 1978, pp. 6-12. Reprinted by permission of Automation Training Center, Inc.

Auditors generally evaluate internal control on the basis of answers to such questions as:

1. Does the agency have a formal plan or organization under which management responsibilities are clearly defined, reasonably aligned and adequately documented by an up to date organization chart?

2. If internal auditors are employed, does the internal audit unit report to an official independent of the operations under review?
3. Are duties separated so that no single individual can control a series of related transactions from beginning to end?
4. Are tangible assets periodically inspected, counted, and reconciled with the general accounting records?
5. Are new management systems properly reviewed and approved by managers before implementation?
6. Are employee training programs adequate?
7. Are employees periodically evaluated by managers?
8. Has a fiscal authority been formally delegated to specific management personnel?
9. Is there a general policy for both security and privacy throughout the entire organization?
10. Is there a top level plan, policies, and procedures for governing the design, implementation, and review of the EDP function?[25]

The auditor will use the data collected to form his opinion as to effectiveness of these controls in achieving internal control objectives.

Two concerns of management that sometimes are discussed within the context of general controls are controls in a computer service facility and controls in a data base management system (DBMS).

Controls in a Computer Service Center

When the client uses a service center, the auditor is particularly interested in service center controls over data transmitted by the client for processing; controls over processing and output; provisions for protection and security such as a disaster recovery plan; and provisions for passwords and authorization control in time sharing systems. Table 4.2 provides the basis for evaluating controls at a service center. The second control concern is data base management systems control.

The auditor will evaluate the third party review in order to determine the extent to which he will examine the input transmitted, the output received, and the extent to which he will rely on extended audit procedures (essentially what is described here is auditing "around" the computer, where the service center is the "Black Box" between input and output).

TABLE 4.2 A CHECKLIST FOR EVALUATING COMPUTER SERVICE CENTER CONTROLS

CONTROL AREA	CONTROL
Input/output scheduling and control	Input/output control group Job handling procedures Scheduling procedures Processing schedules Cutoff dates Job submission/authorization Input/output control group Daily work schedules
Media library controls	Access controls File release Separate library area Physical security Media restriction issuance Media inventory control procedures Media restriction quantity Media use records Handling equipment Security vaults Temperature and humidity control Off-site storage Duplicate file storage Redundancy and backup procedures
Malfunction reporting and preventive maintenance	Procedures reporting Problem documentation System utilization report System utilization reports review Vendor failures logging Resolutions problem logging Trouble reporting responsibility
Environmental controls and physical security	Physical security Access controls Backup for power, cooling, etc. Software backup Hardware backup
Separation of duties	Separation of duties within data processing Separation of data processing from other organizational units Computer programs to enforce separation between systems Automated controls to separate online users
Resources planning	Plan for facilities, equipment, software, and personnel Variance between actual and planned goals

(Cont'd)

TABLE 4.2–Cont'd

CONTROL AREA	CONTROL
User billing/charge-out procedures	Service contracts between the user and data processing Procedures to arbitrate disputes Chargeable versus free services Billing procedures tied to the computerized job accounting system Billing algorithm, periodic user billing statements, rerun cost allocation procedure
Disaster recovery	Disaster plan Disaster scenarios to update the disaster plan Top management's commitment to the disaster plan Maintenance and updating of the disaster plan User responsibility for the disaster plan Testing of the disaster plan User training in use of the disaster plan

SOURCE: SAC Study, p. 91. Reprinted by permission of the Institute of Internal Auditors, Inc.

Data Base Management System Control

Data base management controls are those controls over the data base, its use and management, including access and authorization, error handling, audit trails, monitoring of the data base, etc.

Auditors in evaluating internal control with respect to data base management should evaluate those controls which the data base manager may establish to insure data base integrity, that is, those controls to protect the existence, quality, and privacy of the recorded data.

These controls are defined as definition control, existence control, access control, update control, concurrency control, and quality control. Ron Weber and Gordon C. Everest define them as follows:[26]

> **Definition Control.** Definition control seeks to maintain a continuous correspondence between the database and its definition. The database administrator must attempt to ensure that programs cannot and do not destroy this correspondence. For example, certain disciplines should govern the ways in which application programs are written. These programs should never be allowed to directly manipulate pointers maintained by the database management system. Lyon (1976) states that application programs retrieving the next record along an access path should verify the sequence of the records and their content.

No assumptions should be made about the attributes of the next record retrieved.

Existence Control. Existence of the database is protected by establishing suitable backup and recovery procedures. The procedures must fit within constraints, such as allowable downtime and the cost of backup and recovery.

Access Control. Access controls help prevent unauthorized disclosure of confidential data. The database administrator must determine the required levels and types of access control. Controls may be needed at the data item, group, or file level. There are many types of access controls; e.g., passwords, terminal keys, and magnetic badges.

Update Control. These controls restrict database update processing to authorized users. It is useful to distinguish between permission to add data and permission to change or delete existing data. Further refinements of update control are possible. The user, for instance, may be permitted to add data to the end of the file.

Certain types of updates must be restricted. If a program references only certain data items (fields) within a group or record, it may be permitted to change the values of these data items, but may not be allowed to add new records to the database. Since the program references only certain data items, new records or groups will contain null values (usually blanks or zeros) in the data items that are not referenced. As a result, other programs referencing these data items will process the data incorrectly or will recognize and report error conditions. Obviously, this situation will create confusion for users.

Concurrency Control. Data integrity problems arise when two update processes are allowed access to the same data item at the same time. Consider, for example, an airline reservations system. A clerk accesses the database to determine seat availability, finds one seat unreserved, and informs the potential buyer. At the same time another clerk accesses the same data item, sees the seat is available, and reserves the seat. Meanwhile, the first clerk also activates a reservation transaction. The obvious solution is to lock out the second clerk from the data item while the first clerk is considering the entry of an update. However, in some cases, locking out users can produce a deadlock situation (see Everest [1974]). The database administrator must understand the problems of concurrency and employ various system or administrative controls to avoid resulting data integrity violations or deadlocks.

Quality Control. The database administrator establishes quality controls to ensure the accuracy, completeness, and consistency of the

> data. These controls can take many forms. They include the normal validation procedures applied to input data and batch controls exercised over data while it is in transit. In a database environment, Lyon (1976) points out that proper scheduling of input, processing, and output is essential to the maintenance of data completeness and consistency. Since related input data may be submitted by multiple users, it is important to keep the database in phase with itself. For example, all the data required to cost a job must be submitted before the billing program is scheduled to be run. This kind of scheduling requires global knowledge of user activities. The database administrator should conduct regular audits to ensure that data quality is being maintained.

In the study and evaluation of DBMS controls the auditor will assess the effectiveness of various controls, which among other things, will:

- Insure that the live data base is separate from the data base used for program testing (there should be a test data base).
- Insure that the vendor-supplied specially written utility programs are under the control of the data base administrator. Whenever these utilities are utilized, a log should be kept of who used the utility and when. Utilities for initial loading of data bases, compression of items, and items deleted from data bases should be specially controlled.
- Insure that the computer system operations log (console) and other special DBMS logs are available in order to monitor access and other control features involved with the data base and DBMS software.
- Insure that access to the data base is prevented when the data base is not under the control of the DBMS software. This is especially important because the physical data base would still exist, and might be subjected to an unauthorized copy attempt.
- Insure that there is adequate control over access to the data base, DBMS library, and any other documentation by utility programs, application programs, users, or any other means. Utility programs for listing the data base descriptions, testing the data, or any other type of listing should be specially controlled and continually monitored.
- Insure that there are adequate controls over access to the online data communication network that is being utilized.

FIGURE 4.6 SCHEME FOR CLASSIFICATION OF APPLICATION SYSTEM CONTROLS

TRANSACTION ORIGINATION	DATA PROCESSING TRANSACTION ENTRY	DATA COMMUNICATIONS	COMPUTER PROCESSING	OUTPUT PROCESSING	DATA STORAGE & RETRIEVAL
1. Source Document Origination Controls	1. Data Entry (Batch) Controls	1. Message Input Controls	1. Computer Processing Integrity Controls	1. Data Processing Balancing & Reconciliation	1. File Handling Controls
2. Authorization Controls	2. Data Entry (Terminal) Controls	2. Message Transmission Controls	2. Computer Processing Error Handling Controls	2. Output Distribution Controls	2. File Error Handling Controls
3. Data Processing Input Preparation Controls	3. Data Validation Controls	3. Message Reception Accounting Controls		3. User Balancing and Reconciliation Controls	
4. Source Document Error Handling Controls	4. Batch Proof & Balancing Controls			4. Records Retention Controls	
5. Source Document Retention Controls	5. Transaction Entry Error Controls			5. Accountable Documents Controls	
				6. Output Error Handling Controls	

SOURCE: "Systems Auditability and Control Study," *Data Processing Control Practices Report*, Vol. 2. Altamonte Springs, Fla. The Institute of Internal Auditors, Inc., 1977, p. 45. Compiled by the author, with permission.

- Insure that any input/output access devices located within the computer operations area are adequately controlled as far as physical access and that there is some method of tracing back to see who made which entries through that specific input/output device.

- Insure that specific software controls are utilized to limit access to data bases. Examples of these types of controls are:

  - Tag input requests to identify the terminal, time, and operator from which the input came.
  - Lock out users from parts of the data base that are not needed for the performance of their job.
  - Severely limit changes and updating of data base files with regard to different users.
  - Log all transactions for control, audit, and recovery.
  - Severely control the access when purging the contents of a data base.
  - Severely control the access when reorganizing a data base or compressing data.
  - Limit the number of personnel that can request and have access to test data bases.[27]

Application Controls

Application controls include input controls, processing controls and output controls to provide reasonable assurance that data information fed into the computer is proper, processed completely and accurately, and is distributed to authorized personnel only (Table 4.3, Application Controls).

Controls were discussed in the previous chapter by components, hardware, software, peopleware, service centers, and documentation. The auditor however may find it more useful to study and evaluate controls in the context of processing such as that shown in Table 4.3 which summarizes classification of application systems controls presented in the Systems Auditability and Control (SAC) study.

Transaction Origination. Transaction origination controls are used to insure the accuracy and completeness of data *before* it is entered into the computed application system. That is, the scope of the transaction origination control includes controls up to the point of converting data to a machine readable format.

Transaction origination controls are those controls that govern process in five control areas: (a) source document origination, (b) authorization, (c) data processing input preparation, (d) source document retention, and (e) source document error handling.

A. **Source Document Origination.** These controls include procedures and methods to ensure the proper and timely recording of data. This recording of data may be in a machine-sensible form directly, or may occur after the initial recording of data on a human readable document. Control types include written procedures, source document design, source document storage, and source document handling.

B. **Authorization.** These controls include procedures and methods used to ensure that source data have been properly authorized. Evidence of authorization may be reviewed by manual procedures (internal control group) or computer processing (transactions identification) controls which include separation of duties including the use of a transaction conflicts matrix. Signatures on source documents, written procedures, and evidence of source document approval.

C. **Data Processing Input Preparation.** Controls include those necessary to ensure the accuracy and completeness of data from origination through the data conversion process in preparation for further computer processing. Includes controls over transaction numbering, user identification, scheduling, manual review, batching and batch balancing, logging, and transmittal controls such as packaging, labeling, registry, delivery receipts, and document receipts used to establish audit trails within the system.

D. **Source Document Error Handling.** These controls include procedures and methods used to ensure that all transactions rejected at this point in the system are corrected and reentered in a timely manner. Controls include written error handling procedures, source document correction procedures, responsibility for error corrections, error logging, error notification, verification of reentered data, and monitoring of error corrections.

E. **Source Document Retention.** These controls include procedures and methods used to ensure the proper retention of source documents, including the adequate backup of source data maintained to provide the capabilities to recreate data lost or data destroyed during processing. Procedures include source document retention characteristics, filing of source documents, and retention storage. The identification and filing of source documents facilitate the historical referencing necessitated by statute, company policy, or purposes of recovery.

TABLE 4.3 APPLICATION CONTROLS

CONTROL NUMBER	TYPE	DESCRIPTION
1.	Input	Only properly authorized and approved input, prepared in accordance with management's general or specific authorization, should be accepted for processing in EDP.
2.		The system should verify all codes used to record data.
3.		Conversion of data into machine-sensible form should be controlled.
4.		Movement of data between one processing step and another, or between departments, should be controlled.
5.		The correction and resubmission of all errors detected by the application system should be reviewed and controlled.
6.	Processing	Control totals should be produced and reconciled with input control totals.
7.		Controls should prevent processing the wrong file, detect errors in file manipulation, and flag operator-caused errors.
8.		Limit and reasonableness checks should be incorporated within programs.
9.		Run-to-run controls should be verified at appropriate points in the processing cycle.
10.	Output	Output control totals should be reconciled with input and processing controls.
11.		Output should be scanned and tested by comparison to original source documents.
12.		Systems output should be distributed only to authorized users.

SOURCE: Blish, *op. cit.*

Data Processing Transaction Entry

Transaction entry controls are those controls that govern processes of transaction data entry in the following control areas: (1) data entry (terminal or batch), (2) transaction data validation, (3) batch proof and balancing, and (4) transaction entry error handling. Transaction entry controls are used to insure the accuracy and completeness of data during their entry into the computer application system. The transaction entry process is of particular importance since it involves a data conversion phase. That is, data conversion is the process of converting source data to a machine readable format. Consequently, it is important to establish controls to insure that this conversion is accurately performed. Various procedures are:

a. Transaction (batch) data entry

- Control documentation
- User procedures
- Location of data conversion operation
- Simultaneous recording

b. Terminal data entry

- Security of data entry terminal
- Preformatting
- Interactive display
- Computer-aided instruction
- User application system access
- Terminal authority levels
- Data access matrix
- Master commands
- Terminal sign-on procedures
- Review of terminal assignments
- Terminal features
- Intelligent terminals

c. Transaction data validation

- Key verification
- Preprogrammed keying formats
- Editing and validating routines
- Transaction data cutoff
- Passwords

d. Batch proof and balancing

- Processing schedules
- Turnaround documents
- Cancellation of source documents
- Logging
- Manual check of control figures
- Batch control
- Batch header records

e. Transaction entry error handling

- Error display
- Unauthorized access attempts
- Error listings
- Corrective action
- Warning messages
- Error message
- Corrected data editing
- Control totals and rejects

Data Communication

Data communication controls are those controls that govern the three control areas of message input, message transmission, and message reception and accounting. Data communication controls are primarily concerned with insuring the integrity of data as they pass through communication lines from the message input devices to the message reception devices. These controls are important because most data communication equipment is owned and controlled by organizations other than the sending or receiving organization. These controls are also important because there is a fast-growing trend by many organizations to use data communication services as an integral part of their computer application system. Consequently, to insure the accuracy and completeness of data for the entire application system, auditors are expected to understand and review this area. Controls in this area include but are not limited to:

On-line processing controls. On-line processing controls are necessary since messages from and to the input/output terminal devices can be lost or garbled. It is possible that the terminal will go out of order during transmission or receipt of data. To guard against working with incorrect data under these conditions, the system should provide program routines for checking messages. They include message identification, message transmission control, and message parity check.

Message identification is used to identify each message received by the computer. Message number, terminal identification, date, and message code is the usual information sent which permits directing the data to the correct program for processing. If a message is received with an incorrect identification, it should be routed to an error routine for corrective action or rejection from the system. In general, rejection necessitates retransmission of the entire data.

Message transmission control requires that all messages transmitted are actually received. One method is to assign a number to each message and periodically have the computer check for missing numbers and out-of-sequence messages; unaccounted-for-message numbers are printed for investigation. Another method is the confirmation of all messages received whether through the computer or the input/output terminal.

A message parity check is one which verifies the accuracy of the message sent. Since it originates at the sending terminal, a check digit is added to the end of the message, representing the number of bits in the message. In a similar manner, the receiving terminal compiles a check digit on the number of bits in the message received. If both check digits are equal, a correctly received signal is sent to the terminal or computer. If there is a difference, most systems will ask for a retransmission of the data.

Data protection controls. Data protection controls provide answers to many interactive problems. A typical problem is: what assurance is there that unauthorized personnel are prevented from using the system? The software for data protection controls includes passwords and authority lists.

Lockwords and authority lists are means of preventing unauthorized access to an interactive system. Lockwords, or passwords, are several characters of a data file that must be matched by the sender before access is granted to the file. Since the password may become common knowledge after a period of time, it must be changed periodically. Another type of security is an authority list. In this case, the lockword identifies the sender. When reference is made to the authority list stored in the computer system, it indicates what type of data the sender is permitted to receive.[28]

Computer Processing

Computer processing controls are necessary to insure that complete and accurate information is processed from data entry to output. Processing controls are designed to provide reasonable assurance that EDP has been performed as intended for the particular application, that is, (1) all transactions are processed as authorized, (2) no authorized transactions are omitted, and (3) no unauthorized transactions are added.

In approaching an evaluation of processing controls the auditor should distinguish between (1) computer equipment controls and (2) programmed controls.

Computer Equipment Controls. The reliance on the advances in integrated circuitry technology and the need to produce low cost equipment have resulted in fewer hardware controls.

Overflow, Parity Checks. With succeeding generations there has been a reduction in the number of various checks. Some feel that what is left are overflow and parity checks. What is important are both the manufacturer's and the programmer's software controls.

Programmed Controls. Some of the programmed controls are transaction codes, restart logs (which may provide before-and-after images) run-to-run control totals, file label checks, error routines (i.e., checks for invalid codes, etc.), arithmetic controls such as double arithmetic, overflow checks and reverse multiplication. The documentation and logic should indicate the type of programmed controls. An important source of this data in addition to the flow chart are the operator's manual and the computer program run book.

Computer Processing Error Handling. These controls include procedures and methods used to ensure that all transactions rejected during computer processing are corrected and reentered in a timely manner. Controls in this area provide for the detection of data loss or nonprocessing of transactions. Control error reporting, batch control header balancing, production report of rejected conditions, automated error suspense file, discrepancy report, error serial numbers, destructive update and error suspense reentry.[29]

Output Processing

Output controls take many forms, including control totals that are reconciled back to processing of input, control of the distribution of reports after they are printed, and evidence to ensure that processed data include only authorized data. Output controls are required to insure that the information coming from the computerized record-keeping system is complete and accurate. In addition, output controls insure that the output is distributed only to authorized personnel and that privacy and security of information are maintained. Output processing controls are used to insure the integrity of output data from the conclusion of computer processing until their delivery to the functional user. Output controls, therefore, are those controls that can be used to control the output and distribution of information from the application system (see Table 4.4). One important area is user balancing and reconciliation. User balancing and reconciliation controls are used to insure that the integrity of data has not been lost during the processing by the application system. The user function is normally to perform specific tasks that verify output integrity.

Data Storage and Retrieval

Data storage and retrieval controls are those controls that govern the process of file handling and file error handling. Data storage and controls are important to insure the accuracy and completeness of data during the process of data storage and retrieval. The data storage and retrieval controls should be designed to (1) provide for the protection of data files and programs from loss, destruction, or unauthorized changes, (2) allow for a maximum ease in use of files and programs, (3) allow for backup facilities and procedures for reconstruction of files, and (4) an error handling procedure to insure the detection of errors, correction of error conditions, and timely reprocessing.

Several examples of control techniques in this area are:

1. Keep all sensitive reports in an area so unauthorized personnel cannot obtain copies.

2. Immediately destroy aborted output runs. (Paper shredder for sensitive outputs.)

3. Try to include the following elements in the heading of each report: date prepared, processing period covered, a descriptive title of the report contents, the user department, the processing program's identification job number, how to dispose of the report, and its confidentiality.

4. Label any reports that must be positively and completely destroyed as to their disposal procedures. In other words, a report

that should be returned to a central destruction area should be labeled as such, or it should be labeled to be destroyed in a paper shredder or whatever.

5. Consider filing output records by date so at the end of a calendar year they can be discarded when their retention date has been reached.

6. Insure that there are appropriate waste disposal procedures for the immediate disposal of certain paper products (sensitive output reports).

7. Consider maintaining an independent history file of errors, which is independent of all processing files, and is regularly analyzed to report error trends and statistics by type, source, and frequency of errors within an application system.

8. Insure that error correction procedures are defined in the operations procedures manual.

9. When decollating a sensitive job, insure that the carbon paper is disposed of in a secure manner.[30]

Other techniques include preparation of a log of all application system processing halts and operator interruption, providing backup files for all critical files including offsite storage, and a disaster plan which sets forth the procedures to be invoked in case of application data loss or hardware loss.

While we have discussed one approach as a framework for evaluating internal control there are many published internal control questionnaires and unpublished questionnaires in the auditing industry both private and public.[31]

Based upon the results of study and evaluation of internal controls, the auditor will use either around-the-computer or through-the-computer techniques using various computer-assisted auditing tools and techniques and whatever extended procedures are necessary in the circumstances.

TABLE 4.4 OUTPUT PROCESSING CONTROL STRUCTURE

CONTROL AREA	CONTROL TYPE	CONTROL
Data processing balancing and reconciliation	Data processing control group	Reconciliation Transaction log Computer console log Systems output logs Record of output reports Monitoring process flow Job control card review Graphical charts
Output distribution	Output handling	Handling procedures for computer output Output report distribution Report copies
User balancing and reconciliation	Monitoring procedures	User department changes in master files Report heading Transaction tracing list Internally generated transactions Control totals
	Testing procedures	Statistical sampling of final report List of all transactions
Records retention	User retention and disposal methods	Waste disposal procedures Deletion of unused reports
Accountable documents	Accountable document handling	Negotiable documents storage Printing of additional sequence number on preprinted forms
Output error handling	Error reporting	Independent history file of errors Aging open items Error logging by control groups Output activity review Error correction processing Identification of error correction Correction procedures Responsibility for error correction

(Cont'd)

TABLE 4.4 (Cont'd)

CONTROL AREA	CONTROL TYPE	CONTROL
	Correction reentry	Error logging Verification of reentered data Monitoring of error conditions

SOURCE: SAC Study, p. 83. Reprinted by permission of the Institute of Internal Auditors, Inc.

FOOTNOTES

[1]Bernhard Schwab and Mark Thompson, "Unionism in Data Processing," *Datamation*, October 1974, pp. 61-69.

[2]Cyrus F. Gibson and Richard L. Nolan, "Managing the Four Stages of EDP Growth," *Harvard Business Review*, January-February, 1974, pp. 76-88.

[3]M.A. Mullin, "Computer Security–The Human Element," *The South African Chartered Accountant*, August 1977, pp. 257-259.

[4]American Institute of Certified Public Accountants. *Auditing, Management Advisory Service, Tax Practice As of September 1, 1975*, Vol. 1, AU Section 320.01, Chicago: Commerce Clearing House, Inc., 1975, p. 241. Similarly, U.S. General Accounting Office, *Standards for Audit of Governmental Organizations, Programs, Activities & Functions*, Washington, DC: U.S. General Accounting Office, June 1972 (reprinted 1974), p. 32.

[5]This notion of management's responsibility is reinforced by the U.S. General Accounting Office. GAO refers to internal control as management control and as such the term embodies the policies, procedures, and practices established or encouraged by management, as well as the plan of organization and other measures intended to carry them out. U.S. General Accounting Office, *Standards for Audit of Governmental Organizations, Programs, Activities and Functions,* Washington, DC: U.S. General Accounting Office, 1972 (reprinted 1974), p. 32.

[6]The first supplemental standard for computer related auditing, U.S. General Accounting Office. *Additional GAO Audit Standards for Auditing Computer-Based Systems; Effective Jan. 1, 1980*, Washington, DC: U.S. General Accounting Office, March 1979, p. 2.

[7]Another guide to the study and evaluation of internal control is that furnished by Arthur Andersen & Co. which in addition to objectives and techniques to achieve these objectives includes a discussion of the risks involved when the objectives are not achieved. Arthur Anderson & Co., *A Guide For Studying and Evaluating Internal Controls*, Chicago: Arthur Anderson & Co., January 1978.

[8]The U.S. General Accounting Office in its *Audit Guide* (May 1978) defined these three conditions as low, medium, and high levels of potential risk respectively. U.S. General Accounting Office, *Audit Guide for Assessing Reliability of Computer Output*, Washington, DC: U.S. General Accounting Office, May 1978, p. 89. Another technique that may have applicability is the use of Audit Criticality Measurement. A series of weights are developed for a variety of factors such as technical complexity, impact of systems failure (see Part II–James F. Hubbert, "Audit Criticality Measurement for EDP Applications," *EDPACS*, July 1979, pp. 1-6.

[9]See Kenneth K. Wong, "Management Audit of the EDP Systems' Users," *EDPACS*, September 1979, pp. 9-11; and Standard Research Institute, *Systems Auditability and Control Study*, Altamonte Springs, FL: The Institute of Internal Auditors, Inc., 1977, Chapter 12.

[10]American Institute of Certified Public Accountants, *The Auditor's Study and Evaluation of Internal Control in EDP Systems*, New York, NY: American Institute of Certified Public Accountants, 1977, p. 6.

[11]U.S. General Accounting Office, *Additional GAO Audit Standards: Auditing Computer-Based Systems*, Washington, DC: U.S. General Accounting Office, March 1979, pp. 5-8.

In the revised standards (1981 revision) Objective 2 is changed to include the following: "During the design and development process, the auditor may provide, through formal correspondence, suggested audit trails or other controls to the design/development team. By doing so through formal correspondence the auditor will remain *independent.*" (Emphasis added by the author.)

[12]This discussion is excerpted from the Stanford Research Institute's *Systems Auditability and Control Study, op. cit.*, Chapter 12.

[13]*Ibid.*, pp. 99-102.

[14]Stanford Research Institute, *Computer Abuse*. Prepared for National Science Foundation. Springfield, VA: National Technical Information Service, U.S. Department of Commerce, 1973, p. 5.

[15]Stanford Research Institute, *op. cit.*, p. 36.

[16]These illustrations are just two of the several instances which are presented in an article by Eugene Blish in which he relates cases reported in the Stanford Research Institute's study on Computer Abuse and various general and application controls. A fuller discussion of this article is presented in Part II–*Annotated Bibliography*. Eugene A. Blish, "Computer Abuse: A Practical Use of the AICPA Guide," *EDPACS*, September 1978, pp. 8-9.

The National Bureau of Standards, with support of the General Accounting Office, sponsored an invitational workshop in March of 1977 to explore the subject of "Audit and Evaluation of Computer Security." See U.S. Department of Commerce, *Audit and Evaluation of Computer Security*, NBS Special Publication 500-19, Washington, DC: National Bureau of Standards, October 1977.

[17]This topic is presented more fully in Part II–Annotated Bibliography in the article by Bernhard Schwab and Mark Thompson, "Unionism in Data Processing," *Datamation*, October 1974, pp. 61-69.

[18]Keith R. London, "Figure 4.5: The System Acceptance/Rejection Spectrum," *The People Side of Systems: The Human Aspects of Computer Systems*, NY: McGraw-Hill Book Company, Inc., 1976, p. 89.

[19]Raymond E. Miles and Roger C. Vergin, "Behavior Properties of Variance Controls," *Accounting and Its Behavioral Implications*, eds. William J. Bruns, Jr. and Don R. DeCoster, NY: McGraw-Hill Book Company, 1969, p. 372.

[20]Chester I. Barnard, *The Function of the Executive*, Cambridge, MA: Harvard University Press, 1968, p. 13.

[21]Fremont E. Kast and James E. Rosenzweig, *Organization and Management*, NY: McGraw-Hill Book Company, Inc., 1970, p. 80.

[22]The author is grateful to John E. Murphy of the Office of Personnel Management, Management Sciences Training Center, Washington, DC for sharing with me student reference materials and cases and unofficial solutions from which the above material is based.

[23]Leonard I. Krauss and Aileen MacGahan, *Computer Fraud and Countermeasures*, Englewood Cliffs, NJ: Prentice-Hall, Inc., 1979, p. 26.

[24]American Institute of Certified Public Accountants, *The Effects of EDP on the Auditor's Study and Evaluation of Internal Control*. Statement on Auditing Standards Number 3, NY: American Institute of Certified Public Accountants, December 1974, p. 3. This statement is referred to generally as S.A.S. No. 3.

[25]Jerry Fitzgerald, *Internal Controls for Computerized Systems,* Redwood City, CA: Jerry Fitzgerald & Associates, 1978. Chapter 2, "General Organizational Control Matrix," pp. 9-15. One author describes 49 controls to be examined when reviewing general controls. The AICPA guide provides description, review and tests of compliance for each of 19 general controls discussed. American Institute of Certified Public Accountants, *The Auditor's Study and Evalua-*

tion of Internal Control Systems, New York, NY: American Institute of Certified Public Accountants, 1977, Chapter 3, pp. 25-47. See also Robert J. Thierauf, Robert C. Klekamp, and Daniel W. Geeding, *Management Principles and Practices: A Contingency and Questionnaire Approach*, Santa Barbara, CA: Wiley/Hamilton, 1977. Especially Chapters 2, 8, 12, 16 and 20.

[26]Ron Weber and Gordon C. Everest, "Data Base Administration: Functional, Organizational, and Control Perspectives," *EDPACS*, January 1979, pp. 5-6. The authors quote from Gordon C. Everest, "Managing Corporate Data Resources: Objectives and a Conceptual Model of Data Base Management Systems," Ph.D. dissertation, University of Pennsylvania, 1974. Reprinted by permission.

[27]The importance of controls of the data base management system and the operating system should be apparent from their respective functions (discussed in Chapter 3). Fitzgerald describes sixty-four controls including the above which the auditor might review in his study and evaluation of DBMS. Fitzgerald, *op.cit.*, pp. 72-82. Also see U.S. General Accounting Office's *Data Base Management Systems: Without Careful Planning There Can Be Problems*. Washington, DC: U.S. Government Printing Office, June 29, 1979 (FG MSD-79-35).

[28]For a further discussion and matrix of audit controls in data communication networks see U.S. Department of Commerce, *Audit and Evaluation of Computer Security*, NBS Special Publication 500-19, Washington, DC: National Bureau of Standards, October 1977, pp. 10-4, 10-17.

[29]Fitzgerald, *op. cit.*, pp. 71, 74.

[30]Fitzgerald, *op. cit.*, pp. 50-51.

[31]For example, Dr. Jerry Fitzgerald (*Internal Controls for Computerized Systems*, Redwood City, CA: Jerry Fitzgerald & Associates, 1978) lists over 650 controls organized into nine individual control matrices: general organizational controls; input controls; data communication controls; program/computer processing controls; output controls; online terminal/distributed systems controls; physical security controls; data base controls; systems software controls. Also see by the same author *Designing Controls Into Computerized Systems*. Jerry Fitzgerald & Associates, Redwood City, CA: 1981, 158 pp. This book contains 101 control lists containing over 2,500 specific controls for use during the Systems Development Life Cycle (SDLC).

CHAPTER V
EDP AUDITING TOOLS AND TECHNIQUES

The Systems Auditability and Control Study (SAC) cited above identified some 28 tools and techniques for auditing through the computer.[1] Eleven are discussed in this chapter (Figure 5.1) along with criteria for selecting the best tools and techniques under the circumstances described, adapted from the SAC study.

FIGURE 5.1 ELEVEN SELECTED COMPUTER APPLICATION AUDIT TOOLS AND TECHNIQUES

A. Techniques to test computer application program controls
   1. Test data method (test decks)
   2. Base case system evaluation
   3. Integrated test facility
   4. Parallel simulation

B. Techniques to select and monitor data processing transactions
   5. Transaction selection
   6. Embedded audit data collection
   7. Extended records

C. Techniques for data verification
   8. Generalized audit software

D. Techniques to analyze computer application program
   9. Snap shot
   10. Computer-aided tracing and mapping
   11. Control flowcharting

Techniques to Test Computer Application Program Controls

This category of EDP audit tools and techniques is used to test computational routine, programs or whole applications in order to evaluate controls or verify processing accuracy and continued compliance with specific processing procedures. Such techniques are used for both the evaluation of application systems controls and for compliance testing.

Four such controls are discussed: (1) test data method (test decks), (2) base case system evaluation, (3) integrated test facility, and (4) parallel simulation.

1. **Test Data Method.** The test data method is used to test and verify (1) input transaction validation routine, error detection, and application system controls, (2) processing logic and controls associated with the creation and maintenance of data processing master records, (3) computational routines such as interest, gross pay, or asset depreciation, and (4) incorporation of program changes. The test data method verifies the processing accuracy of computer application systems by executing these systems using specially prepared sets of input data to produce preestablished results, i.e., test decks.

There are some general rules which should be followed in designing test decks bearing in mind that in using the technique the auditor is primarily interested in testing the system and therefore the number of transactions in the test decks has no relationship to the number of transactions being processed:

1. At least one of each type of transaction should be involved in the program.

2. There should be at least one example of each impossible type of transaction.

3. There should be at least one example of each error condition possible.

4. It is not necessary to use all possible combinations of variables within all fields. Unless the variables in different fields are correlated, there is no need to permutate the possible combinations.

5. Only a limited number of the variables which represent quantitative, control break or identification (different account numbers or different dollar amounts) need to be permutated.

6. The final processing results of the transaction should be easily isolated. Thus, if possible, all dummy transactions should be finally cleared to a dummy account. All dummy transactions should be coded to a particular date which no regular transactions would carry.

Whatever isloation or control method is used, it should be something that is not significant to the system so that later confusion will be avoided. One of the simplest approaches is to secure copies of all input forms and complete them so that each condition specified in the test plan is satisfied. This approach can involve preparations of input forms to create a number of master records and then preparing transactions to test the various computation controls and processing logic to be verified. The method does require a lot of preplanning and after-test analysis. Considerable manual effort by the auditor is generally required. The level of effort increases directly with the complexity of the system and the scope of the audit. Extensive data processing expertise on the part of the auditor is not required, but some knowledge of data processing is required.

2. **Base Case System Evaluation.** The base case system evaluation (BCSE) is a technique that applies a standardized body of data (input parameters and output) to the testing of a computer application. This body of data, the base case, is established by user personnel, with internal audit concurrence, as the criterion for correct functioning of the computer application system. A BCSE test package consists of (1) one or more files containing the information necessary to test both valid and invalid conditions established in the design of the system; (2) a predefined set of input transactions that are designed to test every reasonably foreseeable valid and invalid event in systems processing; (3) a precomputed output for each transaction tested which could be provided by an independently prepared report or from terminal output samples; (4) a manual or automated procedure for comparing all files and reports to identify changes; and (5) for online systems, the BC must include transactions that demonstrate those activities normally accomplished on terminals. The BCSE system requires that the data processing user and audit personnel work together.

3. **Integrated Test Facility (ITF).** Integrated test facility is a technique to review those functions of an automated application that are internal to the computer. The auditor's test data are used to compare ITF processing results to precalculated test results. The method is most frequently used to test and verify large computer application systems when it is not practical to separately cycle test data. It is an audit technique that uses a fictitious or dummy entity, for example, a false department or a dummy vendor, within the framework of the regular application processing cycle. The auditor can select the transactions or processing functions to be examined and then apply the transactions to the fictitious entity during the normal processing cycle

along with regular transactions. Normal application processing produces the reports that the internal auditor uses to verify the completeness and accuracy of the functions being evaluated and/or verified. The technique is described as "integrated" because the audit (i.e., fictitious) transactions are processed with production transactions, the audit master records reside on the same files as regular production records. Accordingly, audit checks can be made a part of the normal processing cycle. The ITF input data can be accomplished by preparing such data manually or by using a selected sample of actual data. Each method has its advantages and disadvantages. Manually prepared data, while time consuming to prepare, can be more easily designed to test specific conditions of the particular computer processing system. Actual data, while less time consuming to prepare, must be analyzed and carefully selected to assure that audit objectives are met.

4. **Parallel Simulation.** Parallel simulation is the use of one or more special computer programs to process live data files and simulate normal computer application processing. As opposed to the test data method and the ITF method which process test data through live programs, the parallel simulation method processes live data through test programs. The parallel simulation programs accept and process the same input data as their corresponding application programs. They use the same master files and attempt to produce the same results. This simulation process allows verification of computer applications for correct input data validation and controls procedures, computations and processing logic, master file updating logic, and controls and balancing procedures. This method is described as parallel because all transactions for a particular processing cycle are processed by both a normal application program as well as a simulation program. Simulation results are compared with the application program results to enable an independent and objective check by the auditors. Parallel simulation programs are usually developed using a generalized audit software package or a high-level application language. Even with these powerful and flexible tools, considerable check-out and testing can be expected. The auditor may wish to simulate segments of the application only.

Techniques to Select and Monitor Data Processing Transactions

These techniques include three programs: transaction selection, embedded audit data collection, and extended records. These techniques are used to select and capture production data for subsequent manual audit and verification. Typically, they are used to monitor production activity and select samples as part of continuous auditing activity within the normal production process.

5. **Transaction Selection.** Transaction selection is a technique using an independent computer program to monitor and select transactions for internal audit review. The method enables the auditor to examine and analyze transaction volumes and error rate and to statistically sample specified transactions. Haskins and Sells Audit Tape seems to be an example of this type of procedure. The transaction selection uses software specified or developed by the auditor to screen and select transactions that have been input to the production computer application system. The transactions selection method is implemented as an independent computer application program in which transaction files used as input to the production program are subsequently processed by the transaction selection program which edits and validates input transactions according to criteria established by the auditor. The program can select specified transactions for subsequent analysis. The selection or sampling process can be designed to select by transaction content (for example, all dollar amounts over $1,000), or by a statistical sample. The technique is useful for validating and sampling input transactions but inferences must be drawn concerning how well these transactions represent the entire body or input.

6. **Embedded Audit Data Collection.** This technique uses one or more specially programmed data collection modules embedded in the computer application system to select and record data for subsequent analysis and evaluation. The data collection modules are inserted in the computer application system at points determined to be appropriate by the auditor. This in-line method means that the computer performs the audit data collection function at the same time it processes data for normal production purposes. One note is that the auditor should specify his requirement while the system is being designed so that the cost of retrofitting this technique to an ongoing system can be avoided. The technique involves three elements: (1) the embedded modules themselves, (2) the collection criteria supplied by the auditor, and (3) post-collection processes used by the auditor to analyze and evaluate the collected data. One such version is called SCARF (System Control Audit Review File). This technique provides the auditor and data processing control personnel with the capability to monitor the operation of a particular computer application system on a continual basis.

7. **Extended Records.** The extended records technique gathers together by means of a special program or programs all the significant data that have affected the processing of an individual transaction. This includes the accumulation into a single record results of processing over the time period required for complete processing of the transaction. With extended records, data are consolidated from accounting periods and different computer application systems so that a complete transaction audit trail is physically included in one computer record. The extended record technique provides a comprehensive audit trail for each transaction. From this audit trail data, transactions can be traced from inception to the final disposition on an organization's records or backwards from consolidated totals to the individual transactions. The main benefits derived from the use of the extended records technique are: (1) the auditors are involved in specifying audit trails which bring their expertise into insuring comprehensive audit trails; (2) a complete audit trail exists in one extended record; (3) complete historic data covering different accounting periods are available for analysis by various departments within an organization.

Techniques for Data Verification

Data processing audit tools and techniques such as generalized audit software are included in this category. This is general purpose software which accesses, extracts, manipulates and presents data and test results in a format appropriate to audit objectives. Such generalized file-handling software is usually controlled by parameters or simplified procedural statements that require a minimum of data processing knowledge.

8. **Generalized Audit Software.** Generalized audit software includes such items as special purpose audit programs and terminal audit software which accesses, extracts, manipulates and displays data from online data bases using remote terminal inquiry commands. These software programs include packages which (1) do footings, cross footings and balancing of entire files, (2) select and present detailed data from a file, (3) perform various logical operations on data, (4) stratify data, (5) do statistical sampling and extract information, (6) format reports and prepare confirmation statements, (7) screen specific data elements in a file, including checking for duplicate information, missing information and the range of values present, and (8) compare two generations of the same file from different time periods or two different files with common data elements.

The National Bureau of Standards has prepared a report on the features of seven audit software packages. These are referred to in the bibliography, Part II. The description of the features of software include the audit tape, DYL-260, the EASYTRIEVE, EDP-AUDITOR, HEWCAS, MARK 4/AUDITOR and SCORE.

Techniques to Analyze Computer Application Programs

These techniques, which include snap shot, computer-aided tracing and mapping, and control flowcharting, are data processing audit tools and techniques to evaluate processing logic and procedures internal to application programs, systems of programs, and job control languages.

9. **Snap Shot.** Snap shot is a technique that in effect takes a picture of the parts of computer memory that contain the data elements involved in a computerized decision-making process at the time the decision is made. The results of the snap shot are printed in report format for reconstructing the decision-making process. The snap shot technique offers the capability of listing all the data that were involved in a specific decision-making program. This is an advancement over earlier techniques of what was called a core dump, that is, a complete memory print-out when a program was stopped at a selected point and the data in core at that point was printed out. This was used for de-bugging purposes and to note how various computation routines were acting. One of the important elements is selection of snap shot points. Some of these points are: (1) when transactions enter the computer, (2) when transactions leave a program or complex routine, (3) a point where key decisions are determined, and (4) a point where records are either consolidated or broken into two or more records.

Snap shot routines are coded into the main line of instructions in the computer systems application program. For that reason, the only practical time to install snap shot is during the developmental stages of a new computer application. The auditor as part of a development team can help specify what data are wanted and where snap shot points should be located—for example, the computations and selections in a linear programming operation to determine the variables that went into calculation of the optimal point in a linear programming routine.

10. **Computer-Aided Tracing and Mapping.** Production input data is flagged or marked indicating that it is to receive special audit handling. This technique would normally display such data as it passes through key points in the system. Mapping includes a number of techniques which can be used to determine the logical paths within a pro-

gram and report those that were not used during a process run. The trace listing shows what program statements have been executed and in what order. For example, in processing a payroll record, the tracing may show that instruction statements 1 through 5 were executed, and at that point there was a transfer back to statement 3 because statement 5 was a transfer instruction on high and low, for example, or equal and unequal in a program routine. Tracing, therefore, is an audit technique that provides the auditor with the capability of performing an electronic walk-through of a data processing application system. The objective of tracing is to verify compliance with policies and procedures by substantiating, through examination, the path through a program that a transaction followed.

Mapping analyzes a computer program during execution to indicate whether program statements have been executed. The software measurement can also determine the amount of CPU time consumed by each program segment. It would include a list of any program segments not executed, a list of statistics consuming the most CPU time, a listing of the source program showing the total number of times that each statement was executed.

11. **Computer Flowcharting.** This procedure uses computer program flowcharting techniques to identify and present logic paths and control points within computer application systems. Standard analytical auditing symbols and techniques are used to develop visual profiles of computer applications. These profiles provide useful vehicles for discussion with users and data processing personnel concerning internal application system controls. In addition, the flowcharts serve as an excellent mechanism for training new EDP auditors.

One advantage of this technique is found in the operational auditing of systems to identify lack of control in key areas.

SELECTING COMPUTER AUDIT TOOLS AND TECHNIQUES

William E. Perry, writing in *EDPACS*,[2] provides criteria to consider when selecting a computer audit practice. The criteria are:

1. Computer audit practices must satisfy an audit objective or need in a given situation.

FIGURE 5.2 TRAINING REQUIREMENTS BY KNOWLEDGE AREAS FOR SELECTED COMPUTER APPLICATION AUDIT TOOLS AND TECHNIQUES

	TEST DATA METHOD	BASE CASE SYSTEM EVALUATION	INTEGRATED TEST FACILITY	PARALLEL SIMULATION	TRANSACTION SELECTION	EMBEDDED AUDIT DATA COLLECTION	EXTENDED RECORDS	GENERALIZED AUDIT SOFTWARE	SNAP SHOT	TRACING	MAPPING	CONTROL FLOWCHARTING
1. Data processing principles and concepts	X	X	X	XX	X	X	X	XX	X	XX	X	XX
2. Computer application system structure	–	X	X	XX	–	X	X	X	X	XX	X	X
3. Computer application system controls and procedures	X	X	X	X	–	X	X	X	X	XX	–	XX
4. Data management	–	X	–	X	–	–	X	X	–	X	–	X
5. Computer service center controls	–	X	–	X	–	–	–	X	–	–	–	–
6. Application system development controls	–	X	–	X	–	–	–	–	–	X	–	XX
7. Computer application program	–	–	–	XX	–	–	–	–	–	XX	X	–

Legend: XX = advanced EDP audit training
X = basic EDP audit training
– = not required

SOURCE: Compiled from the various training requirement tables in the *Report of the Systems Auditability and Control Study*, p. 109 and *passim.*

2. It should be cost-effective. If an alternative manual procedure will be just as effective and cost less, the EDP approach should not be used.

3. Auditors must have the resources to perform the practice. Many computer audit practices require the use of special software.

4. The practice can be operational when it is needed. A snapshot application, for instance, can take three to six months before it becomes operational. Thus, an audit which must be completed within four or six weeks cannot utilize snap shot.

5. It can be performed within budgetary limits.

6. The auditor should possess the necessary skill level (Figure 5.2).

The final point, "the necessary skill level," raises the issue of training and education, standards of professionalism, and competencies required of auditors in an EDP environment. These issues are discussed further in the following chapter.

FOOTNOTES

[1]In 1977, the Institute of Internal Auditors, Inc. sponsored a state of the art survey of over 1,500 organizations by interview and mail questionnaire to determine audit and control practices of computer-based information systems. Some of these twenty-eight tools and techniques were used more widely than others. For a complete discussion, see Stanford Research Institute, *Systems Auditability and Control-Audit Practices*, prepared by the Institute of Internal Auditors, Inc., 1977, Chapters 14-25, pp. 109-164.

[2]William E. Perry, "Selecting Computer Audit Practices," *EDPACS*, March 1978, pp. 1-2. Reprinted with permission.

CHAPTER VI
TRAINING AND DEVELOPING EDP AUDIT COMPETENCE

Paraphrasing a statement made once with regard to the public administrator and the computer: There is no question but that the auditor, both internal and external, must have the intellectual accessibility to computers that match their physical accessibility.[1]

Much of the literature addresses the issues of competencies required in EDP auditing, particularly the importance of professional judgment and training and staff development.

The American Institute of Certified Public Accountants, the Institute of Internal Auditors, and the U.S. General Accounting Office have all promulgated standards for auditing in an EDP environment. Basic to each of these standards is the concept of technical proficiency of the audit staff.

EDP Audit Competencies

Several writers have addressed the issue of technical competence required in auditing computer-based systems. Jancura and Lilly stated:

> . . .in order to perform properly the required tasks of reviewing and evaluating internal control and performing subsequent substantive tests of the financial data, the minimum EDP knowledge requirements of the general staff auditor should include:
>
> 1. A basic understanding of computer systems, including equipment components and their general capabilities.
>
> 2. A basic understanding of widely installed computer operating systems and software.
>
> 3. A general familiarity with the file processing techniques and data structures.
>
> 4. Sufficient working knowledge of computer audit software to use existing standardized audit packages.

5. The ability to review and interpret system documentation including flowcharts and record definitions.

6. Sufficient working knowledge of basic EDP controls to

   a. Identify and evaluate the controls in effect in the client's installation.

   b. Determine the extent to which such controls should be tested and to evaluate the results of such tests (although not necessarily to execute such tests).

7. Sufficient knowledge of EDP systems to develop the audit plan and supervise its execution.

8. A general familiarity with the dynamics involved in developing and modifying programs and processing systems.[2]

Although each auditor may not possess the requisite knowledge and skills, the standards require that the auditors assigned must collectively possess adequate professional proficiency for the necessary tasks.

The concept of the auditor calling on a specialist to assist in auditing computers is reflected in the Comptroller General's "Standards for Audit of Governmental Organizations, Programs, Activities & Functions," which states:

> If the work requires extensive review of computerized systems, the audit staff must include persons having the appropriate computer skills. These skills may be possessed by staff members or by consultants to the staff.

Some writers[3] suggest that three proficiency levels are required, namely (1) a general audit staff member, (2) a computer audit specialist, and (3) a data processing professional.

The general audit staff member is assigned audit responsibilities in the examination of financial statements of the client. He should:

1. Understand basic computer concepts.

2. Understand concentration of controls in an EDP environment, e.g., integrated data base.

3. Understand systems flowcharts and description of computerized systems.

4. Understand at least one computer programming language (COBOL or PL/I).

5. Understand in a general way the use of computer auditing software.

6. Understand the concepts of file processing.

The computer audit specialist is basically an auditor and not a data processing specialist. He is a specialist in the sense that his understanding of data processing is greater than that required of audit staff members in general. He should:

1. Demonstrate proficiency as an auditor.

2. Demonstrate ability to review and evaluate EDP internal control (see EDP internal control questions).

3. Understand EDP systems design and operation, i.e., understand flowcharting and systems logic.

4. Have knowledge of programming language and techniques: ability to write a program in at least one language, including design, write, compile test and run moderately complex programs to assist in auditing computer processed accounting records (see audit application practices, especially those requiring advanced knowledge).

5. Be generally familiar with computer operating systems and software.

6. Have the ability to identify and reconcile problems with client data file format and structure.

7. Have the ability to communicate management and EDP personnel concerns to the auditor and auditing concerns to management and EDP personnel.

The data processing professional is a highly trained professional acting as consultant in resolving specific EDP problems. He should be technically competent in such areas as data transmission, programming languages–IMS, IDS, TOTAL, IMAGE/QUERY, file design, multiprogramming, simulation and modeling, data base designs, time sharing. Although the author did not include the following, it would appear that these competencies would also be useful: technical competence in areas of cost accounting, sampling and mathematical model building, operations research and other quantitative methods, and, finally, knowledge of hardware, its reliability and control features.

This knowledge and experience may be gained from (though not limited to) occupations such as operations research analyst, EDP methods analyst, EDP manager, or an EDP systems engineer. Academic background might include computer sciences, mathematics, electrical engineering, etc.

James F. Hubbert[4] offers a profile of a computer audit specialist based upon a composite of computer knowledge, business systems analysis experience and auditing competency. He identifies these competencies as follows:

> *Computer knowledge* can range from that of an electronics engineer with a Ph.D. in computer science to a perfunctory knowledge of a high-level programming language and a functional understanding of computer hardware.
>
> *Business systems analysis experience* ranges from having been a successful project leader on a major integrated business information system to relatively minor participation in the design of second generation systems.
>
> *Auditing competence* would range from successful "big eight" or diversified corporate experience to an undergraduate audit course.

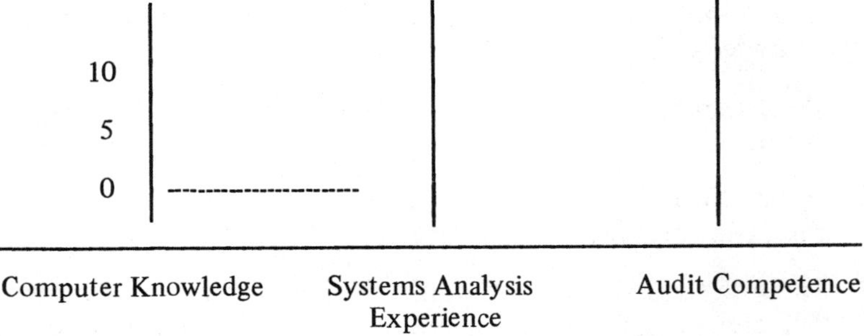

He concedes that it would be rare to find these competencies in any one individual. However, the audit function might be staffed with members each of whom would rate high in one of these areas.

One criterion for judging competencies in each of these functional areas may be through the professional certification process. For example, (1) the Certified Public Accountant (CPA), (2) the Certified Internal Auditor (CIA), (3) the Certified Management Accountant

(CMA), (4) the Certified Information Systems Auditor (CISA), and (5) the certificate in data processing (CDP).[5]

In its report prepared by the Stanford Research Institute for the Internal Auditor's Association, a distinction is made between basic and advanced skills. While these terms are not exactly defined, they are presented as follows:[6]

Basic Skills	Advanced Skills
Data processing principles and concepts.	Two or more years' of experience in either data processing or computer audit.
Computer applications systems structure.	Two or more years in computer systems design or internal audit review of design efforts.
Computer application systems controls and procedures.	A combination of control calculation in new systems and the audit of internal control in existing computerized applications.
Data management.	Experience in extracting data from files plus a knowledge of central data bases and data base management, if appropriate for a practical organization.
Application systems development controls.	A thorough understanding of the systems development life cycle through two or more years' experience.
Computer application programming.	Two or more years experience programming in standard languages like COBOL or PL/I.

One of the important skills required of the auditor is the ability to exercise good judgment.

The Importance of Judgment

Judgment is not the same thing as decision making. The former means drawing an inference from the data and the latter refers to choosing a particular course of action. Judgment takes into consideration not only base rate data but also probability—that is the relative frequency with which an event may occur.

A seminal study of the importance of judgment formulation in public accounting was written some thirty years ago and is presented here in part as having continued relevance.[7]

> Judgment is that mental process by which a person interprets a doubtful situation or problematic experience by referring it to some concept derived from prior experience.
>
> Reflective thinking represents that mental process undertaken to uncover or to infer a significant relation between past experiences i.e., stored-up knowledge, and some new experiences whose existence or use constitutes a problem. *Good judgment is a derivative of experience.* Working hypotheses do not appear from thin air but are based on the reapplication of previous experiences.
>
> Judgment is the mental process wherein an uncertain situation or problem is resolved by reference to ideas stored up from past experience.
>
> The essential function of reasoning is the inducing of a mental reaction to experience that will make these experiences meaningful and subject to inclusion with the thinker's stock of previous experiences as reserve material for further thought.

The facts necessary for the public accountant's appraisal of the fairness of representation in financial statements are embodied in his storehouse of experiences, i.e., knowledge of accounting and auditing theory, of audit techniques and procedures, and of the peculiarities of the particular enterprise under review.

On the basis of this knowledge and on a basis of his appraisal of the client's system of internal control, the public accountant puts himself in contact with the client's records by choosing those techniques and procedures which his broad experience and his observations inform him will adduce the most valid evidence of what the financial representations actually are.

In absence of an occasion to choose among alternatives, i.e., to exercise judgment, there would be little if anything to distinguish the professional man from the skilled craftsman who operates under detailed rules and directives.

Campfield wrote further:

> Only individuals disciplined in the purposes, norms, and techniques of making sound judgments can be expected to direct deliberation toward the resolution of the many problematic and perplexing situa-

> tions that arise out of modern economic activity with which the practice of public accounting is concerned.[8]

At several points in the SAS No. 3 review process the auditor is required to use his/her judgment. Generally important judgmental decisions are required in the following various situations:

1. The potential benefits are substantial, the costs of error are high, and it is difficult to reverse or sabotage a poor decision after action commences.
2. Information is uncomplete or uncertain.
3. Feedback about results is not available until long after the decision has been made.

Specifically, in the preliminary review the auditor is expected to determine the extent to which EDP is used in each significant accounting application and the basic structure of accounting control.

After the preliminary review the auditor may decide (1) to complete the review of controls and, if warranted, place reliance on the system of controls or (2) perform the audit without completing the review of controls and without placing reliance on the controls.[9]

COMPETENCY-BASED TRAINING

The accounting profession has defined competency as "both the technical qualifications of the member and his staff and his ability to supervise and evaluate the quality of the work performed." That is, the auditor implies that he has the necessary competency to complete the engagement according to professional standards, applying his knowledge and skill with reasonable care and diligence.[10]

To this notion of knowledge and skills, I would add understanding and insight, and attitude:

> **Understanding and Insight.** Ability to size up situations, see patterns, develop categories, figure out cause-and-effect relationships, and in general to apply knowledge and thought processes to the analysis and solution of problems.

> **Attitude.** A general tendency of a person to act in a certain way under certain conditions. In the conext of auditing, this requires that the auditor have a belief in the system, that is, avoid having a general mistrust of computer technology and the willingness to serve as an interpreter and communicator to bridge the gap between the needs of management, the auditors and the systems analyst.

A competency-based training system requires (1) an identification of competencies in terms of knowledge, skills, understanding and insights, and attitudes, (2) identification of appropriate training methods, and (3) a way of assessing or evaluating the degree to which the competencies have been acquired. A competency-based training program should begin with an assessment of the job to be done, i.e., job or task analysis. Next is to identify the knowledge required to perform the job. "Skill" as a behavior concept carries both a quantitative and qualitative connotation which would be established by the requirement of the job. The level of skills required or standards can be established by and evaluated by a panel of experts, i.e., those at the level of supervisors of those performing the job or tasks. A model that may be developed and adapted to training auditors in an EDP environment is found in the book, *Self-Directed Learning: A Guide for Learners and Teachers* by Malcolm Knowles[11] (see Figure 6.1).

The Institute of Internal Auditors in the Data Processing Audit Practices report notes that with the growing organizational dependence upon internal auditors, the quality and quantity of EDP audit staff are a concern of top management and audit management. The report states:

> EDP audit training is important because internal auditors are being asked by management to audit *through the computer rather than around it.* This requirement means that internal auditors must understand the concepts of data processing and the tools and techniques available to them to perform a through-the-computer audit. In order to perform this task well, internal auditors must not only become more aware of data processing concepts, they must also keep up with the computer technology and audit tools as they change.[12]

The report continues to point out that the primary objectives of EDP audit training are to:

- Provide the internal audit function with sufficient EDP audit knowledge to effectively audit computer application systems and related data processing activities.

- Develop and maintain an awareness of the best EDP audit tools and techniques available to the internal auditor.

- Develop and maintain an awareness of computer technology as it relates to EDP auditing in order to anticipate new requirements.[13]

FIGURE 6.1 RELATING METHODS TO OBJECTIVES

Type of Objectives	*Most Appropriate Methods*	*Types of Evidence*
KNOWLEDGE (Generalizations about experience, internalization of information.)	Lecture, television, debate, dialogue, interview, colloquy, motion pictures, slide film, recording, book-based discussion, reading, programmed instruction.	Reports of knowledge acquired, as in essays, examinations, oral presentations, audiovisual presentations.
UNDERSTANDING (Application of information and generalizations.)	Audience participation, demonstration, dramatization, Socratic discussion, problem-solving project, case method, critical incident process, simulation games.	Examples of utilization of knowledge in solving problems, as in critical incident cases, simulation games, proposals of action projects, research projects with conclusions and recommendations.
SKILLS (Incorporating new ways of performing through practice.)	Skill practice exercises, role playing, in-basket exercises, participative cases, simulation games, human relations training groups, nonverbal exercises, drill, coaching.	Performance exercises, with ratings by observers.
ATTITUDES (Adoption of new feelings through experiencing greater success with them than with old feelings.	Experience-sharing discussion, sensitivity training, role playing, critical incident process, case method, simulation games, participative cases, group therapy, counseling.	Attitudinal rating scales; performance in role playing, critical incident cases, simulation games, sensitivity groups, etc., with feedback from observers.
VALUES (The adoption and priority arrangement of beliefs.)	Value-clarification exercises, biographical reading, lecture, debate, symposium, colloquy, dramatization, role playing, critical incident process, simulation games, sensitivity training.	Value rating scales; performance in value clarification groups, critical incident cases, simulation games, etc., with feedback from observers.

SOURCE: Adapted from Malcolm S. Knowles, *The Modern Practice of Adult Education*, New York: Association Press, 1970, pp. 110 and 294, with permission.

Based upon the foregoing discussion and a review of other literature, a model of competency for auditors in EDP environment would include internalization of information (knowledge), new ways of performance through practice (skill), the application of information (understanding), feeling better about the task through experiencing greater success because of knowledge and skill development (attitudes), and a positive view of computer technology and its advances and a professional attitude (beliefs and values). In addition to on-the-job training, Campfield has discussed such professional development techniques as reassignments, job rotation and "expanded experience."[14] These techniques include planned rotation among various assignments, jobs, and supervisors; assignment to special studies, committees, etc.; role of understudy or assistant to designated supervisors; and participation in policy and workload planning.

A training program should include (1) a commitment of the firm to a planned program of continuing education, (2) an assignment of authority and responsibility for the planning and implementation of the training program, (3) an appropriate identification of the type of staff member to be trained, and (4) a methodology for identifying training needs, selection of training methods and evaluation of training results.[15]

Campfield indicated that:

> On-the-job training should be used as extensively as possible. Because this type of training is at the scene of staff job performance, it is most realistic. Some of the specific methods and techniques that can be used separately or in combination are:
>
> 1. Direct coaching and demonstrating by a supervisor.
> 2. Observation and analysis by a staff member of performance deemed by a supervisor to meet competency standards.
> 3. Supervising of peer performance under the guidance of a supervisor.
> 4. Participation by staff members with supervisors in on-job conferences for planning and reviewing the job.[16]

In addition to on-the-job training (OJT) and development, there are the various certification organization programs mentioned above; professional societies–American Institute of Certified Public Accountants, EDP Auditors Association, Institute of Internal Auditors; university, governmental, and society seminars and workshops; the Interagency Auditor Training Center, Office of Personnel Management, Washington, D.C.; and various college and university programs.

Separate courses in EDP auditing are only now emerging. In a recent survey which this author undertook of forty schools or departments of accounting only eight of the 21 respondents offered a separate EDP auditing course. Most respondents approach the subject as part of other accounting or auditing courses.

Training and education must keep pace with the advances in information systems and the societal and managerial demands made upon the auditor in this environment.

FOOTNOTES

[1]Herbert Isaac, "Computer Systems Technology," *Public Administration Review*, November/December 1968, pp. 493-495.

[2]E.G. Jancura and F.L. Lilly, "SAS No. 3 and the Evaluation of Internal Control," *The Journal of Accountancy*, March 1977, p. 69.

[3]Richard W. Cutting, Richard J. Guiltinan, Fred L. Lilly, Jr., "Technical Proficiency for Auditing Computer Processed Accounting Records," *The Journal of Accountancy*, October 1971, pp. 74-82. Jerome Lobel, "Auditing in the New Systems Environment," *The Journal of Accountancy*, 1971, pp. 63-67, makes some of the same points as well as James F. Hubbert, "Profile of a Computer Audit Specialist," *EDPACS*, May 1979, pp. 11-14.

[4]James F. Hubbert, "Profile of a Computer Audit Specialist," *EDPACS*, May 1979, pp. 11-14. Reprinted with permission.

[5]The Certified Information Systems Auditor (CISA) is a certification program of the EDP Auditor's Association and the EDP Auditor's Foundation for Education and Research.

The general content of the examination is taken from the 11 job areas of the Information Systems Auditor, including Systems Development Life Cycle (SDLC) review, security review, and information systems audit management.

The Certificate in Management Accounting (CMA) is awarded by the Institute of Management Accounting of the National Association of Accountants. The examination covers: (1) economics and business finance, (2) organization behavior, (3) public reporting standards, (4) auditing and taxes and (5) decision analysis, including modeling and information systems.

The Certificate in Data Processing (CDP) is awarded on the basis of an examination conducted by the Institute for Certification of Computer Professionals. The examination covers: (1) data processing equipment, (2) computer programming and software, (3) principles of management, (4) quantitative methods and (5) systems analysis and design.

[6]William E. Perry, "Skills Needed to Utilize EDP Audit Practices," *EDPACS*, November 1977: p. 3.

Also see Appendix B, *Job Descriptions to Control Objectives–1980*. Published by the EDP Auditor's Foundation. Included are job descriptions for various positions–Senior Computer Audit Specialist, Senior EDP Auditor, EDP Auditor, Supervisor-Computer Auditing. Description includes knowledge and skill requirements.

[7]William L. Campfield, "An Inquiry into the Nature of Judgment Formation and its Implications to the Public Accounting Profession," Doctoral dissertation. An abstract of a thesis. Urbana, IL: University of Illinois, 1951.

[8]Campfield, *ibid.*, p. 9.

[9]Other decision points are presented to the auditor in conducting the SAS No. 3 review. See Jancura and Lilly, *op. cit.*, pp. 73-74.

[10]American Institute of Certified Public Accountants, *Ethics Bylaws of September 1, 1974*, Chicago: Commerce Clearing House, Inc., 1974, p. 4561.

[11]Malcolm Knowles, *Self-Directed Learning: A Guide for Learners and Teachers*, NY: Association Press, 1975.

[12]The Institute of Internal Auditors, Inc., *Systems Auditability and Control: Audit Practices*, Altamonte Springs, FL: The Institute of Internal Auditors, Inc., 1977, p. 47.

[13]*Ibid.*, p. 50.

[14]William L. Campfield, "Insights and Guidelines for Increasing the Proficiency of Accountants," *Singapore Accountant*, Fall 1978, p. 95.

[15]William L. Campfield, "Programming to Training Goals: A Format for the Small Scale Practitioner," *The National Public Accountant,* December 1979, pp. 6-9.

[16]*Ibid.*, p. 7.

PART II
ANNOTATED BIBLIOGRAPHY AND ADDITIONAL REFERENCES

INTRODUCTORY NOTE

Part II consists of some 166 annotated references and additional references–unannotated. Part II is arranged primarily by sections corresponding to the chapters in Part I–Theory and Practice. Secondarily, the annotations within each section are arranged and numbered in chronological sequence from the earliest date to the most recent. Therefore the higher number is the most recent. Annotations within the same year are arranged alphabetically by author.

The chronological sequence was chosen to provide the reader with a sense of the development in auditing thought and practice with respect to the electronic environment.

The additional references are in alphabetical sequence by author.

Sources of Bibliography

The Annotated Bibliography was compiled by the Editor except where otherwise noted in parenthesis. One computerized search was used and included by permission (ABI) and also abstracts from three journal publications, *EDPACS* (EDPACS); *Data Processing Digest* (DPD); and *Accounting Review* (AR). Every abstract was reviewed, and where necessary, was revised or edited. Other sources were the fugitive articles, books, reports and other materials, references in leading articles in the field, professional societies, U.S. government agencies, and from a survey of accounting departments in some 40 universities and colleges.

Selection Criteria

When one begins to review the literature in this field, he is overwhelmed by the abundance of material; quantitatively, there is no shortage of material. More importantly, much of the material that impacts upon practice includes unpublished dissertations, staff documents, memoranda, notes and discussions from workshops and meetings of learned societies, etc., in both government, business and industry files.

Finally, most bibliographies are dated by the time they are published. Nevertheless, certain criteria were applied to provide a workable, qualitative bibliography.

The criteria for the selection of the literature included were to:

1. Insure that a representative sample of the literature is presented;

2. Give priority to literature dealing with the topics covered in Part I—e.g., auditing objectives, evidence, computer systems, internal control, computer auditing technique and training and professional development;

3. Keep manufacturers' material covering hardware and software to a minimum. Also, not to duplicate publications catalogs of professional societies such as that published by the Institute of Internal Auditors, Inc., etc.;

4. Provide references from the 1970s to the present except that earlier materials were selected if they appeared to be seminal literature;

5. Include references furnished by recognized computerized data searches, professional and standard setting bodies, and a survey conducted by the author of accounting departments of universities and colleges.

Selection and editing were purely the responsibility of the author, with apologies to both those who were included and excluded.

Accessing the Annotated Bibliography

The Bibliography can be accessed by referring to the subject matter Index. Page references to Part II are shown in the Index in italics. Books and articles often cover more than one topic; in such cases an arbitrary decision was made to include the work in the topical area in which there appeared to be the most emphasis.

Overview of the Literature

In Section A, Blank, Jancura and Frielink provide an historical look at the impact that automation—from punch cards to minicomputers—has had on the auditing profession. From Blank's article it is apparent that historically to present the audit paradigm has remained grounded in two areas: evidence (the audit trail) and internal control, i.e., the control over the data produced by the client's system whether it be manually produced or computer generated.

While these are internal issues, there are legal and societal issues affecting auditing and the computer such as privacy, security, and federal initiatives such as the Foreign Corrupt Practices Act. Hence computer auditing is impacted by rapidly changing social issues and changing computer technology.

The rapid change in computer technology is evidenced by the writings in Section B. For example, in one article (Bowers' "Analysis of Computer Terminals") the author discusses the status of input/output devices. Writing in 1973 he describes voice-input technology as being in the infancy stage. In 1981 the reader may be aware of the advances made in voice-input technology. Data base management systems (DBMS), operating systems, distributed systems mark other advances in technology.

As indicated by much of the literature reviewed in Section A, the emphasis on auditing continues to be collecting competent evidential matter that is relevant, verifiable, independent, and quantifiable. In Section C John Gallagher, writing in 1967, makes this point as well as many of the later writers. Since it is not possible to perform 100% audits, there continues to be reflected in the literature an emphasis on statistical sampling. Many of the additional references in Section C deal with sampling techniques and other objective methods.

In Section D, the significance of valid data points to the importance of internal controls and management controls. An important role of the auditor is to assess the adequacy of the internal control system as "a plan to ensure that only valid data are accepted and processed completely and accurately and that the necessary information and records are provided."

Many of the references deal with the issue of computer security and abuse as this impacts upon the completeness, accuracy, and availability of the data. The large number of citations indicate the growing importance of this subject. Another issue is the role of the auditor in the Systems Development Life Cycle (SDLC).

As more emphasis is placed on auditing "through" the computer there is a growing use of the computer itself in auditing. In Section E, the literature relates to computer assisted audit techniques (CAAT) including generalized audit software packages (GASP) in addition to test decks, parallel simulation, etc. Selecting the right audit software package requires careful planning (Knowlton's "Audit Software Package Evaluation"). William E. Perry ("Selecting Computer Audit Practices") provides six criteria the auditor needs to take into consideration when selecting a computer audit technique. Several case studies are referenced which are studies in the use of CAAT (e.g., AICPA *Computer Assisted Audit Techniques*).

In order to meet the challenges of the advances in computer and information technology as they impact on auditing it is important that training and education keep pace. William E. Perry ("Skills Needed to Utilize EDP Audit Practices") in Section F outlines the knowledge and skills that are required. These skills are rarely possessed by any single person (Smith) but these competencies should be "resident with the audit team assigned to the engagement" (Cutting, et al.). Several writers point out the type of training that an auditor requires (Mathieson, "Computer Auditing–Some Basic Considerations") and information is provided on various professional certification programs that attest to the prerequisite skills and knowledge.

Sources of Annotated Bibliography

Journals	Frequency Cited
EDPACS	18
Internal Auditor	14
Datamation	12
The Journal of Accountancy	9
Canadian Chartered Accountants	6
The Journal of Systems Management	6
EDP Analyzer	4
Data Management	3
The Magazine of Bank Administration	5
The EDP Auditor	3
Management Services	2
Other journals (26)	34
Total	116

(Continued)

Sources of Annotated Bibliography (continued)

Books and Reports	Frequency Cited
American Institute of Certified Public Accountants	6
Canadian Institute of Chartered Accountants	1
U.S. Government Publications (including public laws)	14
Internal Auditors Association	1
Books and other publications	28
Total	166

SECTION A
AUDITING IN THE ELECTRONIC ENVIRONMENT

ANNOTATED BIBLIOGRAPHY

1. **Blank, Vergil F. "Electronic Data Processing–Programming for the Internal Auditor."** ***Internal Auditor*****, September 1959, pp. 16-22.**

Although written some 22 years ago, the article is relevant today. The author points out that the work of the internal auditor is dependent upon two major segments: (1) internal control and (2) the audit trail. He discusses input controls, processing controls and mechanical controls. The author, writing in 1959, concluded that the internal auditor must possess sufficient training in computers to evolve in his own mind the degree of reliability he may impute to the electronic equipment; he also concluded that the role of the internal auditor is that of an instrument of management.

2. **Frielink, A.B.** ***Auditing Automatic Data Processing: A Survey of Papers on the Subject.*** **Amsterdam, Holland: Elsevier Publishing Company, 1961, 70 pp.**

This survey is an attempt to set forth systematically opinions found in the early professional literature. It is a survey of 71 articles, studies and reports from 1952-1960 (with two references to auditing and punched card accounting, dated 1928 and 1940). The articles cover primarily journals published in the United States, Holland and Scotland. The survey highlights the foundation of the paradigm for auditing in the EDP environment developed during the early days of electronic and automated data processing. Also included is an article on one of the earliest records of computer fraud: James Allan, "Embezzlement By Electronics" (*The Accountants Magazine*, April 1960).

The general thrust of the articles is that the auditing profession will maintain pace with technological advances as evidenced by the profession meeting the challenge of the punched card and EAM equipment accounting.

3. Friedhoff, Stephen H. "The Auditor's Approach to Electronic Data Processing." ***The Canadian Chartered Accountant*****, October 1963, pp. 250-253.**

The auditor will have to adjust to the use of new technical skills. With the advent of EDP, he will still rely upon the basic principles of auditing to formulate an opinion of a client's auditing results. The auditor will maintain the same accepted auditing standards as those formerly used in audits produced on manual and mechanical accounting systems.

The use of the computer does not change the principles of the procedural audit. The auditor must realize that the methods of internal control do not disappear, but change in form only. To understand these changes it is important that the auditor should participate in the planning and development of the EDP system. In this way the accountant can understand the accounting procedures that go into the computer and be satisfied that they will produce a valid accounting result.

The auditor will begin to have at his disposal a series of new aids, available in computer installations. If used wisely these aids can greatly simplify the audit procedures and reduce the extent of audit tests. The auditor will come to realize that there is a system of controls and checks within the system. These controls and checks will be similar to ones familiar to the auditor, including machine, program and clerical controls. Management, as well as the auditor, will have an interest both in computer accuracy and in meaningful reports being prepared on EDP.

While EDP will be a help for the auditor, he can't be lulled into a false sense of security by the accuracy of the computer. The auditor must be as thorough with the EDP system as he was with the manual system. Above all, the auditor must continue to use accepted auditing principles to render a meaningful auditing opinion.

4. Weiss, Harold. "The Programmer Encounters Auditing." ***Datamation*****, September 1963, pp. 31-34.**

Although the article was written 18 years ago, it offers advice that continues to be relevant. The author points out that management has the responsibility for safeguarding the assets of the company, recording all transactions properly in books of accounts, and preparing accurate and adequate financial statements. It is becoming increasingly the role of the internal auditor to assist management in that responsibility through management auditing, systems auditing or operational auditing.

The author points out that what the auditor needs is contained in the Suggested Guidelines for Record Requirements for Taxpayers Utilizing Automatic Data Processing Systems released by the audit division of the Internal Revenue Service, dated March 25, 1963. These guidelines called for a general ledger to be maintained; for the audit trail to be designed so that the details underlying the summary accounting data may be identified and made available to the IRS; for records which provide the opportunity to trace any transactions back to the original source or forward to a final total; for adequate record retention facilities; and for a description setting forth the ADP portion of the accounting system, that is, application standards which should indicate the application being performed, the procedures employed in each application (which, for example, might be supported by flowcharts, block diagrams or other satisfactory support of input or output references), and the controls used to insure accurate and reliable processing. Important changes together with their effective dates should be noted in order to preserve an accurate chronological record, which underlines the need for management to insist upon internal control and audit controls imposed by regulatory agencies. However, these requirements do create problems for the auditor in terms of nonvisible records, loss of historical information, difficulty of access to source documents, loss of human inspection, centralization and concentration processing, and documentation.

Once the programmer is made aware of these needs by the auditor and management, the author gives several suggestions to data processing personnel that may help to promote mutual cooperation. The steps include bringing the auditor into the initial planning phase of the system, involving the internal auditor in systems implementation and testing, giving the auditor the documentation that he and other areas of the business require and which the IRS Guidelines point up, helping in the training of the auditor about EDP, and enlisting the auditor's help in the training of data processing personnel about audit and control requirements.

5. **American Institute of Certified Public Accountants. *Accounting & the Computer: A Selection of Articles from the Journal of Accountancy and Management Services.* NY: American Institute of Certified Public Accountants, Inc., 1966, 356 pp.**

This book is a collection of articles related to accounting and the computer published in *The Journal of Accountancy and Management*

Services between 1962 and 1965. The book provides an introduction and orientation for accounting practitioners who recognize the potential impact of computers on their client's accounting and their own practice. As the editor points out, the book is not intended to serve as a textbook or a detailed guide to practice. The subject is much too vast and complicated to be treated in depth in one comparatively small volume. Rather, the purpose is to present the accounting achievements and potential of computers in fairly broad perspective, to give the reader a general picture of what is happening and what is likely to happen in all phases of practice. The book contains articles relating to computer components and concepts, auditing "around" or auditing "through" the computer, using the computer as an audit tool, the impact of EDP on internal control, evaluating internal controls in the EDP systems, decision making, operations research, statistical analysis, total information concepts, the feasibility study, and EDP equipment selection. Its value is in depicting the "state of the art" in the early 1960s. Of particular interest is the EDP internal control checklist on pages 161 through 166. This checklist includes a series of questions dealing with the organization of the EDP department, standardization of procedures, computer program maintenance, input procedures, computer processing procedures, magnetic tape control, physical condition and maintenance.

6. Cornick, D.L. *The Role of the Federal Auditor In An EDP Environment*. An unpublished report submitted in partial fulfillment for the degree of Master in Public Administration: Technology of Management. Washington, DC: The American University, January 22, 1969, mimeographed, 134 pp.

The author traces the legislative history of federal auditing dating from April 1776 when the Continental Congress in establishing the Treasury Office of Accounts passed a resolution pertaining to the function of an auditor general, to 1968 with various federal acts providing for internal audits and granting various federal acts providing for internal audits and granting various agencies external auditing powers.

The report discusses how various authors from 1940 to 1967 have viewed the impact of the EDP environment on auditing.

As early as 1940 with the advent of machine accounting (EAM), writers were pointing out that the auditor "will continue to rely on segregation of duties and upon test checks."

Subsequently other writers during the 1950s believed that the effects of "Business Electronics" would be minimal since auditing procedures and objectives remain unchanged, i.e., to safeguard against fraud and unintentional errors, and to assess the effectiveness of the data processing method to insure data integrity.

Finally, during the 60s various writers concluded that while there are no changes in the theoretical auditing concepts and objectives, there necessarily will be some changes required in techniques and approaches.

Includes a case study in auditing around the computer in a public utility. The author quotes from the 1966 Air Force Auditor's Guide which prophetically pointed out that the increased value of data being handled, the speed with which the data are processed and the centralization of accounting functions have by no means reached their zenith nor will the pace in technology diminish. The modern day auditor must not only meet the challenge quickly but parallel its future growth. To do otherwise will render the role the auditor plays ineffective, if not futile.

7. Snellgrove, Olin C. "The Management Audit—Organizational Guidance System." *Journal of Systems Management*, December 1971, p. 10. (ABI-72-00151)*

Management audit can provide an objective, impartial, and competent analysis of organizational activities. The audit is a periodic function to evaluate efficiency. The management audit may be used effectively at all levels in the hierarchy and, with decentralization, difficulties of control can be helped. The complete audit must be handled by competent audit personnel who must project themselves into the line organization's position and evaluate deviations from written procedure. Complete audit is a good example of the team-concept—it uses talent from the functional audit group, line management and top management aimed at evaluating and improving operations. Program audit is similar to the complete audit except in scope and direction.

8. Davis, Keagle W. and Donald R. Wood. "Computer Control and Audit." *Tempo*, Fall 1972, pp. 9-20. (ABI-72-03854)

The continuing development of the computer as a tool for the auditor, discussed in two parts, reflects the fact that the profession is ready to refine and develop new techniques and programs for dealing with computers as a normal part of the auditor's function. Part one discusses problems of EDP controls and opportunities; areas of future

*For explanation of special sources of abstracts, see introduction to Part II.

change within the auditing profession are identified. Part two discusses the impact of EDP on audit activities. The planning required for an audit of EDP systems involves total rethinking of audit scope and objectives. Separate consideration is given to the audit of applications, procedures within the installation itself, and system-development methods in use within the organization under audit.

9. **Jancuro, Elise G. and Arnold H. Berger, editors. *Computers: Auditing and Control*. Philadelphia, PA: Auerbach Publishers, Inc., 1973, 498 pp.**

The book is a compilation of articles written in the late 1960s and the early 70s. It complements Frielink (1961), who chronicled the writing of the 50s and the beginning of the 60s. There are several sections and articles of particular importance including those on Computer Auditing Software and Documentation. Other concepts such as evaluation of internal controls and input-output data controls are covered in many other references and texts cited.

10. **Sprigg, J. "Internal Audit in the Service of Management." *Management Services in Government*, November 1974, pp. 209-211. (ABI-74-09793)**

Generally, internal audit has been developing steadily from its traditional role of verifying the accuracy of accounting transactions to its modern more positive function as a service to management. There are two major features which distinguish the more modern internal audit. These are the nature of the audit, and its place within the organization. A significant change in the nature of internal audit also requires changes in attitude and in auditing techniques. Techniques are evolving rapidly. Although attention has been drawn to the auditor's role as an expert on control systems it should be emphasized that it is not the auditor's function to install sound systems of control. The "quiet revolution" has been greatly assisted by a substantial training program which is detailed.

11. ***Privacy Act of 1974*. U.S. Code, title 5, sections 552a (1975).**

The purpose of the Act is to safeguard individual privacy from the misuse of federal records, to provide that individuals be granted access to records concerning them which are maintained by federal agencies. The Act acknowledges that the increasing rise of computers and sophisticated information technology has greatly magnified the harm to individual privacy that can occur from any collection, maintenance, use, or dissemination of personal information. In this regard the law requires federal agencies to provide safeguards to prevent misuse of such information.

Each agency that maintains a system of records shall establish appropriate administrative, technical and physical safeguards to insure the security and confidentiality of records and to protect against any anticipated threats or hazards to their security or integrity which could result in substantive harm, embarrassment, inconvenience, or unfairness to any individual on whom information is maintained.

The Act further states that all records are to be as accurate and complete as is reasonably necessary to assure fairness to the individual. The Act has other provisions, purposes, exceptions, but the above suggest the influence of statutes in the performance of an auditor in an EDP environment.

12. "Auditor's Responsibility for EDP Controls Extended by Courts." *EDPACS*, November 1976, pp. 8-9. (ABI-77-01199)

This past year a court ruling was established that has a great impact on an auditor's responsibility within the area of data processing. The charge by the plaintiffs was that the auditing firm failed to disclose serious problems in the electronic data processing system which proved to be material. The court ruled that the shortcomings in the EDP system seriously jeopardized the validity of reported statistics and that the auditors conducted the audit as if the problems did not exist. Accounting controls and administrative controls are interrelated when viewed from an auditor's point of view. Not disclosing significant EDP deficiencies is contrary to generally accepted accounting principles. The fact that internal control is weak should be of significance to an auditor.

13. Joseph, Anthony M. "Computer Fraud and Sales Audit." *Retail Control*, June/July 1976, pp. 36-41. (ABI-76-08986)

Many companies are paying consulting fees to reformed felons for counsel on security. In the relatively new field of computer security, ex-criminals are also being used as advisors. Although the reformed felon may have the advantage over the rest of us in determining how a system can be cheated, that does not mean that his thought processes cannot be imitated. The controller must imitate this way of thinking if the store's computer security program is to be fully effective.

14. Perry, William E. "Management Support for EDP Auditing." *EDPACS*, August 1976, pp. 5-9. (ABI-76-09968)

The divergence of opinion between auditors and management as to what the electronic data processing (EDP) audit function should be is explored. Management is sometimes alienated by the EDP audit function since some of its characteristics seem to be contrary to many management philosophies. Most of the problems associated with achieving a strong EDP audit function are caused by a failure to communicate. Conflict is a natural outgrowth from the fact that EDP auditing is a change from traditional auditing. Some of the EDP auditor's time should be devoted to resolving this conflict, not by a massive, one-time campaign, but by a continuing educational effort. Responsibility should be accepted by the EDP auditor for educating management about the need for better control over and a stronger audit of data processing. Only then can a solid, healthy relationship be attained between the EDP auditor, audit management, data processing, and financial management.

15. Canning, Richard G. "The Importance of EDP Audit and Control." *EDP Analyzer*, June 1977, pp. 1-12.

The conclusions reached by the U.S. General Accounting Office (GAO) on federal waste, abuse, etc., is presented. For example, federal agency computers cause more than 1.7 billion payment authorizations–checks, bills, requisitions–to be made out each year totalling some $44 billion without anybody reviewing or evaluating whether they are correct. The U.S. General Accounting Office also indicated in 69 cases considered computer crimes the losses totalled over $2.1 million.

The author points out that the GAO studies support the view of some experts in the computer security field that the greatest magnitude of losses come from errors of omission and commission followed by losses due to theft and physical damage. While losses due to theft attract the most attention, it is the system's errors and inadequate internal controls that over a period of time account for the bulk of the losses. The author also describes the research which resulted in the auditability and control study by the Institute of Internal Auditors. The control practices report describes how the systems designer goes about incorporating an adequate set of controls in a new application system.

The report discusses over two hundred specific control procedures which are based on practices in the firms contacted during the study. Of importance to auditors involved with third-party reviews is the discussion of controls relating to: (1) input-output scheduling and control; (2) media library controls; (3) malfunction reporting and preventive maintenance; (4) environment controls and physical security; (5) separation of duties; (6) resources planning; (7) user billing and charge-out procedures; and (8) disaster recovery procedures.

The report lists and describes 28 audit tools and techniques that the study found to be in practical use. The author concludes that the Institute of Internal Auditors (SAC) study which was developed under a grant from IBM will be very helpful to both systems designers and internal auditors in reducing the chance for those types of accidental or deliberate losses that are described in the U.S. General Accounting Office report.

16. ***Foreign Corrupt Practices Act*****. Title 15, U.S. Code (1977).**

This act, among other things, requires every issuer which has a class of securities registered under section 12 of the Securities Exchange Act of 1934 (as amended) and any company that is required to file reports under Section 15(D) of that Act, to keep books, records, and accounts, which in reasonable detail accurately and fairly reflect the transactions and dispositions of the assets of the issuer.

Furthermore, the Act requires that the issuer devise and maintain a system of *Internal Accounting Controls* to provide reasonable assurances that transactions are executed in accordance with *Management's* general or specific authorizations.

Management is held accountable to see to it that transactions are recorded as necessary to permit preparation of financial statements in conformity with generally accepted accounting principles or any other criteria applicable to such statements.

The Act requires that access to assets be permitted only in accordance with management's authorization and that there be a periodic examination of the records.

17. U.S. Government Accounting Office. *Computer Auditing in the Executive Departments: Not Enough is Being Done.* Report to the Congress by the Comptroller General of the United States. Washington, DC: U.S. General Accounting Office, September 28, 1977.

The report discusses the internal audit group's EDP involvement in 12 federal agencies.

The external auditor evaluates the system in terms of the financial statements produced. The internal auditor, additionally, is responsible to management in determining to what extent operations are being carried out economically, efficiently, and effectively.

The report cites the literature which supports the notion that, among other things, auditors have been reluctant to establish strong computer auditing. "The response to auditing computers has been none at all, periodic, responsive, and participative." For example, the resident internal audit staff in one agency had not reviewed and evaluated the adequacy of control over computer processing even though some $7.4 billion in payments were processed by the computer system.

The report examines auditing work in four major ADP areas: systems design and development, equipment acquisition, specific applications and ADP installation management. One important conclusion reached was that terms of auditors with a general ADP background, assisted where necessary by ADP audit specialists, can successfully review both technical and non-technical issues.

The report recommends that, for a proper and effective response to the challenge of computer auditing, the head of each agency require internal audit groups to:

1. Study the effect of ADP on agency operations, expenditures, and program accomplishments.

2. Determine the extent to which computer activities need to be audited (both ongoing system reviews and audits of specific aspects, such as installation of a new computer-based inventory system).

3. Determine whether enough audit resources are available, and if not, get needed resources by training existing audit staff or hiring people with the necessary skills.

4. Develop and carry out audits that will provide enough coverage to determine that ADP resources are used efficiently, economically, and effectively.

5. Periodically review the internal audit coverage of computer-based information systems and adjust resource allocations accordingly.

Finally, the report also observes that computer audit proficiency is not a static matter. The advancement of computer technology must be matched by continuing and broadening auditor knowledge and capability if the challenge to perform to standards is to be met. Even for those most capable audit groups, the task to maintain technical proficiency is unending. Greater management attention is essential to help insure that all internal audit groups throughout the Federal Government develop and maintain needed ADP auditing capabilities.

18. Weiss, Harold. "Computer Audit Survey." ***EDPACS*****, September 1977, pp. 8-15. (ABI-77-15859)**

The results of a questionnaire distributed to registrants at the sixth conference on computer audit, control and security in San Francisco on April 1, 1976, shows that banks and savings-and-loan associations are making greater investments in computer auditing than are other industries. The most common number of EDP auditors per organization in all industries is two. Of all organizations polled, the average salary of computer auditors is approximately $20,000, with bankers paying the lowest salary and retailing and public accounting the highest. The survey also showed that 35 percent of the organizations have their auditors sign off on new systems, while only 19 percent sign off on program modifications. Only 10.5 percent of the audit organizations did code review regularly. Of all organizations, 27 percent did no auditing of systems under development.

19. ***Inspector General Act of 1978*****. U.S. Code, Title 5, Section 8501 (1978).**

The purpose is establishment of an Office of Inspector General with several federal departments and agencies in order to create independent and objective units to:

1. Conduct and supervise audits and investigations relating to programs and operations of the Department of Agriculture, the Department of Commerce, the Department of Housing and Urban Development, the Department of the Interior, the Department of Labor, the Department of Transportation, the Community Services Administration, the Environmental Protection Agency, the General Services Administration, the National Aeronautics and Space Administration, the Small Business Administration, and the Veterans' Administration.

2. Provide leadership and coordination and recommend policies for activities designed (a) to promote economy, efficiency, and

effectiveness in the administration of, and (b) to prevent and detect fraud and abuse in, such programs and operations.

3. Provide a means for keeping the head of the establishment and the Congress fully and currently informed about problems and deficiencies relating to the administration of such programs and operations and the necessity for and progress of corrective action.

It shall be the duty and responsibility of each Inspector General, among other things, to provide policy direction for and to conduct, supervise, and coordinate audits and investigations relating to the programs and operations of those departments and agencies. The responsibilities also relate to management audits, compliance audit and program evaluation audit with such objectives as promoting economy and efficiency in the administration of, or preventing and detecting fraud and abuse in, its programs and operations.

In carrying out these duties and responsibilities each Inspector General shall comply with standards established by the Comptroller General of the United States for audits of federal establishments, organizations, programs, activities and functions and shall take appropriate steps to assure that any work performed by non-federal auditors complies with these standards.

20. Patrick, Robert L. "Auditing and DP: Redressing the Relationship." *Datamation*, November 15, 1978, pp. 139-144. (DPD)

Computer technology has advanced so rapidly that it has all but run off and left the audit profession. A recent Stanford Research Institute study surveyed 1,500 organizations and found that many "common" practices were far from common and, in some cases, were almost unknown from organization to organization. It was also found that training programs for internal auditors neglect to emphasize computer techniques even though 90% of the record-keeping in the U.S. private sector may be in some way computerized.

Understanding how the auditors fell behind the technology will help in devising a solution. Auditors usually grow up as CPA's and follow the CPA continuing education program. After formal training and certification, on-the-job training is provided. There is a lot of "what was good for my father is good enough for me" in these internal training programs.

About 18 years ago, the auditing profession was split by a debate of whether they should audit through or around the computer. In the early '60s when the small accounting machine gained popularity the auditors saw it merely as a replacement for punched card accounting equipment. Many chose to satisfy themselves with reviewing the data put into the computer and the reports that emanated from it. Just about the time auditors decided to audit through the computer, data base management systems were invented. Individual files lost their identity, the simple transaction counts that had sufficed during the punched card years lost much of their meaning, and management information systems were born. About the same time telecommunications entered the computer field. This brought about systems that capture data near the point of transaction and send that data to the computer data base without the paper leaving the point of origination. This meant that auditors would need a whole new control technology. Today those controls are still evolving.

The facts clearly indicate that current audit techniques are not as advanced as the technology being audited. Furthermore, the computer profession shows no signs of waiting while the auditors catch up.

The price of computer electronics is now low enough that middle managers can have their own computers, thus avoiding the standards, the controls, and the audit trails that are so vital to stable business. Also, just breaking on the horizon is a new set of software offerings from several manufacturers which will allow minicomputers to be configured into distributed data processing systems.

There is an opportunity for catching up. With the support of senior management, the auditor can once more play his proper role in the organization. Several years ago concern developed about the economics of programming and the gradual erosion of programmer productivity. Some new systems analysis techniques were invented, and a new look was taken at the programming development process.

The design inspection is an attempt to review program development products at milestones and certify the quality of each one against a predetermined standard. A company that conducts milestones reviews and design inspections during the systems development process has an ideal opportunity to train the audit staff and to build proper audit controls into emerging systems of computer programs. If the auditors can become knowledgeable they can assure that an emerging design contains adequate controls to prevent mistakes, mischief, or malicious activity. Knowledgeable auditors can sit in on milestone reviews to assure the controls being implemented will carry out their intended purpose.

Three things will be required to establish a union between the technicians performing design inspections and the internal auditors: (1) the senior financial executive must lay to rest the auditor's belief that any participation by auditors in the development process would impugn the auditor's objectivity; (2) work priorities for the internal audit workforce must be reviewed and adjusted; and (3) since design reviews are conducted amid an on-going development schedule, the interpersonal reactions are such that an ignorant auditor will not be tolerated. Therefore, it may be necessary to provide some special training or to bring in some special temporary help to augment your audit workforce.

21. DeMarco, Victor F. "EDP Development: Should the Internal Auditor Participate?" *Internal Auditor*, June 1979, pp. 19-25. (ABI-79-10434)

General purpose computers in the U.S. increased almost 300% between 1966 and 1975, and this increase brought greater exposure to risk through error, omission, improper controls, inadequate design, and fraud. Because of these risks, management, regulatory agencies, public accounting firms, and the general public are more often turning to the internal auditor. One of the internal auditor's most important contributions to the organization is independence, but as an overall objective, he can appraise the electronic data processing (EDP) functions and related financial administrative and operational controls to determine the effectiveness of efficiency of operations. A study of perceptions of the internal auditor's independence recommends that internal auditors should be involved in the design phase only in reviewing, testing, and assessing the adequacy of applicable controls, and internal auditors should increase their EDP technical competence.

22. Perry, William E. and H.C. Warner. "Auditing: Expectations vs. Reality." *The Magazine of Bank Administration*, March 1979, pp. 28-32. (ABI-79-06415)

There is a large gap between the auditability and controls for electronic data processing (EDP) systems and the pace of new applications and systems design. Management's increasing dependence on data processing, government reporting requirements, and EDP changes have all made the accuracy of the information provided more critical and therefore have made EDP audits and controls more important. Top management should initiate the study of the adequacy of EDP audits and controls. Current audit and control practices should be periodically checked, new trends in EDP technology investigated, and how current and new programs hold up to audit and control needs should be assessed. In developing controls, written guidelines should be drawn up, more trained EDP auditors should be hired, and top management should stress EDP audits. Internal auditors must become more involved in auditing of computer applications, and there must be a better understanding of the audit's scope between management and the auditor. Graphs.

23. Roberts, Ray. "Internal Controls, It's Not Only the Auditor's Headache." ***Data Management*****, July 1979. (ABI-79-13843)**

While internal controls are still valuable in the context of fraud prevention and detection, they are also critical in ensuring that accounting systems' information is reliable. Recent amendments to the federal securities act provide statutory requirements to "devise and maintain" the system of internal control. Although top management has the nominal responsibility for internal controls, the actual tasks will be delegated to those in electronic data processing (EDP). The existence of a statutory mandate of provisions for internal control may be advantageous for the systems designer, programmer, and the data processing manager because the mandate supports the need for both budget and time to fulfill the requirements. To ensure that a consideration of the myriad controls is accomplished, reference to one of the studies of EDP controls is appropriate. The corporation's independent EDP auditor could also be involved.

24. Ryssdal, Leif. "Future Demands on Auditing." ***International Journal of Government Auditing*****, April 1979, p. 1 (ABI-79-09119)**

Due to the technical possibilities of electronic data processing and current social developments, considerable changes are taking place in accounting and auditing practices. Auditors will be expected in the future to keep EDP accounting systems functioning reliably. Audit departments consisting of specialists in accounts, regulations, EDP, statistics and engineering will be needed to effectively analyze accounts. By establishing standards and guidelines for the presentation of accounts, materials, administration and EDP work, a higher professional standard and uniform procedures will be ensured. A sound national economy requires high productivity but more important is the efficient use of resources. Auditing will become result-oriented auditing as productivity auditing and efficiency auditing is combined.

In the current administration crisis, auditing departments will be required to provide an overall financial view of government tasks. Auditing departments will be performing a necessary social task by demonstrating implementation flaws and helping government solve problems.

25. ***The Dimensions of Privacy: A National Opinion Research Survey of Attitudes toward Privacy*. Stevens Point, WI: Sentry Insurance, May 1979, 104 pp.**

The report concerns privacy vis a vis employment, audit, insurance, medical, news media and government industries. The report also covers the use of computers. In a very real sense, computers are at the heart of the concerns over the loss and potential loss of privacy of personal data. A majority of Americans (54% to 31%) consider the present uses of computers as an actual threat to personal privacy. By an 80-10% majority, the American people agree that computers have made it easier for someone to obtain improperly confidential personal information about individuals. A 52-27% majority disagree that the privacy of personal information in computers is adequately safeguarded (pp. 76-77).

SECTION A. ADDITIONAL REFERENCES

Standards and Legal

26. **Municipal Finance Officers Association of the United States and Canada. *Governmental Accounting, Auditing, and Financial Reporting.* Chicago: Municipal Finance Officers Association of the United States and Canada, 1968.**

27. **Wagner, J.W. "EDP and the Auditor of the 1970s." *Accounting Review*, July 1969, pp. 600-604.**

28. **Newgarden, Albert, ed. "Computer Auditing in the Seventies." Special supplement. *Arthur Young Journal*, Winter/Spring 1970.**

29. **U.S. General Accounting Office. *Standards for Audit of Governmental Organization, Programs, Activities and Functions.* Washington, DC: U.S. General Accounting Office, 1972.**

30. **American Institute of Certified Public Accountants. *Statement on Auditing Standards No. 3*, "The Effects of EDP on the Auditor's Study and Evaluation of Internal Controls." NY: American Institute of Certified Public Accountants, 1974.**

31. U.S. General Accounting Office. *Internal Auditing in Federal Agencies.* Washington, DC: U.S. General Accounting Office, 1974.

32. American Institute of Certified Public Accountants. *AICPA Professional Standards: Auditing, Management Advisory Service, Tax Practice as of September 1, 1976*, Volume I. NY: American Institute of Certified Public Accountants, 1975.

33. Municipal Finance Officers Association of the United States and Canada. *Interpretation 1, GAAFR and the AICPA Audit Guide.* Chicago: Municipal Finance Officers of the United States and Canada, 1976.

34. U.S. General Accounting Office. *Improvements Needed in Managing Automated Decisionmaking in Computers Throughout the Federal Government.* Washington, DC: U.S. General Accounting Office, April 23, 1976.

35. American Institute of Certified Public Accountants. *Management, Control and Audit of Advanced EDP Systems.* NY: AICPA, 1977.

36. Mason, J.O. and J.J. Davies. "Legal Implications of EDP Deficiencies." *CPA Journal*, May 1977, pp. 21-24.

37. McGuire, P.T. "EDP Auditing–Why? How? What?" *The Internal Auditor*, June 1977, pp. 27-34.

38. U.S. General Accounting Office. *Computer Auditing in the Executive Departments: Not Enough is Being Done.* A report to the Congress by the Comptroller General of the United States. Washington, DC: U.S. General Accounting Office, 1977.

39. Arthur Andersen & Company. *An Analysis of the Foreign Corrupt Practices Act of 1977.* Chicago: Arthur Andersen & Company, 1978.

40. U.S. General Accounting Office. *Auditing Computer-Based Systems: Additional GAO Audit Standards.* Washington, DC: U.S. General Accounting Office, March 1979.

Computer Abuse

41. *EDP Physical Security Briefing & Checklist.* Rye, NY: Reymont, 1977. International Business Machines Corp. *The Considerations of*

Physical Security in a Computer Environment. Armonk, NY: IBM 1972. (IBM No. G520-2700-0.)

42. International Business Machines Corp. *42 Suggestions for Improving Security in Data Processing Operations*. Armonk, NY: IBM, 1973. (IBM No. G520-2797-0.)

43. Parker, et al. *Computer Abuse*. U.S. Department of Commerce, Stanford Research Institute, 1973.

44. American Federation of Information Processing Societies, Inc. *Security System Review Manual*, AFIPS Press, 1974.

45. Kuong, Javier. *Computer Security, Auditing and Controls*. Wellesley Hills, MA: Management Advisory Publications, 1974.

46. National Bureau of Standards. Federal Information Processing Standard Publication. *Guidelines for Automatic Data Processing Physical Security and Risk Management*, FIPS PUB 31, 1974.

47. Allen, Brandt. "Embezzler's Guide to the Computer." *Harvard Business Review*, July-August 1975.

48. International Business Machines Corp. *Data Security—Threats and Deficiencies in Computer Operations*. Armonk, NY: IBM, 1975. (IBM No. G320-5446-0.)

49. National Bureau of Standards. Federal Information Processing Standard Publication. *Computer Security Guidelines for Implementing The Privacy Act of 1974*, FIPS PUB 41, 1975.

50. Parker, Donn. *Crime by Computer*. NY: Charles Scribner's Sons, 1976.

51. Romney, Marshall. "Fraud and EDP." *CPA Journal*, November 1976, pp. 23-28.

52. Allen, Brandt. "The Biggest Computer Frauds: Lessons for CPAs." *Journal of Accountancy*, May 1977.

53. National Bureau of Standards. *Audit and Evaluation of Computer Security*. Washington, DC: U.S. Department of Commerce, U.S. Government Printing Office, 1977. (NBS Spec. Publ. 500-19.)

Performance Auditing

54. Suchman, Edward. *Evaluative Research: Principles and Practices in Service and Social Action Programs*. NY: Russell Sage Foundation, 1969.

55. Morse, Ellsworth. "Performance and Operational Auditing." *Journal of Accountancy*, June 1971.

56. Rivlin, Alice M. *Systematic Thinking for Social Action*. Washington, DC: Brookings Institution, 1971.

57. Lindberg, Roy A., and Theodore Cohn. *Operations Auditing*. New York, NY: Amacon Division of the American Management Association, 1972.

58. Rossi, Peter H. and Walter Williams. *Evaluating Social Programs: Theory, Practice and Politics*. NY: Seminar Press, 1972.

59. Weiss, Carol H. *Evaluation Research: Methods of Assessing Program Effectiveness*. Englewood Cliffs, NJ: Prentice-Hall, Inc., 1972.

60. Hatry, Harry P. et al. *Practical Program Evaluation for State and Local Government Officials*. Washington, DC: The Urban Institute, 1973.

61. American Institute of Certified Public Accountants. *Audits of State and Local Government Units–Industry Audit Guide*. NY: American Institute of Certified Public Accountants, 1974.

62. Eifler, Thomas. "Performing the Operations Audit." Management Education Portfolio, NY: American Institute of Certified Public Accountants Professional Development Division, 1974.

63. David, Irwin T. "How to Best Utilize the External Auditor." *Special Bulletin*, Municipal Finance Officers Association of the United States and Canada, December 16, 1976.

64. Knighton, Lemis M. "Information Pre Conditions of Performance Auditing." *Governmental Finance*, May 1976, pp. 22-26.

65. "Performance Auditing: An Untraditional Concept in a Very Traditional Environment." *Governmental Finance*, November 1976.

66. U.S. General Accounting Office. *Assessing Social Program Impact Evaluations: A Checklist Approach*, Exposure Draft. Washington, DC: U.S. General Accounting Office, PAD 79-2, October 1978.

67. U.S. General Accounting Office. *Status and Issues: Federal Program Evaluation*. Washington, DC: U.S. General Accounting Office, PAD 78-83, October 1978.

SECTION B
OVERVIEW OF THE ELECTRONIC ENVIRONMENT

ANNOTATED BIBLIOGRAPHY

1. Martin. W.W. "Flowcharting: Shorthand, Analysis and Model." *Systems and Procedures Journal*, March-April 1966.

Far from being a tedious requirement of systems documentation, charting can be a revealing, adaptable means of pinning down clearly what is happening in the information and discharge of responsibilities. The author defines what flowcharting is and its various uses. Although some of the symbols have since become standardized and are somewhat different from those in the article, it is still a good illustration of systems flowcharting, programming flowcharting, systems flow flowcharting, and document flows. Flowcharting can serve the systems analyst in three ways: as a precise yet convenient shorthand, as a means of analyzing existing processes both quantitatively and logically, and as a model to simulate and test his recommendations.

2. Rudolph, Harley H., Jr. "Flowcharting–A Systems and Control Technique." *Management Services 3*, September-October 1966, pp. 24-30.

Once a specialized industrial engineering technique, flowcharting has become a common tool for systems designers, EDP analysts, and even auditors. This article reviews the basics of its use. The technique flowchart is a prime tool of the computer programmer. The structural flowchart has a wider application as a tool of audit and management advisory service personnel. Since the article was written there has been standardization of flowcharting symbols, yet this does serve as a good background piece to understanding the nature of flowcharting. As the author points out, there are alternative ways of flowcharting but only one criterion, that is, the flowchart must illustrate the pertinent facts in a logical manner. A flowchart is excellent evidence of documentation in evaluating internal control and it is also a helpful tool in analyzing systems, developing improvements, and running procedures.

3. Lobel, Jerome. "Auditing in the New Systems Environment." *The Journal of Accountancy*, September 1971, pp. 63-67.

The author describes four generations of computer technology. The first generation was characterized by electrostatic tubes, magnetic drums, and an emphasis on computing ability rather than upon input-output capabilities. The second generation was characterized by transistorized—or solid state—circuitry and increased input-output capability. The third generation was characterized by integrated circuitry using silicon chips with emphasis upon communication and the need for data transmission over communication lines. Systems capabilities include timesharing and multiprogramming. The fourth generation is described in terms of graceful degradation, advanced memory systems and information utilities.

The fourth generation will affect the auditor in various ways—internal control problems will become critical due to the disappearing audit trail, and unauthorized or accidental data access. For these and other reasons auditors are finally getting involved. They are assigned broader responsibilities and are being directed to participate in EDP systems design at least to the degree that they outline the controls that need to be incorporated in the new system.

The author discusses the need for increased emphasis on internal control evaluations, EDP training for auditors, and need to develop online audit capabilities.

4. Schubert, Richard F. "Basic Concepts in Data Base Management Systems." *Datamation*, July 1972, pp. 42-47.

The article describes the philosophy and terminology of data base management systems and describes the control of data structure, the data base elements, such as physical storage structure, data and control information, and logical relationships among data stored within the data base. It provides the reader with a description of data base languages such as the device media control language (DMCL), which is used to assign and control physical space for the data base. It includes the specification of numbers of cylinders required for the entire data base, page size, etc. It is a good overview for the auditor in getting some notion of data base management software, including data base language systems.

5. Boehm, Barry W. "Software and Its Impact: A Quantitative Assessment." *Datamation*, May 1973, pp. 48-59.

This article deals primarily with the Air Force command and control requirements in the 1980s. The author points out that the Air Force in 1972 spent an estimated $1 to $1.5 billion on software, about three times the average expenditure on computer hardware, and about four to five percent of the total Air Force budget. Of interest to the auditor is the discussion of software reliability and certification. Software certification means providing guarantees that the software will do what it is supposed to do. The author noted that an average of one software error per day was discovered in one large system which contained about 2.7 million instructions. The lack of certification capabilities makes it virtually impossible to provide strong guarantees on security or privacy for sensitive or personal information.

One of the problems is that a program provides so many paths through which data can go. For example, the author points out that even in a simple operation, the number of different paths through a program could be in the magnitude of about ten to the twentieth power, and if one had a computer that could check out one path per nanosecond (10^{-9} seconds), and had started to check out the program at the beginning of the Christian era (1 A.D.), the job would be about half done. Fortunately, most of the data goes through a relatively small number of paths that can be checked out, but the unchecked paths still have a probability of occurring. The author reports that one organization paid $750,000 to test an 8,000 instruction program and even then couldn't be guaranteed that the software was perfect, because testing can only determine the presence of errors, not the absence.

The article concludes that 30 percent of the labor force must deal with computers in their daily work, but only 15 percent of the labor force is required to have any understanding of computers. Extrapolating this trend into the 1980s, it is estimated that almost 75 percent of the labor force will be working with computer systems but by 1985 only 40 percent will be required to have some knowledge of how computers work, which indicates that perhaps 40 percent of the labor force will be trusting implicitly in the results produced by computer software.

6. Bowers, Dan M. "An Analysis of Computer Terminals." *The Office*, October 1973, pp. 89-93, 135-136.

The author begins by defining a computer terminal. To simplify, he proceeds to define it as those devices which present data directly to and take data from humans. There are two major equipment categories: (1) expensive systems which prepare large batches of data for input to a computing system, and also systems which prepare large batches of data for humans; and (2) the system which accepts data directly from the human who originates it, submits the data to the computer for immediate processing, and immediately returns the data to the human, which the author states as being a true computer terminal. The usefulness of computer terminals is as real-time devices. Some of these devices are the teletypewriter (which was first), strip-and-list printers (not very popular), character displays, alpha-numeric CRT displays (with or without keyboards), and voice input-output (infancy stage). Bowers analyzes the advantages and disadvantages of the devices. The teleprinters are inexpensive and give printed copies of data; the CRT has higher speed, is more expensive than the teletypewriter, noiseless operation, and good where printed copy is not required; graphic CRT is expensive but sometimes is used in place of numbers.

7. **Feidelman, Lawrence, and George B. Bernstein. "Advances in Data Entry."** ***Datamation*****, March 1973, pp. 44-48.**

The authors of this article stress the importance of data entry. Data entry accounts for 40 to 50 percent of data handling dollars. This article describes the data entry system in terms of hardware, software, and the people who use the equipment.

Data entry, according to Feidelman and Bernstein, involves personnel considerations, data preparation procedures, forms design, equipment communication, and computer interface. The three types of data entry systems are: keypunch, keypunch replacements, and source data automation.

The keypunch is the most common form of data entry and is a slow means of data entry. It requires a rigid format and is costly when used in a multi-keypunch installation. However, there is the case of punching small jobs, ease of data insertion, and resistance to change.

Keypunch replacement came about as an attempt to increase the efficiency of the keypunch operation and lower data cost, without changing data preparation procedures.

The source data automation goal is to capture data at its point of generation or origin. This can be accomplished by keyboard entry, optical readers, voice input, magnetic readers, and multimedia systems.

The selection of a data entry system should meet the organization's input, processing and output needs. The other aspects of cost are reliability and maintenance.

8. **House, David L. "Micro Level Architecture in Minicomputer Design."** ***Computer Design*****, October 1973, pp. 75-80.**

Micro-level architecture allows the microprogrammer to mold a processor to be what the system requires. The microprocessor architecture must be such that it does not restrict software architecture.

In order to do this, the microprocessors must be flexible, possess speed, and be cost-beneficial. In the area of flexibility, the general registers must be plentiful, the branch conditioners must be extensive, shift modes and end conditions must be exhaustive, and I/O and memory systems must be extremely flexible.

Considering speed, cycle time should be optimized with *an eye on cost and reliability*. The microprocessor should be designed to operate as fast as is reasonably possible, using parts which are readily available in mass production; thus resulting in a design that is producible, reliable, and serviceable.

9. **Best, David P. "Minicomputer Software Primer."** ***Automation*****, April 1974, pp. 64-67.**

Best focuses upon some key concepts toward understanding software and its basic characteristics. Software includes the programs and coded instructions which determine how a computer will process input data. Software can be divided into two broad categories; namely, operating systems and application programs. The former are developed by the manufacturer and the latter by manufacturer and/or EDP personnel.

The main factors in considering minicomputer software is the availability of high-level language, e.g., BASIC and FORTRAN; the ability to support equipment such as microprocessing devices; system response time; a back-up power system; and priority interrupts.

The author includes a glossary of software terms.

10. **"Problem Areas in Data Management."** ***EDP Analyzer*****, March 1974, pp. 1-12.**

Data management systems are thought to be problem-free, but some of the areas where problems existed before have been found to still be problem areas.

Some of the thought-to-be benefits were data redundancy, data independence, automatic relation of data items, data security, and data integrity.

Mayford Roark of the Ford Motor Company questions cost benefits when looking at core requirements, mass storage requirements, and processing time. Data bases have much to offer, but it may be advisable to keep systems simple, or wise to use the simplest sequential files.

11. Wieselman, Irving L. "Choosing Proper Computer Output Systems." *Computer Design*, December 1974, pp. 63-67.

The value of this article is the description of printers, computer output microfilm (COM) and CRT display terminals. Also, it points out that cost, among other factors, is a consideration in computer hardware selection.

12. Awad, Elias M. *Business Data Processing*, 4th ed. Englewood Cliffs, NJ: Prentie-Hall, Inc., 1975, 713 pp.

The author presents the types, makeup and source of information flow generated by a business firm. Information flow is discussed in terms of data origination (source documents) data input, data processing (classifying, sorting, calculating and recording, summarizing), data reporting and communicating and data storage and retrieval. Information flow is described in manual and machine processing terms and techniques as an introduction to computers which in effect follows these same processes. Several chapters are devoted to computer hardware, MICR, computer output microfilm, printers, disks, visual display terminals, etc.

One feature of the book is the discussion of minicomputer systems (chapter 13), particularly the definition and description of the four broad areas of telecommunication-remote concentrators, front-end communicator processors, message switching, and intelligent terminals.

The author provides a critical path schematic for the installation of a computer system which may be of interest to auditors involved in systems design and pre-installation evaluation.

Included are a glossary of EDP terms and a list of various computer organizations, and selected periodicals.

13. Anderson, William S. "Where are We Going with Future Technology?" *Data Management*, January 1975, pp. 20-29.

The computer is finding its way into everyday life, supermarkets, self-service banking, and many other aspects of public life. The development of microelectronics has accelerated the pace at which the computer will go to the public. There has been a dramatic decrease in memory and processing costs. The quest for information at all levels has created problems that our society did not anticipate at the beginning of the computer age. Now, we can see the application of the computer in education, medicine, transportation, urban planning and welfare. The trend toward miniaturization and high-processing speeds will continue to grow, which will open up whole new areas for use of computers at lower costs.

Tomorrow's computer will have increased storage capacities and call for more advanced equipment, such as scanning devices.

14. Boillot, Michael H., Gary M. Gleorow, and Wayne L. Horn. *Essentials of Flow Charting*. Dubuque, IA: Wm. C. Brown Company Publishers, 1975, 114 pp.

Easy-reading book on flow charting, especially various routines such as counting, end of file (EOF) checks, file updating, report writing, sorting.

15. Wilkinson, Joseph W. *Accounting with the Computer: A Practice Case and Simulation*, 3rd ed. Homewood, IL: Richard D. Irwin, Inc., 1975, 64 pp.

This is a very readable and understandable practice case designed for the student in his or her first accounting course. The student learns how the computer accepts data, processes and outputs the data, and prepares accounting statements. This is done by following two month's accounting transactions through in a step by step, simulated computer processing. One feature is a list of error messages that might well be included in processing controls that would be of interest to an auditor in an EDP environment.

16. Withington, Frederick G. "Beyond 1984: A Technology Forecast." *Datamation*, January 1975, pp. 54-73.

The computer industry's products are clearly in a state of transition, and many users faced with decisions about commitments to today's products need to know whatever they can about possible future successors. In early 1974 Arthur D. Little, Inc. prepared a comprehensive forecast of the nature of future data processing equipment, software, data communications services, and their costs for the Electronic Systems Division of the U.S. Air Force, for use in a project called SADPR-

85, which dealt with base-level data processing operations through 1985. A substantial effort involving 25 investigators, the study produced a 284-page report with a bibliography of over 500 titles. The full report is available to qualified defense contractors from National Technical Information Services, 5285 Port Royal Road, Springfield, Virginia. It is Appendix VI, in Volume 3, of the six-volume report—*Support of Air Force Automatic Data Processing Requirements Through the 1980's*, document number AD-783-768.

This article summarizes the contents of that report, adding new material derived from subsequent studies and industry developments. Like the report prepared for the Air Force, this updated summary focuses on commercially available, general-purpose, administrative data processing hardware and software. It covers the full spectrum of sizes and types, but omits specialized tools for scientific, industrial process, or dedicated commercial applications. Its objective is to provide forecasts of processing modules—computer, file and I/O subsystems, etc.—that can be used as building blocks in studying alternative configurations.

Each building block requires a specific forecast of functions, power, and costs, but not a detailed discussion of the components within it. Therefore, the discussion of technologies as such is limited to those likely to be available in proven, commercially available modules by 1982. Also, in cases where alternative technologies might be used in a module without materially changing its price/performance, no effort is made to determine which will be the technology of choice. Constant dollars are used; no allowance is made for inflation. Forecasts for each type of module are made for two target years, 1977 and 1985. Included is a discussion of hardware, micro-coding, multiprocessing, auxiliary storage, batch I/O equipment, OCR station, and terminals.

17. "Systems and Audit Aspects of the Data Dictionary." *EDPACS*, May 1976, pp. 1-12. (ABI-76-06682)

Data dictionaries define data elements, records or segments, and the data base or files. They allow for greater data definition control, assist auditors in conducting audits, and help in designing and implementing data base management systems. However, they do take much time and effort to write, and require a lot of upkeep. When planning a data dictionary, such factors as naming and numbering conventions, dictionary contents, and the reports to be generated should be considered. Data dictionaries usually include hierarchy diagrams, segment libraries, detailed documentation, and indexing. Other topics discussed are the implementation steps involved with data dictionaries, data dictionary maintenance, security and control considerations, and audit considerations. Tables and diagrams.

18. Gibbs, Thomas E. and Valdu Silbey. "Documentation Standards and the Internal Auditor." ***Internal Auditor*****, August 1977, pp. 27-32. (ABI-77-11909)**

An old tool, documentation, is often overlooked when electronic data processing is added to the body of knowledge for internal auditors. Without system documentation, the organization runs the risk of improperly scheduling, monitoring, maintaining, and controlling the complex EDP operations. Establishing documentation standards is a prerequisite to designing and implementing any system. To insure proper documentation, there must be control over the documentation standards system. Because documentation standards are part of the EDP control system, they are the internal auditor's concern. Documentation standards are the criteria against which all system documentation (developed throughout the system development cycle) is to be evaluated. Without adequate documentation standards, the auditor has no assurance that documentation will be consistent, accurate, and accessible. The auditor must take an active role in the development of a sound system.

19. Patrick, Robert L. "Sixty Ingredients for Better Systems." ***Datamation*****, December 1977, pp. 171-189.**

This article is based on a National Bureau of Standards special publication, *Performance Assurance and Data Integrity Practices*. Current hardware has far fewer error-checking features because the componentry is more reliable. Partly in pursuit of lower prices, computer manufacturers have convinced themselves that partial checking is now adequate. Also, the state of the art in current software is worse. Many operating systems, compilers and utility programs simply do not work as promoted. Software vendors are pressured both by their customers and by their competition. As a result, they continuously seek to offer more function with less memory and faster execution speed. To achieve needed code compression, it is not uncommon to strip out most of the software checking mechanisms that could provide increased reliability. The author states, "it is not surprising that we have undetected errors or that we have had to devise a set of application techniques to 'plaster over' the cracks left by the hardware and software vendors."

Dynamic error checking and correcting is achieved only as a result of building a hierarchical set of checks and balances into the hardware, operating systems software, application programs, and manual procedures that make up a computer system. Audit trails require careful design if they are to remain unbroken in all circumstances. Files must have controls designed in. Mathematics may require special attention, too, and more and more it is becoming apparent that a data processing system requires that careful design attention be given both to computer processing and to manual processing such as data capture, balancing, error correction, reports distribution, that surround the computer system.

If a data system taxes the hardware, involves careful consideration of individual privacy, or is geographically distributed, the challenge is greater. The designers need to measure the error frequencies and their impact, review the basic design and reaffirm the design goals. There is a discussion of 60 elements to control for better systems. Among these elements are such items as: provide for operator feedback; logs of before and after images for restart; maintain error suspense files; build redundancy into the system such as check sums; use quality flags; maintain update controls; review of the mathematics; perform parallel check calculation; pilot test the input system; establish limits; use good processing practices, quality control, staff, and many other techniques to try to make systems more error resistant.

These 60 elements can be used as a systems checklist in evaluating internal controls. A yes or no answer to these may be of benefit to the auditor in evaluating internal controls.

20. Kelley, Neil D. "Entering More Than Just Data." *Infosystems*, December 1978, pp. 46-48. (DPD)

Keying data, especially at a central site, is decreasing—succeeded by data entry with terminals and systems which are used also for other applications. Users interested in future equipment will want to inquire if terminals and systems are capable of text processing, word processing, report generation, user-to-user message switching, electronic mail, transaction or real time processing, both central and local file inquiry, and remote-site to remote-site computer communications, or other requirements they might want to consider. For example, Data Point has a distributed configuration which can also manage and monitor telephone systems.

A trend in data entry is the use of multiple terminals in a multifunction system, managed by a minicomputer or "cluster controller" or "data concentrator," capable of communicating with a larger host computer. Terminals may also provide multiple methods of entering data—such as by keyboard or OCR. Distributed data entry will come with the trend toward distributed processing. Other new features include portable terminals having keyboards or scanning equipment, voice recognition systems, and multifunction keyboards/CRTs linked to a cluster controller. Users will want data entry where data is generated, performed on operator-oriented terminals smart enough to prompt operators on how to use them.

Both display and printing terminals will have intelligence features for editing and off-screen storage before data is transmitted to the computer. This avoids the problem of the controller going down and shutting down all the terminals linked in.

Data entry is taking on many different forms, driven by the trend toward distributed computing, multifunction systems, online processing, and the trend toward entering data at the source where it is collected.

21. Malcolm, Robert E. and Joseph L. Sardinas, Jr. "Operating Systems and the Internal Auditor." ***The Internal Auditor*****, June 1978, pp. 73-78. (EDPACS)**

The article explains the functioning of operating systems including the linkage editor. While IBM oriented, much of the treatment is of broad applicability. The operating system is an integrated package of highly sophisticated and complex programs. It controls all operations which occur within the machine. Through the operating system, one can suppress computer activity logs, insert modules in programs, bypass security routines, and modify computer audit packages so they are ineffective, yet give the impression they are operating properly. Some of the hazards in the operating system are: (1) any variable an auditor sees in a source listing may not be the variable being used in the object module; (2) if a source program has an audit module, the programmer can deactivate it by specifying that it not be translated; (3) any modules in a library can be incorporated into a source program and hence into object code 5 during link edit, subroutines with any name in a private library can be included in the object module. A programmer need only CALL a fradulent module for inclusion in the load module. Only the CALL instruction will appear on the printout.

Improper modifications to operating systems may seriously impair processing. Internal auditors must familiarize themselves with the capabilities of operating systems as well as procedural controls *not* in the system.

22. Rinder, Robert. "ACS Is Coming." *Datamation*, December 1978, pp. 95-99. (DPD)

ACS is a shared, switched data communications network service. It provides for: (1) sharing communication facilities; (2) interfacing incompatible terminals and computers; (3) various data communications capabilities from which users can select as needed; and (4) the managing and reporting of network performance.

The advantages of shared facilities are reduced costs and ease of data exchange between system users. Compatibility is a major problem for forms that have implemented various systems in a piecemeal fashion, application by application. ACS won't eliminate this problem, but will greatly reduce it. Provision will be made for interfacing terminals and computers having different data rates, protocols, and character sets. Any terminal in ACS can talk to any other terminal or any computer. ACS will allow users to configure their own virtual subnetworks, selecting from all available features those applicable to their requirements. In ACS the task of fault detection, isolation, and recovery will be performed, as they should be, by the network vendor, A.T.&T., rather than by the user. In addition, many of the reports that users require for monitoring performance will now be provided by ACS.

One can apply minimum effort to become operational in ACS. But if you want to take advantage of the system's full capabilities, design and programming effort will be required.

Customized services will be available in several areas: formatting CRT screens for data input and message preparation; validating data entered; message preparation aids; editing functions; and message handling. Customizing will be by customer programs via A.T.&T. supplied high level languages.

As to the impact of ACS on the future, it is clear that: (1) A.T.&T. has embarked on a major program that marks a distinct departure from past practices of exclusivity; (2) ACS is a major advance in data processing; and (3) ACS is a challenge to the industry.

23. Weber, Ron. "Database Administration: Functional, Organizational, and Control Perspectives." ***EDPACS*****, January 1979, pp. 1-10. (DPD)**

The database administrator is responsible for managing an organization's data resource. The auditor needs to work very closely with him because the quality of database administration has a direct impact on the quality of the database environment; and since much of the communication in a database environment is channeled through the database administrator, he constitutes an important source of information about system strengths and weaknesses. Also, the database administrator can provide technical and managerial information the auditor needs.

To evaluate the database administrator, the auditor needs to know the following information: what functions should be performed, how it should be organized, and how it should be controlled.

Database administration involves five major functions: defining, creating and retiring data; making the database available to users; maintaining integrity; monitoring operations and improving efficiency; and providing information to and servicing users.

To maintain database integrity, the database administrator should carry out definition control, existence control, access control, update control, concurrency control, and quality control. The database administrator must monitor the database management system to identify opportunities for improving efficiency. Four major elements have an impact on efficiency:

1. The database itself. As data usage patterns change, it may become necessary to reorganize the database.

2. Application programs. These may be inefficient when they are first written or become inefficient due to changes in the structure of the database.

3. System software. Software should be monitored and changed as necessary to improve efficiency.

4. Operating procedures. The database administrator should conduct regular procedures audits designed to detect opportunities for improvement.

The authority and responsibilities of the database administrator must be designed to meet the needs of the organization at each stage in its evolution of the database management system.

The database administrator has a position of unique power which could be abused, and which runs contrary to the fundamental principles of sound internal control. The auditor must be aware of the potential control weaknesses associated with the database administration position and the remedial measures which can be used to reduce the effects of these weaknesses.

Two aspects of the database administrators' role represent direct threats to data integrity: the breadth of functions violate the traditional control principle of separation of duties; and the database administrator's wide knowledge of the database environment and its tools can be used to override established controls. Some potential control measures include: assign appropriate seniority to the position; separate duties to the extent possible; maintain logs; train each member of the group in different duties and rotate those duties.

24. Thierauf, Robert J. and George W. Reynolds. *Systems Analysis and Design: A Case Study Approach*. Columbus, OH: Charles E. Merrill Publishing Company, 1980, 509 pp.

The authors stress an interactive and distributed data processing approach to systems.

Several chapters of the text are devoted to a typical systems design case study—namely, the ABC Company—whereby students are shown how to design an order-entry system. Based upon this illustrated case, they are then required to design a finished product inventory system or an accounts receivable system that complements the one presented. Thus, students are exposed to the underlying principles and practices of systems analysis and design, as well as given an opportunity to design an interactive computerized (management information) system in a distributed processing environment, in a batch processing mode.

The structure of the book follows a logical sequence to insure comprehensive treatment of systems analysis and design. The major areas covered are described below.

Part I: An overview of systems analysis and design. Chapter 1 provides an introduction to systems analysis and design, and chapter 2 discusses the standard tools employed by system personnel. In chapter 3, an overview of the major subsystems of the ABC Company (the master case study) is presented.

Part II: Systems analysis of present business information system. The introductory investigation of a system project is the subject matter of Chapter 4. In Chapter 5, the detailed investigation of the present system, or systems analysis, is examined, along with the concluding investigation phase of a system project, resulting in an exploratory survey report to top management. Chapter 6 focuses on analyzing the present order-entry system of the ABC Company.

Part III: Systems design of new management information system. An overview of systems design is treated in Chapter 7. In contrast, Chapters 8 and 9 center on the design of system output and data files, respectively. This material provides the background necessary to design the required output reports and data base (Chapter 10) for the order-entry system of the ABC Company. Similarly, Chapters 11 and 12 set forth the important design criteria for input and procedures, respectively, and Chapter 13 applies these criteria to the ABC Company. Lastly, Chapter 14 examines the design of system controls, and Chapter 15 relates this area to the ABC Company. Hence, all important design criteria from theoretical and practical viewpoints have been presented in sufficient detail to give the student a link between system theory and practice.

Part IV: Beyond systems analysis and design. In Chapters 16 and 17, equipment selection and system implementation are presented, respectively. These areas complete the essential parts of a typical system project.

Chapter 14, design of control systems, which deals with internal control, is of particular interest to auditors in an EDP environment. The text includes charts, tables of interest.

SECTION B. ADDITIONAL REFERENCES

25. Martin, James. *Design of Real-time Computer Systems.* Englewood Cliffs, NJ: Prentice-Hall, Inc., 1967.

26. Magie, F. Stuart, Jr. "EDP Documentation: Ten Ways." *Administrative Management*, 30 June 1969, pp. 62-64.

27. Laurie, Edward J. *Modern Computer Concepts: The IBM 360 Series*. Cincinnati: South-Western Publishing Company, 1970.

28. Davis, Gordon B. *Computer Data Processing*. 8th ed. NY: McGraw-Hill Book Company, 1973.

29. National Bureau of Standards. Federal Information Processing Standard Publication. *Flowchart Symbols and Their Usage in Information Processing*, FIPS PUB 24, 1973.

30. Thierauf, Robert J. *Data Processing for Business and Management*. NY: John Wiley & Sons, Inc., 1973.

31. Spier, Michael J. "A Pragmatic Proposal for the Improvement of Program Modularity and Reliability." *International Journal of Computer and Information Sciences*, 4 June 1975, pp. 133-149.

32. National Bureau of Standards. Federal Information Processing Standard Publication. *Guidelines for Documentation of Computer Program and Automated Data Systems*, FIPS PUB 38, Washington, DC: U.S. Department of Commerce, 1976.

33. Phister, Montgomery, Jr. *Data Processing Technology and Economics*. Santa Monica, CA: The Santa Monica Publishing Co., 1976.

34. National Bureau of Standards. *Features of Seven Audit Software Packages, Principles and Capabilities*. Washington, DC: U.S. Department of Commerce, U.S. Government Printing Office, 1977. (NBS Spec. Publ. 500-13.)

35. Akresh, Abraham D. and Michael Goldstein. "Point-of-Sale Accounting Systems: Some Implications for the Auditor." *The Journal of Accounting*, December 1978, pp. 68-74.

36. Patrick, Robert L. and Robert P. Blanc. *Computer Science and Technology: Performance Assurance and Data Integrity Practices*. Washington, DC: U.S. Department of Commerce, National Bureau of Standards, 1978.

SECTION C
THE AUDITOR'S TASK IN AN EDP ENVIRONMENT

ANNOTATED BIBLIOGRAPHY

1. **Gallagher, John F. "Systems and Auditing: The Case for More Interaction." *Systems and Procedures Journal*, March-April 1967, pp. 22-27.**

Although almost 14 years old, this article does point out the early history of internal auditing and the functions of internal auditing. The author points out that the internal auditor is to determine the adequacy of the system of internal control, investigate compliance with company policies and procedures, verify the existence of assets, see that proper safeguards of assets are maintained to prevent or discover fraud, check on the reliability of the accounting and reporting system, and finally to report findings to management and provide corrective action where necessary. The data processing system is also a subset of the Management Information System (MIS) along with the internal audit function.

The systems analyst and the internal auditor are often in conflict. The conflict stems from the auditor's responsibility for policing and evaluating what the systems analyst develops. In this sense, it can be said that the systems analyst exercises a creative faculty, while the internal auditor exercises a critical faculty. The systems analyst is involved in installing a system under the pressures of time and task, whereas the auditor is more apt to place stress on the needs for control. There is a point of optimum tradeoff and it is over the determination of this critical point that there may be conflict.

However, the author points out the possibilities for cooperation between internal auditors and the systems analyst in the area of internal controls. The systems department should bring the internal audit department in on any proposed system development early in the game. Each should participate in cross-training and sharing of information which will benefit the other. If the company can afford it, there should be at least one member of the internal audit staff who has a very high degree of expertise in systems and computers. Systems personnel should assist the internal audit staff to develop a basic approach to testing computerized transactions and aid them in the actual audit test.

Management audits of any magnitude should be performed as a joint venture of systems analysts and internal auditors, since both groups have something to offer.

2. **Jancura, Elise, G. "Electronic Data Processing–Evidential Matter in the Audits of Computerized Records." *The Woman CPA*, July 1975, pp. 15-16. (ABI-75-07865)**

The collection and subsequent use of competent evidential matter is vital to the proper execution of an audit. The introduction of computerized records does not change the need to collect and assess the reliability of that evidence. In deciding which procedures should be executed for each of the steps in the audit process and the extent to which those procedures should be executed, the auditor must make judgments regarding the materiality of individual items under examination. The four standards set forth in "A statement of basic accounting theory" by the American Accounting Association provide the criteria to be used in evaluating evidential matter. These are: (1) relevance; (2) verifiability; (3) independence; and (4) quantifiability.

As always, the major criterion in evaluating evidence is the source from whence it originated.

3. **Perry, William E. "How to Plan an EDP Audit." *EDPACS*, November 1976, pp. 108. (ABI-77-01198)**

The detailed nature of data processing requires that data processing audits be more detailed than traditional financial audits. The first phase should be to plan the audit. The first requirement is to select the parts of the system that need to be audited. This should be followed by probing to learn more about the area being audited. The third step is to define the audit objectives, which should be stated in quantifiable terms. The fourth step is to define the data requirements which will meet the stated objectives. Included will be the sources and the uses of the data. Fifth, a methodology should be defined which will include the sampling plan, types of tests, audit techniques, and preliminary paperwork. Finally, the different aspects of the administration of the audit, including audit skill, frequency of audit, and composition of the audit team, should be established. Tables.

4. **Clinch, J. Houston M. Jr. and Charles E. Johnston. "Auditing EDP Efficiency." *The Magazine of Bank Administration*, May 1977, pp. 56-59. (EDPACS)**

Part of the internal audit's basic mission, as defined by the Institute of Internal Auditors, is the evaluation of EDP efficiency. Several EDP performance measurements are presented: meeting deadlines, accurate and complete output, quick responses to user requests, budget performance, absence of wave-making, use of cost/benefit analysis in selecting projects, long-term planning, appraisals by the immediate, non-EDP superior executive, aggressive promotion of new EDP ideas, quality of personnel, knowledge of the company's business, user reaction to EDP, use of latest technology, and low personnel turnover.

EDP activity divides into four functions: operations, system development, feasibility studies, and planning. Each has special factors that must be considered during the operational audit. These are partially listed in relation to these four functions: physical layout of the EDP facility, operator efficiency, training, and backup, documentation, scheduling, preventive maintenance, hardware utilization, job accounting and charge backs. Also review of standards, compliance with standards, quality control procedures, user participation, planning procedures, and compliance with procedures.

To carry out a successful operational review, the auditor must be tactful and cooperative at all times. He must support his reports with documented facts and build a lasting rapport with data processing's line management. It will be a difficult but rewarding task that should benefit the organization.

5. Morris, Richard II. "The Internal Auditor and Data Processing." *Internal Auditor*, August 1978, pp. 75-81. (ABI-78-12280)

The data processing department has become one of the primary organizational units within corporations. Management can utilize the information in its decisionmaking process that is furnished by the computer. In fact, management has come to rely on the output of the machine so much that incorrect information placed in the system often results in incorrect management decisions that are costly to the organization. The internal auditor is often used to provide an independent verification of the firm's internal flow of information. As dependence on the computer increases, the auditor must develop expertise in electronic data processing to provide internal auditing services to management. The successful development of data processing audit methodology and its implementation will help internal and external auditors assure themselves and management that the risk of loss due to fraud has been reduced. The constant threat that fraud will be discovered is a deterrent in itself.

6. **Perry, William E. "Who's In Charge, You or Your Computer?" *Computer Decisions*, February 1978, pp. 38, 39, 41. (DPD)**

Systems auditability and control has become increasingly important for a number of reasons. Managers have become more dependent on data processing for their information needs. The expansion of businesses has intensified their need for communication of data. Data are now being interchanged among previously unrelated management information systems. Governmental regulations and associated reporting requirements have increased the amount and kinds of information that organizations must collect, process, and retain. New accounting standards and guidelines impose substantial new requirements on computer-based information systems. Not only are there more computer systems, but new capabilities and user applications are continually being developed and refined.

Managers must evaluate their organization's audit and control capabilities in the data processing environment in conjunction with internal auditors.

The five important aspects of computer control and audit that managers should consider are: (1) the expanded role of the DP audit group; (2) the development of DP audit staff skills; (3) audit independence; (4) the use of DP audit and control techniques; and (5) methods of DP audit and control.

The ultimate responsibility for internal controls rests with top managers, but at lower levels the responsibility for internal controls tends to be fragmented, with the responsibilities divided among line managers and users.

Internal controls associated with a computer application system are frequently fragmented and not evaluated within the context of total computer application system requirements because of the varying types and levels of knowledge held by the participants.

Internal auditors are becoming increasingly involved in evaluating internal controls relating to computer application systems. The role of the auditor is to judge the adequacy of controls and to recommend control improvements.

Little quantitative information is available to reflect either present levels of expenditures or anticipated trends in costs associated with auditing computer-based information systems.

7. **Perry, William E. and Henry C. Warner. "Systems Auditability: Friend or Foe?" *The Journal of Accountancy*, February 1978, pp. 52-60. (DPD)**

The data processing function typically includes three basic elements of internal control: computer application systems, computer service center operations, and application systems development. The responsibility for internal control tends to be fragmented among users (responsible for establishing the requirements for controls within the computer phase of an application system) and data processing management (responsible for designing and implementing the controls governing automated phases of computer application systems and the controls governing other phases of data processing activities). Unfortunately, controls are often established without being evaluated within the context of the total computer application system and its associated control objectives.

Three powerful allies to the independent auditor are the internal auditor, computer-assisted audit techniques, and control point identification. Internal auditors are involved in evaluating internal controls relating to computer application systems. However, the responsibility for internal controls properly resides with data processing and the user groups. The role of the internal auditors is to judge the adequacy of controls and recommend control improvements. The computer is an ideal instrument for keeping records and producing information about its own activities and the nature of its work. Such records, statistics, and analyses can often be compiled concurrently with the main tasks it performs. If these capabilities are deliberately exploited by the auditor, they can be very powerful and useful tools for this work. It may be possible for the auditor to create computer programs designed to do major audit analyses that otherwise would have been performed manually or not at all. If internal auditors participate in the design of a major computing system, they can aid in creating provisions for automatic real-time monitoring and checking facilities which will be operative during routine operations on the system.

While still not widely used, control documentation and the identification of specific system control points is now becoming recognized by auditors as well as many system designers as an essential element to computer system understanding.

Top management should initiate periodic assessments of their organizations' audit and control programs pertaining to the data processing environment. CPAs should provide input to these periodic evaluations. Here are some areas of improvement needed in computer auditing:

- Greater internal audit involvement in the data processing environment.

- EDP audit staff development.
- New tools and techniques for EDP audit.
- Participation by internal auditors in the system development process.

CPAs can help by including specific recommendations in their management letters that are supportive of an aggressive and organizationally independent internal audit function which is both skilled and involved in data processing.

8. **Webb, Richard D. "Audit Planning—EDP Consideration."** ***The Journal of Accountancy*****, May 1979, pp. 65-75. (ABI-79-10089)**

Many organizations use computers to process significant financial data, and the auditor should determine its impact in the context of a systematic audit approach. EDP-related planning tasks include initial planning, systems description, compliance tests, substantive tests, review and evaluation of financial statements considering audit evidence gathered, and issuance of accountant's report. Audit objectives do not change because the company computerizes its accounting systems, but computer-related considerations must be incorporated into overall audit planning. Such considerations include: (1) going concern risk; (2) use of computer-assisted audit techniques; (3) potential for fraud; and (4) operating recommendations. Planning pays for itself in better use of audit personnel by identification and performance of only the necessary audit procedures. The plan also offers a measure for managing the engagement. Tables. Graph.

SECTION C. ADDITIONAL REFERENCES

9. **Mautz, R.K. "Evidence, Judgement, and the Auditor's Opinion."** ***Journal of Accountancy*****, April 1959, p. 43.**

10. **Campbell, Donald T. and Julian C. Stanley.** ***Experimental and Quasi-Experimental Designs for Research*****. Chicago: Rand McNally College Publishing Company, 1963.**

11. **Cochran, William G.** ***Sampling Techniques*** **2nd ed. NY: John Wiley & Sons, Inc., 1963.**

12. Cornick, D.L. "The Role of the Federal Auditor in the EDP Environment." Prepared for the Seminar in Technology of Management. Washington, DC: The American University, 1969 (mimeograph).

13. Cornick, D.L. and Robert Elkin. *Analyzing Costs in a Residential Group Care Facility: A Step by Step Manual*. NY: Child Welfare League of America, 1969. Especially uses of random moment and random day sampling techniques.

14. Fox, David. *The Research Process in Education*. NY: Holt, Rinehart and Winston, Inc., 1969.

15. Aly, H.F. and J.I. Duboff. "Statistical versus Judgement Sampling: An Empirical Study of Auditing and the Accounts Receivable of a Small Retail Store." *Accounting Review*, January 1971, pp. 119-128.

16. CODASYL "Data Base Task Group (DBTG) Report 1971." NY: Association for Computing Machinery, April 1971.

17. Holmes, Arthur W. and Wayne S. Overmeyer. *Auditing: Principles and Procedures*. Homewood, IL: Richard D. Irwin, Inc., 1971.

18. Ijiri, Y. and R.S. Kaplan. "A Model for Integrating Sampling Objectives in Auditing." *Journal of Accounting Research*, Spring 1971, pp. 73-87.

19. Willingham, John J. and D.R. Carmichael. *Auditing Concepts and Methods*, 2nd ed. NY: McGraw-Hill Book Company, 1971.

20. Elliot, R.K. and J.R. Rogers. "Relating Statistical Sampling to Audit Objectives." *Journal of Accountancy*, July 1972, pp. 46-55.

21. Miles, Lawrence D. *Techniques of Value Analysis and Engineering*. NY: McGraw-Hill Book Company, 1972.

22. Smith, K.A. "The Relationship of Internal Control Evaluation and Audit Sample Size." *Accounting Review*, April 1972, pp. 260-269.

23. Anderson, Rodney J. "Audit Uses of Statistical Sampling." *Internal Auditor*, May/June 1973, pp. 31-41.

24. Anderson, R. J. and A.D. Teitlebaum. "Dollar-Unit Sampling." *CA Magazine*, April 1973, pp. 30-39.

25. Kaplan, Robert S. "Statistical Sampling in Auditing with Auxiliary Information Estimators." *Journal of Accounting Research*, Autumn 1973, pp. 238-258.

26. Kaplan, Robert S. "A Stochastic Model for Auditing." *Journal of Accounting Research*, Spring 1973, pp. 38-46.

27. Lippitt, Gordon L. *Visualizing Change: Model Building and the Change Process*. Fairfax, VA: NTL Learning Resources Corporation, Inc., 1973.

28. Loebbecke, J.K. and J. Neter. "Statistical Sampling in Confirming Receivables." *Journal of Accountancy*, June 1973, pp. 44-50.

29. Meigs, Walter B., E. John Larsen and Robert F. Meigs. *Principles of Auditing*. Homewood, IL: Richard D. Irwin, Inc., 1973.

30. Arkin, Herbert. *Handbook of Sampling for Auditing and Accounting*, 2nd ed. NY: McGraw-Hill Book Company, 1974.

31. Deakin, Edward B. and Michael Granoff II. "Regression Analysis as a Means of Determining Audit Sample Size." *Accounting Review*, October 1974, pp. 764-771.

32. Roberts, Donald M. "Statistical Interpretation of SAP No. 54." *Journal of Accountancy*, March 1974, pp. 47-53.

33. American Institute of Certified Public Accountants. "Advanced EDP systems and the Auditor's Concern." *Journal of Accountancy*, January 1975.

34. Bedingfield, James P. "The Current State of Statistical Sampling and Auditing." *Journal of Accountancy*, December 1975, pp. 48-55.

35. Defliese, Philip L., Kenneth P. Macleod and K. Roderick. *Montgomery's Auditing*. New York, NY: The Ronald Press Company, 1975.

36. Kaplan, Robert S. "Statistical Sampling in Auditing with Auxiliary Information Estimators." *Journal of Accounting Research*, Autumn 1973, pp. 238-258.

37. Kinney, William R., Jr. "A Decision Theory Approach to the Sampling Problem in Auditing." *Journal of Accounting Research*, Spring 1975, pp. 117-132.

38. Loebbecke, J.K. and J. Neter. "Considerations in Choosing Statistical Sampling Procedures in Auditing." *Journal of Accounting Research*, Supplement 1975, pp. 38-68.

39. Neter, J. and J.K. Loebbecke. "Behavior of Major Statistical Estimators in Sampling Accounting Populations. *Auditing Research Monograph No. 2*. NY: AICPA, 1975.

40. Teitlebaum, A.D. and C.F. Robinson. "The Real Risks in Audit Sampling." *Journal of Accounting Research*, Supplement 1975, pp. 70-97.

41. Cook, James W. and Gary M. Winkle. *Auditing: Philosophy and Techniques*. Boston: Houghton Mifflin Company, 1976.

42. Jenkins, A. Milton. and Ron Weber. "DBMS Software as an Audit Tool: The Issue of Independence." *Journal of Accountancy*, April 1976.

43. Selltiz, Claire, et al. *Research Methods in Social Relations*, 3rd ed. NY: Holt, Rinehart and Winston, Inc., 1976.

44. Anderson, Rodney J. *The External Audit 1*. Toronto: Pitman Publishing, 1977. Especially Chapter 13, "Statistical Sampling" (pp. 330-377) and Chapter 22, "Supplement on Statistical Sampling Theory" (DUS, pp. 610-627).

45. Barkman, Arnold. "Within-Item Variation: A Stochastic Approach to Audit Uncertainty." *Accounting Review*, April 1977, pp. 450-464.

46. Barrett, M.J. and D.E. Ricketts. "The Statistical Auditor." *The Internal Auditor*, February 1977, pp. 32-37.

47. Champine, G.A. "Sinx Approaches to Distributed Data Bases." *Datamation*, May 1977.

48. Felix, W.L., Jr. and R.A. Grimlund. "A Sampling Model for Audit Tests of Composite Accounts." *Journal of Accounting Research*, Spring 1977, pp. 23-41.

49. Hansen, D.R. and T.L. Shaftel. "Sampling for Integrated Objectives in Auditing." *Accounting Review*, January 1977, pp. 109-123.

50. Reneau, J.H. "Auditing In a Data Base Environment." *Journal of Accountancy*, December 1977.

51. Cushing, Barry E. *Accounting Information Systems & Business Organizations*, 2nd ed. Reading, MA: Addison-Wesley Publishing Company, Inc., 1978.

52. Roberts, Donald M. *Statistical Auditing*. NY: American Institute of Certified Public Accountants, 1978.

53. Wilkinson, Joseph W. "Evaluating Controls in Advanced Computer Systems." *Internal Auditor*, October 1978.

54. Cardenas, A. *Data Base Management Systems*. Boston: Allyn and Bacon, Inc., 1979.

55. Cornick, D.L. "Towards an Action/Contingency Theory of Budgeting." Doctoral Dissertation, Los Angeles: University of Southern California, 1979.

56. Robertson, Jack C. *Auditing*. Homewood, IL: Richard D. Irwin, Inc., 1979.

57. Taylor, Donald H. and William G. Glezen. *Auditing: Integrated Concepts & Procedures*. NY: John Wiley & Sons, Inc., 1979.

58. Bodnar, George H. *Accounting Information Systems*. Boston: Allyn and Bacon, Inc., 1979.

59. Cerullo, Michael J. "Security Measures for Computer Systems." *The EDP Auditor*, Summer 1981, pp. 15-27.

60. Scott, George M. "Auditing the Data Base." *The EDP Auditor*, Summer 1981, pp. 37-49.

SECTION D
THE ROLE OF INTERNAL CONTROL IN EDP AUDITING

ANNOTATED BIBLIOGRAPHY

1. **Price Waterhouse and Company.** ***Use of Computers in Auditing: A Professional Development Course in Electronic Data Processing*****, New York, NY: Price Waterhouse and Company, (undated, circa 1962), 88 pp.**

This historical pamphlet contains six case studies in auditing with EDP (Part VI): Bank Reconciliation, Accounts Receivable, Physical Inventories, Materials and Supplies, Payrolls and Expense Analysis. The payroll case illustrates the use of error and exception routines, for example: codes for bona fide new hire, bona fide termination, etc. plus the information printed out with each code.

2. **Bower, James B. and Bruce J. Sefert. "Human Factors in Systems Design."** ***Management Services*****, November-December 1965, pp. 39-50.**

The article deals with some ways to minimize the human problems in systems design and change. The way in which the analyst goes about introducing the system can result in resistance to change on the part of the three levels of employees, i.e. non-supervisory employees, middle management, and top management.

Some of the steps that might be taken are: (1) having top management make assurances about job security, salary retention and opportunity for training and the rules to be followed in reassignment; (2) using a project team made up of representatives of the various departments affected, operating with or under the analyst. This has the advantage of perhaps producing a sounder systems design and also creates greater system acceptance by team members and others; (3) recognizing the responsibility for educating management about systems in general and the particular system; (4) being receptive to suggestions for the design and implementation of the system.

The systems analyst should be cognizant of the fear of loss of self esteem and status, and counter this by stressing the increased importance of each manager or supervisor through his part in supplying better information for decision making.

3. **Boutell, Wayne S. "Auditing Through the Computer."** ***The Journal of Accountancy*****, November 1965, pp. 41-47.**

This article seeks to focus upon the differences between auditing around the computer and auditing through the computer. Whenever there is an audit examination, the central focus is review and evaluation of the internal control system. The auditor must be aware of and concerned with the three basic elements–input, processing, and output–of the accounting system. When auditors tried to audit around the computer, the processing step was largely ignored. This meant that all the records that were maintained *before* automation had to be in effect maintained to provide a sufficient "audit trail." In other words the computer was essentially ignored.

The advocates of auditing through a computer felt that the auditor does not require the use of the traditionally maintained accounting records. The following arguments are offered for auditing through the computer.

(a) it is compatible with the requirements of efficient system design.

(b) it uses the client's computer to assist with the examination,

(c) it is consistent with the American Institute of Certified Public Accountants' evaluation requirement, and

(d) it is less expensive in terms of actual audit time.

Two major ideas have been suggested to implement the philosophy of auditing through the computer. The general idea of the first, test decks, is to test the client's program for converting inputs to outputs. The second idea is borrowed from operations research which is to essentially contructs a model of what *should* happen and compare it to what *actually* occurs. The auditor in effect substitutes his computer program for that of the client. The model approach allows the auditor to rigorously apply his professional experience and judgment so that it becomes the basis for for evaluation of computer-processed portions of the accounting system. Boutell believes that the model approach seems to offer more promise for the future since it can be expanded to include limited decision-making ability and the actual development of the audit program itself.

The author feels that the philosophy of auditing through the computer would permit optimal system design and satisfactory assurances and safeguards for the auditor.

4. International Business Machines Corporation, *Management Control of Electronic Data Processing*. White Plains, NY: International Business Machines Corporation, 1965, 33 pp.

Although published in 1965, the pamphlet contains an excellent definition of internal control as it relates to EDP systems. It discusses management's responsibility for controlling the EDP system. Rephrasing the broad definition of internal control in terms of EDP controls may be described as a plan to ensure that only valid data is accepted and processed, *completely* and *accurately*, and that the *necessary information* and *records* are provided. The report defines these italicized terms. "Valid" means correct *and* authorized, "completely" means remaining intact throughout processing, and being fully processed through all *appropriate* computer operations. "Accurately" means without undetected errors and that the processing fully accomplishes its purposes *and* is in accordance with *management's* policies and instructions. "Records" means an information trail and retrievable data storage adequate for the reconstruction (if necessary) of current records for processing or to meet the needs of third parties, customers, auditors, Internal Revenue Service, and other outside agencies (page 1).

The pamphlet describes input, output and processing controls. Included are two cases to illustrate effective controls in an EDP system. Also included is a summary checklist for reviewing the adequacy of controls.

5. Davis, Gordon B. *Auditing & EDP*. NY: American Institute of Certified Public Accountants, 1968, 344 pp.

The book was the output of a special auditing EDP task force of the American Institute of Certified Public Accountants. It is organized into three major sections. Section I, Chapters 2-7, discusses typical procedures and preferred practices utilized in the organization, administration and control of data processing. It provides some of the background to enable the auditor to "understand and utilize an EDP system review questionnaire" as illustrated in Appendix E to the book (p. ii). Section I covers such topics as organization, documentation standards, hardware controls, programmed controls and safeguard of records and files. Program documentation is frequently the best source of information on control features in the computer program and, accordingly, review of control may depend in part on adequate documentation of programs. "The absence of adequate documentation probably indicates a lack of administrative controls which may influence the auditor's evaluation of internal control."

Section II, Chapters 8-12, discusses specific audit procedures–evaluating internal control and the audit trail, performing audit tests with and without using the computer. The author discusses certain criteria which may be used in deciding to audit without using the computer (auditing "around" the computer).

Generally, auditing around the computer may be used if the system is a batch controlled system having detailed audit trails and is characterized by: (1) batches sorted and run sequentially against a master file; (2) recording of transactions manually, followed by conversion to machine-readable form; and (3) numerous printouts–often at each processing run. The feasibility of auditing without using the computer depends upon the auditors ability to obtain evidence by means of tests on the input and output, sample computations, tests of controls, etc. Conditions which complicate this last criterion are: (a) summarized end-product output so that individual items are not identifiable by manual means; (b) large volume of transactions and transaction types; and (c) integrated system in which the output of one application becomes input into another application without human intervention. Illustration of both types of auditing is provided as well as a discussion of Generalized Audit Software.

Section III, Chapters 13-15, discusses problems arising from integrated systems, service centers, time sharing and the training requirements for the CPA auditing EDP systems. Appendix A, an overview of computer data processing, Appendix B, example of documentation, and Appendix C, flow charting, provide the reader with clear, simple approaches to understanding these topics. Appendix E provides a questionnaire for evaluation of internal control in electronic data processing. Each item may be answered yes-favorable, no-unfavorable and is coded A, B, or C in order of the item's importance to the auditor.

This book, published in 1968, is still cited frequently in the current literature.

6. U.S. General Accounting Office. *Review Guide for Evaluating Internal Controls in Automatic Data Processing Systems*. Washington, DC: U.S. General Accounting Office, 1968, 45 pp.

Discusses input, output and processing controls. Section II is a questionnaire for use in review of internal controls in ADP systems. The questionnaire emphasizes the methods of internal control rather than specific procedures of auditing. The pamphlet describes some of the early computer assisted auditing software, such as Haskins & Sells Auditape, Flexible Audit selection technique (FAST), Selecting Audit Transactions Electronically (SATE) and the Utility Program for Selecting Data.

7. The Canadian Institute of Chartered Accountants. *Computer Control Guidelines*. Toronto, Canada: The Canadian Institute of Chartered Accountants, 1970, 135 pp. (and Vol. II, 182 pp., 1975).

Volume I is the first part of a two-part study of computer control and audit guidelines designed to assist management, data processing personnel and internal and external auditors in evaluating the controls in computer-based data processing systems. Volume I is divided into seven chapters: (I) Pre-Installation Controls; (II) Organization Controls; (III) Development Controls; (IV) Operations Control; (V) Processing Controls; (VI) Documentation Controls; and (VII) Outside Data Centre Controls.

Pre-installation Controls (Chapter I)

The process of considering computer processing requires a series of defined and disciplined steps in order to ensure that the preliminary studies are complete and accurate, and to form a sound basis for management decision. Pre-installation controls refer to controls required to ensure a sound, well organized approach to the work preceding the installation of computer systems and equipment. This chapter reviews the conduct of a preliminary survey under the direction of a management committee and the subsequent carrying out of a feasibility study and other pre-installation tasks under the direction of a computer steering committee.

Organizational Controls (Chapter II)

Standards which should be adhered to in a plan of organization are similar for all levels of systems, manual or computer. However, the design and operation of a computer system and the high degree of concentration of processing in the computer center are two new factors which affect the organization structure of a company installing a computer. The purpose of this chapter is to outline the organizational controls required in a computer environment. It reviews the division of duties, both outside and within the EDP department, the functions of a data control gorup, and the method of reporting to senior management.

Development Controls (Chapter III)

The development of computer systems and programs and their maintenance during subsequent operations calls for the combined efforts of personnel in the EDP department and other departments of the organization. Effective systems development requires that certain procedures be followed and necessary controls applied for that phase of the work which deals with the actual development of the detailed system and programs, their testing, and the conversion of the system to the computer format. The development controls included in this chapter cover the planning of new applications on the computer and the establishment of standard procedures for systems design and programming, authorizations and approvals, testing of systems and programs, control over conversion of data in initial operations, and control over subsequent changes.

Operations Controls (Chapter IV)

Operations controls include those methods and procedures which must be established in order to produce an environment intended to ensure effective production by the operations section and to provide physical security for machine-sensible records maintained in the computer room. This chapter covers standard operating instructions, the handling of computer files, and security against accidental destruction of records or equipment.

Processing Controls (Chapter V)

Computer data processing should generate accurate, complete and valid information on a timely basis. The production of this information during a given unit of time, such as a day, can be thought of as a processing cycle. (The processing cycle is usually associated with a specific period of time which must be predetermined for scheduling purposes.) The complete processing cycle includes procedures both in source and user departments and in the EDP department. Since control techniques for the processing cycle often exist in several alternative forms (e.g. visual editing versus computer editing), a discussion of control requires that all controls over the processing cycle be dealt with together. This chapter discusses processing controls which are commonly described as hardware controls, input and output controls, and programmed controls, and are necessary to ensure the completeness, accuracy and authorization of data processed by the computer and to ensure the adequacy of management trails.

Documentation Controls (Chapter VI)

Adequate documentation of computer systems, programs, and operating procedures is necessary for a complete and accurate understanding of computer processing activities and the impact of such processing on user groups. The documentation controls covered in this chapter include problem definition, the establishment of documentation standards, systems documentation, program documentation, operators' manuals, and the documentation of file maintenance and file protection operations.

Outside Data Center Controls (Chapter VII)

In the preceding chapters, computer data processing controls have been presented from the view of a user who has equipment on his own premises. An alternative to "in-house" data processing is the use of services provided by an outside data center, either on a complete or partial data processing basis. The controls included in this chapter cover the commitment for and selection of data center services, organizational requirements for data center operations, input and output controls, management and audit trails, and the security and protection over customer data records and reports.

Chapters VI, Documentation Controls and Chapter VII, Outside Data Centre Controls should be of particular interest to ADP auditors because there is a paucity of literature on both and because of the growing importance (particularly third party reviews) of the latter and the importance of the former in a complete and accurate understanding of the computer processing activities.

Outside data center controls should be developed which among other things should include criteria for data center selection, should provide for a review of the center's organizational and procedural organization, should include a plan to ensure that only authorized persons have access to customer's data, records and reports, and provide for adequate protection of documents, reports and files against theft, fire or other damage or destruction.

Volume II (Chapters VIII-XIX), *Computer Audit Guidelines*, is designed to assist auditors of computer-based processing systems—both for internal auditors who are conducting reviews on behalf of management and external accountants who are performing an attest function in relation to an organization's financial statements.

Chapter XVIII includes a Control Evaluation Guide, recommended for use by both external auditors and management auditors in evaluating and verifying controls in a computer based system. The steps in completing the guide are: (1) verify the control techniques (Chapter XI); (2) based on the verification, evaluate each control technique as *good, adequate, poor* or *absent*; (3) with respect to those items having *attest* significance, revise substantive tests and/or conduct other specific compensating procedures to establish that material errors have not occurred despite the weakness in control (Chapters IX, X, XI, XIII & XV); (4) make recommendations in improvements.

Chapter XIX includes a Control Evaluation Guide for evaluating and verifying controls in a system involving computer processing by outside data centers. The steps in completing the guide are essentially the same.

8. Baron, C. David. "Audit Opinions on the System of Internal Control of Governmental Units." ***New York CPA*****, October 1971, p. 743. (ABI-71-00665)**

The CPA, in auditing a governmental entity, apparently does not give adequate attention to administrative (management) controls, in contrast to the consideration of accounting controls. Yet the administrative controls have an importance of unique interest to users of government reports, citizens and others. Therefore, the author urges, for the reasons he cites, an extension of the internal control examination. Internal control systems for managing the financial affairs of governmental units are basically similar to those of commercial enterprises. For this reason, the development of audit field-work and audit reporting standards to support a proposed extension of the attest function in the governmental setting can draw heavily from similar attempts in corporate reporting.

9. Bergart, Jeffrey G., Marvin Denicoff and David K. Hsiao. ***An Annotated Cross Reference Bibliography on Computer Security and Access Control in Computer Systems.*** **Columbus, OH: Ohio State University, November 1972, 62 pp.**

The paper represents a study of published works on computer security and access control in computer systems. The study includes a selected annotated bibliography of some 85 important published results in the field of computer security. These papers analyze the state of the art and are among the early works dealing with the state of the art.

10. Barrington, J.D. "Audit Through Management Control Systems." ***Canadian Chartered Accountant*****, October 1973, pp. 44-48. (ABI-73-05305)**

Audit through management controls (ATMAC) has been effective in identifying the areas of critical importance to the auditor. In case situations where ATMAC was used in parallel with traditional approaches, the audit of the management control system highlighted all major weaknesses in internal control. The approach is efficient–little time is wasted on weak management control systems because they are readily identified at the onset of the work. The use of ATMAC has been fully justified on the grounds of its contribution to the audit. With the use of ATMAC the auditor can provide a better quality service to the client, one which is more in line with the client's own priorities because the emphasis is on management control, not on accounting. The assessment of a management control system is in essence no different than an assessment of an accounting system. In each case information must be collected on how the system operates.

11. Davis, Gordon B. ***Computer Data Processing*****, 8th ed. NY: McGraw-Hill Book Company, 1973, 662 pp.**

The book is divided into six parts. Parts 2, 3, 4, 5: *understanding how a computer works, development of computer data processing applications, the computer system in use*, and *understanding assembly-level programming* are of most concern to the EDP auditor.

The book is well illustrated with pictures, graphs, and very easy to read. It proceeds in a step by step basis from the explanation of a punched card through time sharing and remote processing.

The nature of control is presented in terms of quality control; that is, the author points out that errors may result from any one or all of the following: bad input data, program errors, operator mistakes, improper distribution of output.

Quality control over computer data is achieved by a series of controls applied at different stages of processing. Application or processing controls are part of top management's responsibility for overall organizational controls over data processing. This later responsibility includes establishing a system for authorizing system additions or changes, post installation review of actual cost and effectiveness of systems projects; review of organization and control practices of the data processing function, and monitoring of performance.

The author points out the need for establishing "Audit trails" in random access systems where the old data are destroyed by the updated processing of new data. Audit trails are established by use of "logs" which provide a record of input transactions from terminals.

The book meets the author's objectives of providing a text that is sufficiently broad that the reader is exposed to all of the important topics in computer data processing in generally non-technical terms. The author provides selected references, a guide to computer organizations and periodicals, certificate programs, a glossary of terms, and information on data processing standards for those who wish to go into the subject in greater depth.

Provides a guide to computer organizations and periodicals, and a glossary of EDP terms.

12. Louderbeck, Peter D. "Audit and Control of Off Premises EDP Systems." *Bank Administration*, March 1973, pp. 31-33. (ABI-73-00875)

There has been considerable interest among bank audit groups on the subject of responsibility for auditing and controlling a data center operated by a second party, e.g., a servicer, correspondent facilities manager, etc. The author discusses the AICPA standards pertaining to off-premises EDP services which were issued in draft form at the time of his writing. These standards would require auditors to assume responsibility for audit and control of off-premise EDP centers and on-premise centers operated by a facilities manager or another second party. Several cases where a bank service center was responsible for serious problems at the bank being serviced are outlined. The type of trainined needed for an EDP center review and a description of the approach to the review are described.

13. Martin, James. *Security, Accuracy, and Privacy in Computer Systems*. Englewood Cliffs, NJ: Prentice-Hall, Inc., 1973, 626 pp.

Data security refers to protection of data against accidental or intentional disclosure to unauthorized persons or unauthorized modifications or destruction. Privacy refers to the rights of individual and organization to determine for themselves when, how, and to what extent information about them is to be transmitted to others. If computers are to assume such vital functions in our society and industry, one assumption must be demanded, namely, *the data processing function shall not lose vital data, introduce errors into them, or permit data to be read or modified without authorization*.

The design of a tightly controlled computer system is not enough by itself. It must be surrounded by layers of control *external* to the system design—physical security, administrative controls, and legal and societal controls.

Each security exposure must be attacked in three ways: (1) minimize the probability of it happening at all; (2) minimize the damage if it does happen; and (3) design a method of recovering from the damage. The author presents an expected value approach to assessing risk; that is, the probability times the loss equals the expected value of the risk.

Figure 32, Sources of Computer Errors (p. 23), is an excellent visual of possible sources of errors—hardware, software, application, operation, data input, inappropriate program design and questionable system philosophy.

Part II, Chapters 5-23, provides the reader with a discussion, and liberal graphics, of various controls for accuracy and authorization in batch processing, terminal-online, real time processing, and structure of authorization tables.

In Part III, which concerns the design of physical security, the author discusses eight steps essential in the maintenance of psychological security: (1) information and training; (2) ensure that security is taken seriously; (3) monitor the observance of security rules; (4) morale; (5) knowledge of the individual employees; (6) care when firing employees; (7) controlling outsiders; and (8) example-setting by higher management.

The author in discussing the auditor's role emphasized that the auditor's requirements must be built in at the design stage. The auditor sets objectives for the design of the controls and later evaluates the design. He must act as the "devil's advocate" on behalf of top management. Also, he must not be responsible for enforcing the procedures, but must judge the effectiveness with which somebody else enforces them.

There are a number of techniques that auditors can use in an operational system: (1) general questioning; (2) questions and checklists; (3) spot checks; (4) sampling; (5) use of erroneous transactions; (6) attempt security violations; (7) test records, pseudo transactions and a mini company; and (8) special programs. For example, the auditor should keep original copies of programs, rerun them on a surprise basis and compare the results with current programs with such techniques as computerized flow charting. The author provides in Appendix D a variety of checklists and summaries intended to assist the reader in the design and auditing of procedures for security, accuracy and privacy. There is A Specimen Checklist for Auditors and A Specimen List of Invalid Transactions which an auditor may feed to a system to test validity checks.

14. Nolan, Richard L. "Plight of the EDP Manager." *Harvard Business Review*, May-June 1973, pp. 143-151.

Firings and terminations in this profession are running high. Why are EDP managers and companies so unhappy with one another? The general remedy for this manager's plight is a closer collaboration and more sympathetic collaboration between the EDP manager and top management. To resolve the problem it is incumbent on top management to understand better the EDP management challenges and create an organizational climate in which the needs of the EDP manager can be met. It is incumbent upon the EDP manager to take a larger and more organizational view of his job. The EDP manager's role is one of linking the efficiency of new computer technology with the needs of his organization. His effectiveness is determined by how well he can bring about organizational changes suggested by advancing technology, recognizing that knowledge of advancing technology is only one small part of his job.

The auditor should bear in mind the role of the EDP manger in the areas of conflict that may exist between EDP management and the organization. This may have some bearing on computer abuse, security and internal control.

15. Stanford Research Institute. *Computer Abuse*. Prepared for National Science Foundation. Springfield, VA: National Technical Information Service, U.S. Department of Commerce, 1973, 131 pp.

This study deals with computer abuse which is defined as "all types of acts distinctly associated with computers and data communications in which victims involuntarily suffer or could have suffered losses, injuries or damages, or in which perpetrators receive or could have received gain."

The report includes a summary of 148 reported cases of computer abuse on file at the time the study was conducted (Appendix A). Roughly, there are 26 cases of vandalism, 49 cases of information or property theft, 50 cases of fraud or theft and 23 cases of unauthorized uses or sale of services. The study points out that the computer may be: (1) the object of abuse; (2) as the environment for abuse–theft of and unauthorized uses of programs and data; (3) used as a tool itself in committing fraud; or (4) as a symbol.

The study is extensively documented with some 67 references which provide the reader with a bibliography on the subject.

One of the important features of the study is the description of perpetrators. From a review of the study it is apparent that the following factors are often involved:

1. access to a computer;
2. access to data files;
3. access to computer programs;
4. systems knowledge;
5. means of converting fraudulent activity to personal gain.

In addition, there is a description of perpetrators which the study states (pp. 49-50) are white-collar amateurs rather than emotional or professional criminals. Few women have been encountered, and when involved, they tend to be accomplices employed as keypunch operators or clerks. Most perpetrators are 18 to 30 years old. A few of the embezzlers are older.

The principal threat against whom protection is required is the perpetrator who knows as much about the system as the designers do.

Motive is a less helpful means of identifying potential perpetrators. Just the challenge of penetrating systems is attractive to many programmers and has produced a small population of so-called "system hackers," most of them in university environments. Most perpetrators have rationalized part or all of their acts. In fact, they often put more effort into rationalizing their acts than in planning them.

Perpetrators' acts often tend to deviate in only small ways from the accepted and common practices of their associates. In one case of program theft through a terminal, it was revealed in the trial that programmers in both the victim's firm and perpetrator's firm were gaining access to each others's computers frequently.

Another commonly found rationalization is the Robin Hood argument. Perpetrators tend to differentiate between doing harm to individual people, which is immoral, and doing harm to organizations, which they believe is not immoral in certain circumstances. In fact, they often claim they are just getting even for the great harm organizations do to society. One perpetrator has said that he was motivated to perform his acts to make money, for the challenge of seeing how far he could go, and to get even with the victim company which he believed at that time did great harm to society.

Among traditional motivating forces in crime, the challenge aspect seems to be much stronger in computer-related acts. Among several perpetrators interviewed and almost universally among university student perpetrators, the challenge of seeing how far they could go or "beating the system" ranks high in reasons given for the acts. In some cases claims of victims that their computer systems were safe and could not be penetrated encouraged eager young programmers who look upon their work as an intellectual challenge to pit their minds against the intransigent machine.

It appears that perpetrators strongly fear unanticipated detection and exposure. This makes detection as a means of protection at least as important as deterrence and prevention.

Perpetrators tend to be amateur white-collar criminal types, for whom exposure of activities would cause great embarrassment and loss of prestige among their peers, in contrast to many professional criminals, who want their peers to know of their accomplishments.

One approach to security is a cost-effective approach, i.e., to determine the value of the loss of assets against expenditure of resources on security. Another approach is to reduce the population of potential perpetrators to as few trusted people as possible.

16. Wasserman, Joseph J. "Audit Questionnaire for Computer Libraries and Back-up." *Internal Auditor*, March-April 1973, pp. 57-61. (ABI-73-01031)

Unless management develops and implements an effective computer security program, they may be exposing their companies to a potential catastrophic loss. In addition, officers and directors may find themselves legally liable for a stockholders suit because they have not taken reasonable precautions to protect and prevent losses due to neglect or inadequate security measures being employed at their EDP facility. The objective of this audit is to ensure establishment of effective levels of security to protect all aspects of the corporation's computer assets—hardware, software, data, personnel, etc. From environmental conditions, theft, fraud, intentional or unintentional errors and system failures develop.

17. Palme, Jacob. "Software Security." ***Datamation*****, January 1974, pp. 51-55.**

The safe operation of a computer can be disturbed either by unintentional errors or by intentional interference such as illegal access to data; illegal modification, addition or destruction of data; and interference with the ordered working of the computer.

Illegal access to data may be controlled through personal keys in which the number of combinations in the key are large; the key should be randomly selected from all the combinations and it should be easy to memorize since the risk of unauthorized use is larger if it has to be written down. Once the user is identified he can be prevented from reaching data other than that for which he has need and the authority to have. This is accomplished through a table lookup, a hierarchical or levels of authorization.

Authorization should not be strictly access or no-access, but rather the right to read, or to add, change and delete data and/or execute change in program.

There are four oft-occuring weaknesses in operating systems: (1) legality not checked; (2) the user changes the message after it is checked by the O/S but before it has been performed; (3) misuse of openings in the O/S and used improperly later; and (4) change of data in the user memory area. The author stresses the importance of the operating systems, "the central point of security on a computer is the operating system and the basic hardware." Finally, cryptography, as a method of transforming data to make it unreadable without a key, is discussed. (Note: the term is called data encryption, enciphering, scrambling and privacy transformation.)

18. Davis, Ruth M. "Privacy and Security in Data Systems." ***Computers and People*****, March 1974, pp. 20-27.**

Privacy is the right of an individual to decide what information about himself he wishes to share with others. Confidentiality is the status accorded to data which has been agreed upon between the person or organization furnishing the data and the organization receiving it and the degree of protection which will be provided. Security is the protection of hardware, software and data through the imposition of appropriate safeguards. Security relates to protection against destruction, disclosure, access both intentional and unintentional. The author discusses data encryption. A table lists eight threats and 13 categories of countermeasures.

19. Gibson, Cyrus F. and Richard L. Nolan. "Managing the Four Stages of EDP Growth." *Harvard Business Review*, January-February 1974, pp. 76-88.

The authors show how issues change shape as a company moves through four stages of development. The four stages are: (1) initiation; (2) expansion; (3) formulization; and (4) maturity. In stage one, initiation, there are problems such as behavioral aspects, e.g., job displacement anxieties and open employee resistance. The initiation phase may also be characterized by lax management (the EDP organization is under the department of the first application), and lack of controls over user priorities.

In stage two, expansion, there is a proliferation of applications into various functional areas–cash flow, general ledger, budgeting, etc. There is growth in EDP personnel. Systems analysts and programmers are assigned to work in various functional areas. Controls are lax. In order to engender applications development, few standards are developed and there is informal project control. The technicians run the shop. Management priorities guidelines are not well articulated and there is a crisis atmosphere. During this period, there may be neglect of current programs, i.e., program maintenance, and data base development which could lead to a common data base for all of the applications. During this stage, the emphasis is on separate applications.

In stage three, formalization, there may be a moratorium on new applications and emphasis on control. The staff is concerned with control and effectiveness assurance. This stage is characterized also by control-oriented management: programming controls, documentation standards, management reporting systems, project management, and quality control policies for computer systems design, programming and operations. Maintenance programming and systems programming become the dominant activities. The EDP moves out of the functional area of first application and becomes a functional specialty.

Stage four, maturity, is characterized by data base applications, online query systems, and more sophisticated technology such as teleprocessing and continued growth in EDP specialized personnel. It is further characterized by the refinement of management controls, elimination of ineffective control techniques, and further development of others, and the introduction of data base policies and standards. The organization attempts to strike a balance between organizational stability and keeping up with technological changes or the technological imperative.

Knowing where the organization is with respect to these four stages may help the auditor in an EDP environment assess the degree to which controls may exist, and how sophisticated the hardware and software may be.

20. Renninger, Clark R. and Dennis K. Branstad. *Government Looks at Privacy and Security in Computer Systems*. A summary of a conference held at the National Bureau of Standards, Gaithersburg, MD, Nov. 19 and 20 1973. Washington, DC: National Bureau of Standards, February 1974, 46 pp.

The publication summarizes the proceedings of a conference held for the purpose of highlighting the needs and problems of Federal, state and local government in the safeguarding individual privacy and protecting confidential data contained in computer systems from loss or misuse. The paper discusses the need for technological guidelines and standards for assuring uniform compliance with legislative requirements, management guidelines for identifying and evaluating threats to security and improved technological methods for controlling access to computer systems. Cost implications of providing security measures are also discussed.

21. Schwab, Bernhard and Mark Thompson. "Unionism in Data Processing." *Datamation*, October 1974, pp. 61-69.

The authors discuss the emerging importance of unionism in data processing. They warn that management should examine any contract to insure that undue restrictions inadvertent or intentional do not hinder data processing operations. The potential for strikes and threats of strikes would have some bearing on security of EDP operations. Unionism may also cause some restriction on work assignments, which means that there may be some limitations on management's right to assign employees which could seriously inhibit the efficiency of the operation. It could impact upon the area of separation and segregation of duties and responsibilities which could impact upon internal control features. Therefore, the interest of this article for auditors is that the auditors might need to participate early in collective bargaining between management and the EDP personnel. This may be particularly important when managerial and supervisory personnel may take over the essential parts of EDP operations during a strike. The authors point out that feelings can become quite bitter and emotions will run high in strike situations. When a militant union sees its bargaining position eroded, the possibility of sabotage and other illegal actions on the part of disgruntled employees can become quite real. Thus, the issue of security can take on new dimensions when a union enters the scene, and thorough preplanning for a contingency is just as important to mitigate the effects of downtime suffered from work stoppages as it is in the case of fire. Possible trend towards unionization will provide a changed environment with new challenges. The changes need not be all bad; it will be up to management to insure that they are not. In the same vein that this presents a challenge for management, it obviously presents a challenge to the EDP auditing profession.

22. Bushkin, Arthur A. *A Framework for Computer Security*. Revised ed. Santa Monica, CA: System Development Corp., June 1975, 158 pp.

This document presents an overview of the computer security problem and a model for a structured approach to the computer security problem. The model discusses standards and measures in the area of systems design, procurement specifications, daily operations and assessment of existing systems with a special emphasis on the attainment of an acceptable level of risk. It discusses such items as threat evaluation, computer program documentation, risk analysis and auditing.

23. Cook, James D. "An Operational Audit of EDP and a Review of Internal Controls." *The Magazine of Bank Administration*, April 1975, pp. 18-26A. (ABI-75-04091)

As EDP systems become more sophisticated and integrated management information systems are designed with common data banks, the auditing function becomes maintained around and through the computer. The auditor's primary responsibility is to determine that controls and operating procedures are functioning in a way to protect the bank's assets by carrying out tests and procedures that establish the validity and activities of the bank. EDP auditing at American National Bank and Trust Company in St. Paul uses an internal control questionnaire during an installation review. Various controls can be instituted, such as segregation of duties, application controls, standards and procedures controls, and processing controls. Threats to computer security, such as fire, water, tornado, accidental or deliberate damage and fraud are covered in the questionnaire. A through-the-computer audit trail using EDP programs is the predicted evolution of this approach to auditing.

24. Palmer, Frederick B. "Auditing for the Future, Audit Review of Systems Development." ***The Internal Auditor*****, March-April 1975, pp. 61-67. (ABI-75-03253)**

Audit review of systems during development is a very rewarding activity for the auditor and a real service to management. It should help produce better functioning, documented, and controlled systems which create output that will be used to its full potential, and with understanding, by all users. A system survey is a very broad look at the objectives of the system to be developed and possible strategies for building the system. Refining cost and time estimates on various approaches and a recommendation on the best approach are part of a feasibility study. During the specifications phase logical descriptions and requirements for the systems are provided through heavy involvement with the user. Systems design, the technical development of the system, covers logical file design and detailed processing flow and physical aspects of the system. Programming, testing, conversion, start-up and operation follow these steps.

25. American Institute of Certified Public Accountants. ***Guidelines for Development and Implementation of Computer-Based Application Systems.*** **Management Advisory Services. Guidelines Series. Number 4. NY: American Institute of Certified Public Accountants, 1976, 52 pp.**

The guidelines present a step-by-step approach to the development and implementation of an EDP application system. They are procedural rather than technical, i.e., they explain what to do, not how to do it. There are 87 system development tasks classified as follows:

Phase 1: Requirements Definition and Alternative Approaches (Tasks 1-19).

Phase 2: General Systems Design (Tasks 20-26).

Phase 3: Detail Systems Design (Tasks 27-45).

Phase 4: Program Specifications and Implementation Planning (Tasks 46-52).

Phase 5: Programming and Testing (Tasks 53-57).

Phase 6: Systems Testing (Tasks 58-64).

Phase 7: Conversion and Volume Testing (Final Testing) Tasks 65-73).

Phase 8: Implementation (Tasks 74-82).

Phase 9: Post-Implementation Evaluation (Tasks 83-87).

Each task is defined and discussed in terms of output and purpose and the suggested form the output is to take (e.g., memo, worksheet, flowchart, contract, etc.). The following is an example of the format used in presenting the tasks:

In Phase 3 (Task 31) – *Detail Systems Design*, the task is to develop system and subsystem processing flow and interfaces with other existing systems. The output, purpose and suggested form is as follows:

Output and Purpose	Suggested Form
System Flowchart. To provide a schematic representation, work flow, and general information about the system.	Flowchart
Subsystem Flowchart. To provide the detail design for each subsystem, its data flow, and its interfaces with other subsystems, files, and processes.	Flowchart
System and Subsystem Narrative. To provide in narrative form the logic requirements of the system and subsystem design.	Worksheet

The guide includes a flowchart of the system development tasks network (pp. 18-28).

26. Mair, William C., Donald R. Wood and Keagle W. Davis. *Computer Control and Audit*, 2nd ed. Altamonte Springs, FL: The Institute of Internal Auditors, Inc., 1976. (AR)

This text deals effectively with the development, control, and audit of electronic data processing (EDP systems as they are used in business in working with financial information. It provides a logical framework for those who wish to solve the problem described in the sub-title on the dust jacket, "How to reduce management exposure to computer traps." Although the work provides no great advance to state-of-the-art knowledge, nor could it be considered a compendium of answers to all computer-related management problems, it is worth owning for any reader who wishes to strengthen his knowledge of computer auditing and control. Best suited for readers who are knowledgeable in auditing and familiar with elementary EDP systems, it is most effective when considered from the point of view of the internal auditor, in his involvement in the control and audit functions. It is also of potential value for those concerned with the external audit function or overall management.

The authors take a practical and logical approach to the analysis and audit of a variety of internal controls used in both computerized and manual information systems.

The authors include advanced topics such as: (1) online systems; (2) data bases; (3) minicomputers; (4) computer abuse; and (5) operational auditing.

The text is divided into six major sections. The first (Chapters 1 through 5) gives an overview of the elements of control and audit. For instance, Chapter 2 develops the concept of control as it relates to the reduction of exposures: practices such as "erroneous record keeping, unacceptable accounting, fraud and embezzlement . . ." (p. 11). The authors construct an elementary matrix with various controls as the rows and causes of exposure as the columns. Where each control intersects a cause of exposure, a ranking of the control's effectiveness is assigned, with the scale ranging from 0 to 3, with 3 the most effective. This approach facilitates an organized method of evaluating current internal controls or pointing out effective controls for newly constructed systems. The first section does an adequate job of covering the topics of EDP organization, control, and compliance of an EDP system.

The second section (Chapters 6 through 10) deals with business information applications systems. The input, processing, and output activities are presented and potential audit exposures are discussed in detail. In Chapter 7 an extensive table depicts the application controls, explains each control, and gives an example of each. This table is a valuable contribution of this book. Chapter 8 deals with application audit tools and general purpose audit software.

The third section of the text (Chapters 11 through 14) includes discussions of systems development activities and controls and audit functions. Chapter 11 has extensive tables and sample forms to aid the auditor in the systems development activity. The authors stress the need for accurate and complete documentation of the system as a major audit tool and audit technique. A point well made by the authors is that the auditor must gather basic information, but beyond this, the auditor must evaluate and test this information. The auditor's opinion must emerge from the evaluation and tests.

The fourth section (Chapters 15 through 19) describes the information processing facility itself. Here the authors detail the activities, operating and hardware/software controls, security, recovery and audit of the EDP facility. While this section provides the structure for good, sensible analysis, the presentation is of a general nature, and, in my opinion, there is insufficient emphasis on methods of recovery from minor system failures and of the operation of the facility even with a minor degradation of the system's service. These kinds of problems are more likely to occur than the major disasters, such as a fire in a computer center, which the authors treat more extensively.

The last two sections cover advanced topics and audit management. The former (Chapters 20 through 23) uses the same approach as the three preceding sections. The emphasis is placed upon defining the activities, causes of exposure, controls and audit techniques. The reader is not inundated with highly technical solutions and controls but is presented with a sound, organized approach to the complex problem. The final section consists of only one chapter, which deals effectively with the topic of audit management.

In summary, this text provides a sound treatment of the development, control, and audit of computerized business financial information systems.

27. Morris, William and Hershe Anderson. "Audit Scope Adjustments for Internal Control." *The CPA Journal*, July 1976, pp. 15-20. (ABI-76-08014)

A problem has always existed in relating the degrees of reliance on internal control with the requirement that opinions be based on sufficient evidential matter. This includes determining which aspects of control need to be reviewed by the auditor and the stability of the control system. A study was conducted of three CPA firms to determine how evaluations of internal controls affect audit procedures. The results of the study showed that there is no change in the amount of evidence obtained on an engagement due to an evaluation of the internal control system. Internal control was generally evaluated over time to see how it changed. Of major concern in determining the amount of evidence required was the inherent risk in not exercising due professional care. The nature of the company, including age, type of business, and reputation, were major factors. Tables.

28. Myers, Glenford J. *Software Reliability: Principles and Practices*, NY: John Wiley & Sons, Inc., 1976, 360 pp.

The author defines software reliability and analyzes the major causes of unreliability, the design of reliable software, software testing, and development of reliable software. The author defines software error as present "when the software does not do what the user reasonably expects it to do." A software failure is an occurrence of a software error. Software reliability is the probability that the software will execute for a particular period of time without failure, weighted by the cost to the user of each failure encountered.

Hardware can become inoperative because of three types of problems—design error, manufacturing error, and failures (i.e., problems arising out of operations such as heat, friction, radiation, etc.). Software reliability however is entirely in the design; it is seldom manufacturing error and is not due to failure.

All design principles and practices can be grouped in four categories: Fault Avoidance, Fault Detection, Fault Correction, and Fault Tolerance, which the author defines and discusses in several chapters.

Important to the auditor is "the myth of Path Testing." For example, a statement followed by a two way *IF* followed by a second *DO* statement could result in approximately 10^{18} unique paths through the particular model which leads the author to state the following:

> If your goal is to show the absence of errors,
> You won't discover many.
> If your goal is to show the presence of errors,
> You will discover a large percentage of them.

The book also provides some testing axioms (191-195):

> A good test case is a test case that has a high probability of detecting an undiscovered error, not a test case that shows that the program works correctly.
>
> One of the most difficult problems in testing is knowing when to stop.
>
> As the number of detected errors in a piece of software increases, the probability of the existence of more undetected errors also increases.
>
> Testing, as almost every other activity, must start with objectives.

The Index to the book will provide the reader with an indication of the wide range of important topics covered.

29. Parker, Donn B. *Crime by Computer*. NY: Charles Scribner's Sons, 1976, 308 pp.

The author says that auditors who deal with fraud involving computer manipulation (as contrasted with data alterations) "must have an in-depth technical understanding of computers because the integrity of the computer system has been threatened and attacked. The auditor must deal with the problem of correctness of computer programs and data files stored and used within the computer."

The book presents comprehensive case descriptions of computer fraud, the result of intensive research by the author.

Parker speculates that the increased application of countermeasures may reduce the number of computer frauds, but expects the losses per incident to increase. Auditing capability is one of the significant measures in controlling fraud. Parker believes EDP auditing for security against fraud is the principle barrier for the "next few years until more powerful technological solutions are achieved."

30. Tharp, Marvin O. "Auditor and the Systems Audit." *Journal of Systems Management*, April 1976, pp. 29-33. (ABI-76-04138)

As computers are increasingly being used in accounting and financial systems, data processing managers must become more aware of the audit function and know the procedures involved in the systems audit. Audits review and evaluate an organization's internal control procedures and evaluate the EDP records produced. How the DP system's controls are supposed to work and how they ideally work are compared. Seven areas are usually examined in a system's audit—organizational control, system documentation, hardware controls, file safeguards and security, input and output controls, processing controls, and the audit trail. The auditor then tests and evaluates the system for compliance. A six-step outline of a good audit plan and a summary of 10 minimum controls needed for a basic batch system are also included. Tables.

31. ***Accounting Controls In a Minicomputer Installation*****. NY: Price Waterhouse, 1977, 12 pp.**

This 12-page booklet was written for auditors to help them tailor information to their minicomputer installation from existing audit programs for computerized systems. The booklet was prepared by Price Waterhouse. The booklet discusses accounting control ojbectives and the problems an auditor may encounter with small EDP departments. Price Waterhouse also prepared a complete EDP guide as a part of its series, Guide to Accounting Controls. For information on obtaining the Guide and the booklet, write to National Office Distribution Department, Price Waterhouse, 1251 Avenue of the Americas, New York, NY 10020.

32. **Allen, John Robert. "The Auditor's Relationship to the Development of Data Processing Controls."** ***Management Accounting*****, November 1977, pp. 39-42. (ABI-77-17217)**

Electronic data processing systems must be properly tested before they are implemented or changed, and adequate controls must be built into these systems from the outset. Contrary to much stated opinion, the internal auditor is neither responsible for testing the systems nor for developing the controls. Auditors should be knowledgeable about computer systems and involved at an early stage of their development, but it does not follow that the auditor should develop or implement these controls. Rather, controls are the responsibility of user and data processing managements as they would be for any factory or processing facility. The problem facing internal auditors is that they must be independent and objective during post completion audits of data processing systems, but often their ideas are needed during systems development because the auditors are considered the corporate control experts.

33. American Institute of Certified Public Accountants. *The Auditor's Study and Evaluation of Internal Control in EDP Systems*. NY: American Institute of Certified Public Accountants, 1977, 67 pp.

The basic objectives of the guide are: (1) to describe and recommend procedures to be performed by an independent auditor in the auditor's study and evaluation of EDP accounting controls as part of the overall review of the accounting control system; (2) to provide the auditor with information for meeting the requirements of *Statement of Auditing Standards No. 3*; (3) to outline some examples of the typical tests of compliance that can be applied to EDP accounting controls; and (4) to discuss in general terms, the possible effect of a weakness in EDP accounting control.

The guide is geared toward batch processing as the dominate EDP orientation and of interest to the largest number of auditors. It reviews the essential characteristics of internal accounting control and outlines procedures for its review—the preliminary phase (a system walk-through which may be based on the review of the system flow charts), assessment, test of compliance and evaluation. Evaluation involves determining for each significant accounting application: (1) the type of error or irregularities that can occur; (2) the existence of effectiveness of the accounting control procedure that prevent or detect such errors; and (3) the type and extent of substantive tests to be conducted.

Nineteen general controls are identified: Organization and Operation Controls (1-3); Systems Development and Documentation Controls (4-10); Hardware and Systems Software Controls (11-12); Access Controls (13-15); and Data and Procedural Controls (16-19). Each control is described in terms of objectives and the various review and compliance test procedures related to each test. The audit effect of the weakness of various controls is discussed also. For example, in discussing the audit effects of a weakness in systems development and documentation controls (general controls 4 to 10 – Documentation), the guide states that usually this weakness will require the auditor to devote more effort to the evaluation of other accounting controls within significant accounting applications (pp. 36-37).

In Chapter 4, twelve (12) application controls are similarly described and discussed.

34. Earl, Michael J. "Program Auditing: A New Approach to Computer Audit." *EDPACS*, December 1977, pp. 5-14. (ABI-78-04319)

An external auditor is basically involved in substantive auditing, while the internal auditor is concerned with compliance auditing. Program auditing involves an examination of the text of the computer program itself in order to become familiar with the actual processing steps. Program audits answer the questions: (1) can the system correctly handle valid data? (2) can the system deal properly with invalid data? (3) are all the steps the system takes legitimate? (4) is the system reviewed the one normally used? (5) is the system effective and efficient? (6) is the system operationally reliable and secure? Known applications for program audit include: (1) followup on queries raised by other techniques; (2) audit of sophisticated programs; (3) checking of complex and critical program functions; and (4) efficiency audits. Financially significant programs are obvious candidates for program audits. The method deserves serious consideration. Charts.

35. Mullin, M.A. "Computer Security–The Human Element." *The South African Chartered Accountant*, August 1977, pp. 257-259.

This article concentrates on the human aspects of computer security. In the final analysis, computer problems can usually be traced to people.

The advent of online data base systems offer a number of very useful facilities but also impose a number of human-related limitations; such systems require a high level of technical skill. Someone with such skills can compromise the system. An unskilled person can easily damage or destroy it. Many users now have direct access to the system. This increases the risk of security failures.

Some basic principles should be observed to enhance computer security: (1) management action should be designed to foster an employee awareness of the importance of EDP security; (2) computers should be used within a framework that allows the staff to realize their own potential in an ethical environment; (3) controls should be designed to detect and report security violations; and (4) computer criminals should be prosecuted promptly.

36. Perry, W.E. "Computer Audit Practices." *EDPACS*, July 1977, pp. 1-9. (ABI-77-14362)

In 1974, the Stanford Research Institute conducted an IBM-funded study of computer audit and control, called "systems auditability and control (SAC)." Three main conclusions result from the SAC Study: (1) once learned a given technique is used to satisfy many objectives;

(2) audit tools and techniques are primarily debugging practices; (3) most techniques are sophisticated ways of auditing around the computer, not involving an analysis of the adequacy of computer internal controls. Five tools or techniques topped the list for auditing of both systems development and modification as well as production systems: (1) parallel operations; (2) test data methods; (3) manual tracing and mapping; (4) flagging transactions; and (5) generalized audit software. As a result of the SAC study, a total of 29 different techniques have been classified into seven categories. Table.

37. Smith, John H. and Wilfred C. Uecker. "Internal Audit Activities in EDP System Design, Testing and Control." ***Internal Auditor*****, February 1977, pp. 57-62. (ABI-77-01977)**

This article reports the results of internal audit activities in the design and development of EDP systems, the test of controls before beginning an operation, the controlling of changes in programs and operations, and in the audit tests of controls. Responses were received from 113 internal auditors in the midwest area who were questioned about the above items. The results of this study indicate that internal auditors have not yet contributed much toward the design of effective, well controlled EDP systems. Auditors, however, have become involved in the control and testing of existing systems but not in their design. Continued and increased pressure must be maintained to persuade management that control must be an integral part of any EDP system and that this control must involve auditors at both the design stage and the operating stage. Tables.

38. Stanford Research Institute. ***Systems Auditability and Control Study*****. Three volumes. Prepared for the Institute of Internal Auditors, Inc. Altamonte Springs, FL: Institute of Internal Auditors, Inc., 1977.**

The systems auditability and control (SAC) research study is in three volumes: (1) *The Executive Report*, (2) *The Data Processing Audit Practices Report*, and (3) *The Data Processing Control Practices Report*.

The purpose of the report is to provide a compendium of various proven controls and techniques to the auditing and data processing communities. More specifically it is to provide practitioners with practical solutions to the known current problems associated with computer audit and control.

The title of the study—Systems Auditability and Control—reflects the interrelationship between internal audit and control. The auditability of computer-based information systems refers to the features and characteristics needed to verify the adequacy of controls as well as to verify the accuracy and completeness of data processing results. Systems control pertains to the mechanisms within the total system environment that ensure the accuracy and completeness of the computer-based information system and its output. Thus, the scope of this study includes both internal audit and internal control, two separate but closely related subjects.

The Data Processing Audit Practices Report presents information on auditing in the data processing environment.

Part I of the report describes the state of the art of EDP auditing. This section discusses the importance of the EDP audit function and outlines a comprehensive role for internal audit as it relates to the data processing function. Information is also presented on establishing an EDP audit staff, selecting individuals for that staff, and training of EDP auditors.

Part II discusses the three areas of audit activity in the data processing environment. These areas are auditing computer-based information systems, auditing computer service centers, and auditing computer-based systems development. Discussions relate to what various organizations are doing in each of these areas.

Parts III through VI discuss the various audit tools and techniques being used by large organizations. The descriptions of these tools and techniques are designed to provide internal auditors with enough background information to evaluate the applicability of implementing these techniques in their organizations. Each technique contains a table showing the data processing knowledge level required by internal auditors to use the tool or technique effectively. A brief evaluation of the effectiveness of the technique is included as part of each description. SRI has identified 28 EDP audit tools and techniques.

The Data Processing Control Practices Report presents information relating to control techniques applicable to computer-based information systems, computer service center operations, and the system development process. It provides an overview of data processing control practices and describes specific controls and techniques identified during the study. This report is written for system analysts, computer programmers, data processing users, internal auditors, and others concerned with effective auditability and control in the data processing environment. This report complements the information presented in the Data Processing Audit Practices Report.

Computer information systems are presented in six phases: transaction origination, data processing transaction entry, data communication controls, computer processing, data storage and retrieval, and output processing. Each phase is further subdivided into control areas and the control types that SRI found in use in organizations visited. The controls listed are not all-inclusive but, rather, are representative of the types of controls currently implemented in data processing operations.

Part I of the report discusses the state of the art of EDP auditing and the importance of the EDP audit function, and outlines a comprehensive role for internal audit in the data processing environment.

Part II describes specific controls for computer-based information systems. Controls are presented for each of the six control phases listed above.

Part III describes general controls applicable to the computer service center and application systems development. Internal auditors or data processing management can use this part of the report to review the general controls in their computer service centers and systems. While this refers to EDP departments within organizations, the material is of use to those auditors involved in third-party reviews which is of growing concern due to the increase in commercial computer facilities and time sharing.

39. Wilkinson, Bryan. "An Application Audit." *Datamation*, August 1977, p. 51. (EDPACS)

The objective of the article is to assist data processing managers who have little contact with auditors, understand how auditors perform their work. The article discusses the five work steps in a typical audit: pre audit; around-the-computer audit; through-the-computer audit; audit wrap-up; and post audit. The balance of the article takes a more detailed look at each of these five phases.

Pre audit. The auditor in making his decision on which application to audit first is often based on an informal approach. Payroll is a logical first audit. Basically audit attention will be directed toward applications that control major assets, produce management reports, update important master files, contain many programs, or use a major portion of available computer resources.

In the around-the-computer phase the auditor uses a check list to interview the data processing manager and later a number of other people in the installation. The steps generally are to ask different people the same questions and comparing the answers, comparing work paper data with answers given and comparing observation to check list answers. This approach serves to provide the auditor with detailed knowledge in a short time.

Often the auditor will find it useful to employ a computer audit software package to sample files and verify their content, i.e., through-the-computer audit. When the field work is complete, the auditor wraps up the audit by reviewing and evaluating his findings and preparing his recommendations. The article presents nine categories around which recommendations can be grouped: (1) project and change control; (2) operational and administrative controls; (3) manual controls; (4) programmed controls; (5) online system controls; (6) controls over service bureaus or outside facilities; (7) safety, security, and backup provisions; (8) asset protection; and (9) efficiency and effectiveness. The post audit consists of a review, six months to a year later, to review the results of the corrective action.

40. Bequai, August. *Computer Crime*. Lexington, MA: D.C. Heath and Company, 1978, 224 pp.

This book examines the criminology of computer crime. The author defines computer crime and discusses traits of computer criminals as well as the lack of deterrence for this modern day crime. A detailed description of system vulnerability is presented next along with a review of the categories of crimes involved. One of the initial chapters covers securing the computer with a description of certain aspects of personnel and physical security.

Chapters 4 and 5 address the issues of federal and state laws and how they can be applied in the fight against the spread of computer crime. Also presented are legal definitions for various offenses involving habitation or property. Two chapters are devoted to the investigatory resources which are available at local, state, and federal levels.

Chapters 9 through 13 present a description of the legal problems involved in the prosecution and conviction of computer felons. Numerous legal cases are cited throughout these chapters and the following two chapters which illustrate the problems which face prosecutors and defenders in computer crime cases. The final chapter examines crimes of the future in the world of the Electronic Funds Transfer System (EFTS).

41. Burger, Albert D. "EDP Audit: Don't Forget the User." *Internal Auditor*, February 1978, pp. 20-26. (ABI-78-02484)

The primary objective of an electronic data processing (EDP) operational audit is to assess the overall performance of the data processing department. Since most corporate data processing departments view themselves as service organizations dedicated to filling the information processing needs of various user departments, it seems logical that the EDP auditor would be interested in seeing if this goal is met. One successful communication technique is the user evaluation survey sheet. The survey questionnaire, accompanied by a cover letter explaining the auditor's request, is sent to all users of DP services. The user evaluation survey sheet allows the auditor to quantify user satisfaction. By determining where the user thinks a problem exists, the survey alerts the EDP auditor to potential communication problems or functional shortcomings. With additional investigation, the auditor can pinpoint the problem and solve it. Charts.

42. "Computer Fraud and Embezzlement." ***EDP Analyzer*****, September 1978, pp. 1-14.**

The article states that while there is no assurance that an embezzler can be detected in advance of the crime based on behavior characteristics, there are some things that managers can do to reduce the risks of embezzlement. Management can: (1) make an inventory of the person's financial needs; (2) check on prior arrest and convictions; (3) review the job history to make sure that all time intervals are accounted for; (4) check for persons who never take a two-week vacation or longer or any vacation, who refuses promotion or rotation, who is always on the job when the end-of-period accounting is done; (5) identify persons who have access to records or the computer, and/or can authorize transactions and get at the assets; (6) identify those who have access to company's premises when no one else is working, for example, a third-shift type or a weekender.

The opportunities for embezzlement or fraud are enhanced by sloppy record keeping and poor controls. With many errors in the data file, it may be impossible to tell if an asset is missing or if it is simply carried in the wrong account. If the error rate is high, theft may very well go on undetected.

A program for controls should consist of identifying the assets and analyzing the potential threats to the assets. This would include location of assets; identification and tracing the flow of removable assets and information as it moves through the organization, good preemployment checks, limited access to certain areas such as the computer room and tape vaults, separation of duties to be strictly enforced for operators, programmers, librarians, data entry clerks and data control clerks, rotation of those with sensitive duties, establishment of an internal audit capability and establishment of strong internal control systems. Some of the techniques for testing the internal controls are to introduce deliberate errors and procedural violations by the internal auditor to see if the controls are working, computer program review, that is, to study the sensitive programs to look for unexplained branch points (the use of an automatic flowcharter might be helpful for displaying all of the actual branch points in a program and not just the ones shown by the programmer on a flowchart). Computer-assisted audit packages can be used to perform calculations, compute interest, age accounts receivable, compare results for a group of records, or compare and reconcile two different files. The article also discusses how to handle the situation after the fraud has been detected.

43. Diroff, T.E. "The Protection of Computer Facilities and Equipment: Physical Security." *Data Base*, Summer 1978, pp. 15-24. (DPD)

The objective of physical security should be to minimize the probability of an event happening to the greatest extent possible with the given resources.

The first step in systems security planning process is the proper delegation of planning authority to a single individual in the organization who, in turn, can study and initiate related security planning activities and help pinpoint responsibility areas for his organization. The individual responsible for security should be a member of, or report to, top management.

The second step in a good systems security plan is the identification of the specific organizational risks, goals, and priorities associated with the protection of its information and the physical system that stores or processes its data. This concept is known as risk analysis, which consists of: (1) identifying computer installation threats; (2) estimating the cost of the possible loss to the organization; and (3) estimating the possible frequency of the losses. Installation counselling is available from several hardware manufacturers and many consulting firms. One can use checklists to determine threats facing the installation and the corresponding weaknesses that need to be corrected. User associations can be contacted to learn what other companies are doing.

The following personnel may be included in identifying and evaluating threats: data base administrator, physical security officer, insurance officer, legal officer, personnel officer, data processing manager, line managers of the departments which use the computer and the head of the internal audit team.

Two goals of computer installation access control are: restricted access of outsiders to computer data and restricted access of computer personnel to unauthorized data. These goals can be achieved through a series of physical devices and operating procedures. Regular access to system and facilities must be limited to a specially designated elite. A list of authorized personnel should be maintained and reviewed at regular intervals. . . .A guard force is the first line of defense against an intruder. A buffer zone can be established at essentially no cost by proper layout of the facility. A simple key lock on the door to the computer room can buy a lot of security for a small price. A popular improvement on the lock is a card reader mechanism. There are several other types of detectors that may be used to detect an intruder's presence.

A security program needs to be reviewed on the basis of current effectiveness, continuing appropriateness, level of complexity, and readiness status.

44. Fitzgerald, Jerry. *Internal Controls for Computerized Systems*. Redwood City, CA: Jerry Fitzgerald & Associates, 1978, 93 pp.

The book is a working tool containing an abundance of controls that can be applied to the various components of the organization's computerized systems. It identifies over 650 controls and is organized into 10 chapters which divide the data processing function into its basic components. Each chapter contains a matrix of controls that interrelates the organization's concerns/exposures with the specific resources/assets that must be reviewed. These chapters and accompanying matrices cover:

	Number of Control/ Safeguards
• General organizational controls (Chapter 2)	49
• Input controls (Chapter 3)	68
• Data communication controls (Chapter 4)	91
• Program/computer processing controls (Chapter 5) (Chapter 5)	92

- Output controls (Chapter 6) 43
- On-line terminal/distributed systems controls (Chapter 7) 68
- Physical security controls (Chapter 8) 108
- Data base controls (Chapter 9) 64
- System software controls (Chapter 10) 68

This book can be used in numerous ways; it is useful in designing new or enhancing current computerized systems, conducting internal control reviews, evaluating risk analysis, developing EDP audit plans, and developing organizational control standards.

The matrix approach subdivides a sophisticated data processing system into its specific components, such as the data communication network. Then the controls that relate to each component of the system are reviewed.

The book is a practical "how to" manual. The various controls might be incorporated into an internal control checklist by adding a "yes/no" column to each of the 651 controls.

45. Fitzgerald, Robert J. "Organizing for an EDP Internal Audit." ***Journal of Systems Management*****, September 1978, pp. 12-17. (ABI-78-15017)**

The determination of what constitutes audit adequacy in the area of EDP security and internal control can be established during the initial stages of organizing the internal audit function. A risk oriented EDP audit planning program should be developed which estimates time and cost requirements to meet future objectives on both a short and long term basis. A risk evaluation entails reviewing those data processing systems which have accounting or financial significance, such as accounts payable, payroll, general ledger, etc. with regard to the impact they have on the overall financial statements of the corporation. Each defined EDP audit area should be evaluated for time, cost, and potential savings, and estimates should be developed. With the use of tables and charts the priority of the major areas for an EDP audit program can be developed. Environmental audits include: (1) administrative audits; (2) operational audits; and (3) technical support audits. Application audits include: (1) participation in design; (2) systems audits; (3) audit test development; and (4) audit test processing. The nature of the corporation will determine the approaches to planning and organizing, of which there are many. Charts.

46. Grooms, David W. *Computer Information Security and Protection: Citations from NTIS Database*. Springfield, VA: National Technical Information Service, August 1978, 357 pp.

This document contains the bibliography of federally-funded research projects covering the various aspects of computer information security and computer privacy. Some of the topics included are: reliability of security procedures, natural disasters, audits, electronic crime and implications of the Privacy Act of 1974. This updated bibliography contains over 350 abstracts and is a good source of issues and topics on computer networks, risk, reliability, records management and auditing in a computer environment.

47. Lee, Gerald W. "Rethinking Terminal Security Requirements." *EDPACS*, October 1978, pp. 1-10. (DPD)

This article reviews terminal system exposure and recommends solutions to their control problems.

Terminal system security and control is a complex topic. It involves hardware, software, and the need for a company-wide awareness program that stresses the need for adequate data security and control.

Vendors have not solved the terminal security problem because they concentrate on meeting the demands of their customers. Users have not demanded good terminal security systems. Systems designers have had problems creating effective controls for terminal security systems within the available technology.

Security and control programs can use much of the existing hardware and software. Some areas, however, would still benefit from technological advances. We need better methods of user identification and improved encryption technology for high speed data transmission lines.

The EDP auditor and the data processing designer should determine what is needed now and, more importantly, what will be needed in the future as the company's online terminal systems expand. We need to rethink our terminal security requirements.

A good starting point for rethinking terminal security requirements is to review the security and internal control systems that existed in the manual systems. The EDP auditor and the system designer should begin to see that many of the controls which existed in the manual environment have been lost in the terminal system. However, many of the basic control features identified in manual systems are relevant control objectives for a terminal security system.

Some of the issues to be addressed in rethinking terminal security requirements are:

1. User identification.
2. Authentication.
3. Application independence.
4. Compatible functions.
5. Maintenance of the security system.
6. Security system administration and monitoring.
7. Auditability.
8. Program and maintenance personnel.
9. Terminal operator training.

There are at least five alternatives which EDP auditing and data processing management can consider in their efforts to achieve the necessary levels of control: (1) return to manual controls; (2) separate terminal systems for each application; (3) front-end minicomputer for security; (4) custom designed security system; and (5) generalized security system. The generalized security system approach seems to be the most efficient method for most companies. When a company chooses the generalized approach, whether based upon a minicomputer or the host computer, new applications can be handled without the need for changes in the conceptual design of the security system.

48. Pritchard, John. "Computer Security–What is the Auditor's Role." *Accountancy*, November 1978, pp. 81-82. (ABI-79-01709)

Computer based accounting and information systems have become an integral part of the operations of most business concerns. Reliability on computer systems has increased significantly in recent years. However, many companies have failed to provide adequate security measures for their systems. An adequate security plan should include three items: (1) physical security of the facilities should be provided, including security from both accidental and intentional acts; (2) contingency plans of operation; and (3) periodic audit review of the security system which may be performed by either internal or independent auditors. In designing the security audit, the auditor must be especially aware of the differences between electronic and conventional manual records processing. Particular problems confronting the auditors include: (1) the lack of visible records; (2) the concentration of large quantities of data in a single location; and (3) the high concentration of expensive electronic equipment and highly specialized staff.

49. Roussey, Robert S. "Third-Party Review of the Computer Service Center." ***The Journal of Accountancy*****, August 1978, pp. 78-82. (DPD)**

The EDP auditing standards subcommittee of the American Institute of CPAs surveyed a number of public accounting firms to determine the effectiveness and reliability of the third-party review concept as applied to computer service centers.

The computer service center may service many industries or may be devoted to one basic industry. Industry-oriented service centers process data for banks, brokerage houses, hospitals and other organizations and can provide almost complete transaction accounting services. In addition, some centers process shareholder data for mutual funds and similar organizations, and others process corporate and individual income tax returns.

The AICPA saw that the growth, importance and complexity of service centers could have a significant effect on the processing of data and could affect an auditor's examination for clients using service centers. The guide discusses the audit approach, typical controls, compliance testing and third-party review of service centers.

In the third-party review, one auditor, the third-party auditor, would review the descriptions of a center's system, procedures and controls and issue a report describing the scope of review and extent of testing performed.

The AICPA survey requested information on additional auditing procedures, if any, considered by the user auditor in connection with the use of third-party reports. Sixty-two percent indicated that they had visited and in some instances called the third-party auditor to discuss the procedures and results further. Fifty-seven percent indicated that they found it necessary to visit the service center and perform additional reviews.

Sixty-seven percent of the firms indicated that the report gave them sufficient data.

In questions related to the independence of third-party auditors, the majority of the respondents stated that the third-party reviews used by them were performed by large national CPA firms. The user auditors implied that the independence and reputation of these auditors were not a problem.

In considering the possible future of the third-party review concept, three important factors should be explored: cost, utility, and need.

Will the need to rely on service center controls increase? Service centers are becoming more complex and, in certain situations, are recording transactions and making calculations outside the control of the user organization. These situations require the attentions of the auditors of the users of these service centers. This will surely result in increased attention to the third-party concept.

50. Stevens, Barry A. "Audit and Control of Performance in DP." *Journal of Systems Management*, August 1978, pp. 40-47. (ABI-78-13296)

Performance management is controlled in the areas of: (1) forecasting; (2) capacity analysis and resource planning for hardware and personnel; (3) measurement tools and techniques in both development and operations; (4) problem resolution procedures; and (5) organizational reporting. Systems managers should: (1) establish a process for concluding formal agreements on work; (2) establish forecasting methods based on user units of work; (3) complete the definition of service level criteria for development and operations; (4) extend problem resolution procedures to include a broader definition of problems; (5) compare actual service levels to objectives; (6) strengthen planning procedures; and (7) ensure that project management data and workload tracking data are consistently prepared. The insurance of good service to all users must be the primary objective of performance management. Formalization of procedures is mandatory. Chart.

51. Patrick, Robert L. and Robert P. Blanc. *Computer Science and Technology: Performance Assurance and Data Integrity Practices*. Washington, DC: U.S. Department of Commerce, January 1978, 45 pp.

This report identifies the approaches and techniques now practiced for detecting, and when possible, correcting malperformance as it occurs in computer information systems.

The report is addressed to two audiences: to the systems designer and to the manager who wishes to chronicle the deficiencies in an existing system prior to improving it. The report enumerates 67 items of current practices which prevent computer malperformance.

The ideas are grouped into the following four categories:

A. Data processing systems analysis.

B. Scientific systems analysis.

C. Implementation (testing).

D. Environment (organization structure)

52. U.S. General Accounting Office. *Audit Guide for Assessing Reliability of Computer Output*. Washington, DC: U.S. General Accounting Office, May 1978, 94 pp.

The reliability assessment guide is to assist the auditor make an appropriate examination when a determination is made that the reliability of computer output is important in accomplishing assignment objectives.

The guide includes a schematic overview of the reliability assessment approach, followed by a discussion of the steps outlined.

Computer processed data includes not only reports, checks, etc. prepared *by* the computer, but also reports which are *manually* prepared from computer generated information.

There are three uses of computer data identified: (1) as background information; (2) as a tool for audit planning; or (3) as support for findings. An example of this is a case where a GAO report may cite data from an agency's computer system to show the status of a worker protection program. Inaccurate or incomplete data could result in a distorted picture of program results.

Several questionnaires are included: (a) a user satisfaction questionnaire–processed products; (b) computer operations controls; (c) access controls; (d) file controls; (e) disaster recovery controls; (f) application system inventory; (g) application systems documentation and program modification controls; (h) data input control; (i) data error controls; (j) batch processing controls; (k) telecommunication processing controls; (l) data output controls; (m) computer application control profile. Glossary. Selected Bibliography.

53. Ussher, Albert. "The Computer Service Center: Should it be Visited?" *The South African Chartered Accountant*, December 1978, pp. 423-425, 427-428.

Although the article concerns service centers in South Africa, the growth of service centers in the U.S. makes this a timely article.

The author reports on a survey of auditor involvement in all service bureaus. Several findings of the study are: (1) only three percent of client auditors ask for access to the bureau to observe their clients' processing; (2) 18 percent look at administrative controls or documentation relating to the processing of their client's record; (3) 57 percent of the bureaus were visited by fewer than 25 percent of their clients' auditors; (4) 85 percent of the clients' auditors said they did not visit the bureau at least once during each audit; (5) 78 percent of the bureaus felt that a majority of their clients' auditors did not have the technical expertise to assess the work of the service bureau.

Some of the problems of third party review are: (1) timing the audit–the service bureau may not coincide with the audit of the client; (2) audit approaches–client and third-party auditors may have different audit approaches.

A great responsibility is placed on the auditor to evaluate clients controls particularly at the client-service bureau interface.

54. American Institute of Certified Public Accountants. *Controls Over Using and Changing Computer Programs.* NY: American Institute of Certified Public Accountants, 1979, 27 pp.

The American Institute of Certified Public Accountants has published a guideline designed to help CPAs decide when they can rely on a company's computer data in performing audits. It also contains much information for management in planning a program to prevent unauthorized use of computer programs.

55. Bailey, Andrew D., Jr., Michael Gagle and Andrew B. Whinston. "A Coordinated Approach to the Use of Computers in Auditing." *The EDP Auditor*, Spring 1979, pp. 27-42.

Auditing is a systematic process of objectively obtaining and evaluating evidence regarding assertions about economic actions and events to ascertain the degree of correspondence between those assertions and established criteria and communicating the results to interested users. This definition can relate to any audit setting involving evidence gathering and evaluation. The audit process, then, is describing, reviewing, testing, and evaluating internal control systems; performing substantive tests of details and balances, and evaluating data opinion on the fairness of the financial reports. The authors present a software model for evaluating control systems in complex organizations which is known as TICOM (The Internal Control Model). The advent of the accounting data base systems contribute to the auditor's functions by placing significant portions of the accounting information in computer readable sources; hence, the auditor is placed in a position of being able to access vast amounts of data efficiently. The article contains flowcharts of the auditing process plus references to auditing many of which relate to the use of auditing computer software. Those references are:

Cash, J.L., Jr., A.D. Bailey Jr. and A.B. Whinston. "A Survey of Techniques for Auditing EDP-Based Accounting Information Systems." *The Accounting Review*, October 1977, pp. 813-832.

Cash, J.L., Jr., A.D. Bailey Jr. and A.B. Whinston. "The TICOM Model–A Network data Base Approach to Review and Evaluation of Internal Control Systems." *American Federation of Information Processing Societies Conference, Proceedings, AFIPS*, June 1977.

Haseman, W.D. and A.B. Whinston. *Introduction to Data Management*. Richard D. Irwin, Inc., Homewood, IL, 1977.

56. Bracey, Randolph D. and Michael G. Walker. "Developmental Auditing Gauges Process Risks." ***Data Management*, July 1979, pp. 13-18. (ABI-79-13842)**

The electronic data processing (EDP) developmental auditing function is an operations-type audit, as opposed to an internal financial audit. The developmental audit is chiefly concerned with the managerial and technical aspects of large-scale computer systems development. Computer Sciences Corporation audits the development of its work to ensure that developmental risks are within tolerable limits. Auditing controls used by the company are separated into three major areas: (1) management controls; (2) conceptual controls; and (3) specific technical controls. Since few controls can be imposed on a development project after it is already underway, it is imperative that these controls be established beforehand. The systems development life cycle is a conceptual control that allows developers, auditors, and ultimate users to visualize computer system development. The life cycle is divided into five phases: (1) requirements definition; (2) preliminary design; (3) detailed design; (4) implementation; and (5) testing. A testing group independent of the program developers is used to add objectivity. References.

57. *Guide to Accounting Controls: EDP Guide No. 3*. NY: Price Waterhouse & Company, 1979, 40 pp.

The guide provides the reader with a basic understanding of the difference between minicomputers and traditional computers. Control problems in a minicomputer installation may include: lack of segregation of duties, inadequate software processing controls, ready access to data files and/or programs, inadequate file and program backup procedures, lack of control over program changes. Controls which address these concerns are discussed.

The cost benefit approach is discussed. It may be used in establishing priorities for system development projects, modifying an existing EDP system, eliminating duplicate controls which exist in both the user and EDP departments, etc.

Independent auditors consider the information gained from reviewing and evaluating prescribed controls to be tentative until tests have been made to provide assurance that the prescribed controls are actually in effect. Compliance testing includes sampling and use of test deck and controlled reprocessing. This technique is one in which the auditor controls the computer during a processing run of actual data using a program that has been developed or tested under his control. The objective is to determine that the output of the reprocessing under the auditor's control is identical with the output generated by normal processing procedures. Various other tests are described. Controls are discussed under internal accounting controls, procedural controls, data processing controls, and risk considerations.

58. Jarocki, Stanley R. and Eric J. Novotny. "Data Security/Privacy Requirements in Federal Bureaus." *The EDP Auditor*, Summer 1979, pp. 35-66. (DPD)

ADP security refers to the administrative, operational, technical, and physical safeguards employed to protect the Bureaus' ADP resources. Security safeguards are designed to minimize losses to the Bureaus that could be caused by delays, unauthorized disclosures, destruction of resources, and unintentional or deliberate acts of data modification.

Unless the rationale for security is identified, most organizations run the risk of over- or under-controlling existing threats. Security requirements should be based on a need that justified the time and expense required for implementation. For this reason, three sources of security requirements are identified: external requirements, user-specified requirements, and requirements based on risk assessment.

Various levels of security requirements are imposed on Bureaus by departmental or other executive authorities pursuant to law or executive order. Most of the current external security requirements arise from regulations written in support of the Privacy Act of 1974.

In addition to the current laws and regulations affecting the Bureau, at least three other sources of new requirements may affect the Bureau in the near future: revisions in the Privacy Act, Federal Computer Systems Protection Act (S. 1766), and federal ADP reorganization.

While the current and anticipated regulations set the stage for security requirements, the actual controls need to be specified, either from user requests or from the results of risk assessment and vulnerability surveys.

The DDP has a major responsibility under OMB Circular A-71 to provide an adequately documented and tested contingency plan. This should include an alternative processing service in case of emergencies or disasters. The establishment of user application priorities for the processing after a local outage is also needed.

Prudent management requires that the risk of natural hazards, accidents, and attacks be evaluated and that appropriate security controls be installed.

Two appendices follow the article. Appendix I summarizes federal regulations affecting security and privacy practices. Appendix II summarizes current federal regulations affecting ADP procurement.

59. Nearing, G.H. "Computer Master File Audit—A Systematic Approach." *The Magazine of Bank Administration*, July 1979, pp. 52-57. (ABI-79-12550)

A computer master file audit is necessary for direct verification of the information on the computer's data files to make certain no material errors have occurred. Periodic audits of computer data are not sufficient to test data validity unless personnel performing them understand the ways in which data can be manipulated and unless control procedures are adhered to rigidly. A systematic, generally applicable approach to the computer audit function is presented. Areas which should be considered include: (1) direct file manipulation; (2) indirect file manipulation; (3) computer audit objectives and elements; and (4) audit methodology. Execution of the computer audit takes place in three phases: (1) load phase; (2) balance comparison phase; and (3) verification phase. The control techniques suggested will greatly reduce the likelihood of unauthorized file tampering and allow data processing to report accurately the financial status of the bank. Charts. Figure.

60. Pomeranz, Felix. "Preemptive Auditing: Future Shock or Present Opportunity." *Journal of Accounting, Auditing & Finance*, Summer 1979, pp. 351-356. (ABI-79-11335)

The time is right for implementation of "preemptive" audits—those done before a transaction is completed so that the auditor can make suggestions about how best to reduce costs and improve revenues. A preemptive audit would focus on the review of the system and its controls with an eye toward future transactions. It would involve containing risk through system design, providing management with timely decision-making information, and altering management to budget and plan deviations while correction action is still possible. Preemptive audit techniques emphasize understanding the risks confronting the business and how to avoid, shift or mitigate them through controls. Computer analysis or simulation may be used to achieve this. The logic of computer programs will be checked and appropriate systems will be developed incorporating the proper audit trails and controls. Electronic data processing (EDP) applications would be developed to see if user needs are being met, and controls and their objectives would be evaluated.

61. Robertson, Jack C. *Auditing*. Revised ed. Dallas: Business Publications, Inc., 1979, 732 pp.

The revised text reflects changes and events in the accounting and auditing profession since 1976. The author cites 11 of these events including the Foreign Corrupt Practices Act of 1977, Quality Control Standards Committee report and the Commission on Auditors Responsibilities recommendations.

The author states that the auditor is one who must possess the inquiring, questioning mentality of a problem solver and hence discusses auditing in terms of the scientific method: (1) *recognize* the assets, problems and preliminary data required to formulate a testable hypothesis statement; (2) *formulate* the hypothesis in such a manner that either acceptance or rejection of it yields a useful auditing decision; (3) *collect* competent evidence that contributes to the decision; (4) *evaluate* the evidence relative to the decision choice; (5) *make* the decision to accept or reject the problem-related hypothesis. This last statement implies a formulation of a judgment on the conformity of the assertion with reality as the auditor perceives reality at the time of the evaluation of the evidence.

Chapters 8 and 9 are devoted specifically to auditing EDP, namely, "auditing internal control in an EDP environment" and "generalized audit software."

The author distinguishes between evaluating internal accounting control and using the computer to perform audit work. The purpose of the internal control study and evaluation is to determine whether general controls in a computer facility are satisfactory and whether application controls are properly designed and operate effectively. The purpose of using the computer to perform audit tasks, operating on machine-readable records, is to obtain sufficient competent evidential matter pertaining to the fair presentation or usefulness of output information.

Six pages are devoted to generalized system software, including discussion and description of STRATA, a Touche, Ross computerized audit software package.

Bibliography. Exercises and problems.

62. Ross, Steven J. "Distributed Systems Security." ***The EDP Auditor*****, Spring 1979, pp. 17-26.**

Data security is defined as the assurance that management's goals with regard to EDP will not be undermined due to faulty or malicious practices. Therefore, the placement of small or distributed data processing systems must proceed with full attention given to the requirements of data security. Questions relating to hardware should be asked of the vendor when purchasing a small computer. Can disk files be date protected? What is the technique for scratching a disk? Can access to that technique be restricted? Does the system utilize standard tape labels? Does the drive recognize an end-of-volume condition? Does the printer recognize paper jams and end-of-form conditions? Does the CPU, central processor, have parity checking? As to software, is there an operating system? The important items to check are the methods for invoking programs and accessing data. Do all programs reside in protected files or libraries access to which is limited, based on passwords, terminal identifiers or other restrictive devices? The authors warn that with the advent of PROMs or EPROMSs, that is, erasable or reprogrammable memory chips, it is possible to alter physically the control mechanisms of the computer itself. Therefore, the auditor may run the files under review on an independent main frame to increase the reliability of his findings.

63. Scott, Ronald L. and Jon A. Booker. "A Three-Phased Approach to the Systems Development Audit." ***Internal Auditor*****, June 1979, pp. 26-31. (ABI-79-10435)**

Internal auditors have generally recognized the need to be involved in the systems development audit (SDA), but many tasks are involved over a multiyear period. A phased organization of audit activities is helpful in managing and controlling such an audit. The primary objective of an SDA is to review and evaluate the application controls which ensure the reliability, accuracy, and completeness of data. The audit phase activities can be organized into initial planning and analysis, design, and development and implementation. Specific activities associated with a given audit phase will depend on the objectives stated by audit management. Special training may be required to provide auditors with the necessary electronic data processing education because of changes in the technology of information processing. The completion of each phase marks an audit control point which provides an opportunity to evaluate the effectiveness and progress of the audit and to review documentation collected and produced. Tables.

64. Statland, Norman. "Data Security and Its Impact On EDP Auditing." ***EDPACS*****, October 1979, pp. 108. (DPD)**

This article is essentially a checklist for auditors in assuring data security. The three principles of data security are stated:

1. Access Control: Don't let an interloper get at your computing resources.

2. Use Control: If he gets at them, don't let him use them.

3. Threat Monitoring: If he gets at them and uses them, you had better know about it.

The check lists are detailed under the following headings: (1) threats to data; (2) security ground rules; (3) programming for security; (4) online control procedures; (5) audit of online systems; and (6) audit involvement in online system design.

The external auditor should help his client to establish data security procedures as an extension of the traditional audit of computer systems. The small cost will be more than paid for in the benefits.

65. U.S. Department of Commerce. *Guidelines for Automatic Data Processing Risk Analysis. FIPS PUB 65*. Washington, DC: U.S. Department of Commerce. National Bureau of Standards, August 1, 1979.

Risk Analysis is a method of quantifying the impact of potential threats on organizations supported by Automatic Data Processing. Risks may be to data integrity, data confidentiality and EDP availability. The hazards are natural disorders, environment (e.g., explosives, flammable products), facility housing, access, work scene (e.g., employee/management relationship), data value (unauthorized disclosure of data, incorrect data).

The loss is determined in "expected value" terms, that is, the probability or frequency of an event occurring *times* the impact of the loss. Annual loss exposure (ALE) is the product of estimated impact in dollars (I) and estimated frequency of occurrence per year (F). In determining estimated frequency, if an event may occur five times daily, then (F) is 1825 times a year and if the estimated frequency is once every five years, then loss exposure is one-fifth (1/5th).

Applying the formula presented the impact of a $1 million loss which might occur once in 300 years the loss in terms of expected value would be $3,000. The risk analysis task is better approached from the standpoint of cataloging each of the data files or application systems on a work sheet on which the results of the analysis can also be noted. The work sheet might be a matrix application by data integrity, data confidentiality and processing availability. Several problems may be encountered in completing the analysis, two of which are identifying the risk and estimating frequency of occurrence. Intuition, experience, common sense and technical knowledge can assist in dealing with both problems.

The report comments on the conclusions which seem to be emerging from the growing body of statistics on computer crime.

- The vast majority of white collar crime is committed by employees defrauding their own employers.

- In general, employees who defraud their employers do so using resources to which they have access in the course of their jobs.

- The best deterrent to white collar crime has proved to be curtailment of incentive, i.e., limiting the profit potential of dishonest activity to the minimum consistent with the assigned task. If employees can expect no more than minimal gain from unscrupulous acts, they will be less likely to attempt them. The second-best deterrent is the fear of getting caught. If employees know there is adequate surveillance of activity, they will be less apt to place themselves in jeopardy.

A case is presented using a hypothetical government agency to show some of the facets which must be considered in a risk analysis.

The appendix lists several situations to which applications systems are vulnerable, grouped by eight (8) variables: (1) falsified data input; (2) misuse by authorized end users; (3) uncontrolled system access; (4) ineffective security practices; (5) procedural errors within the ADP facility; (6) program errors; (7) operating system flaws; and (8) communication systems failures. There are roughly nine problems under each of the eight classifications which could form the basis of a control questionnaire. References and suggested readings.

66. U.S. General Accounting Office. *Questions Designed to Aid Managers and Auditors in Assessing the ADP Planning Process*. (An Exposure Draft.) Washington, DC: U.S. General Accounting Office, August 1979, 85 pp.

The guide identified in question and answer format approximately 58 elements which are considered essential to the operation of an effective ADP planning process. By comparing the actual management of ADP planning with these criteria an assessment can be developed of the quality of the planning process.

These criteria include organizational involvement, direction, structure, control and reporting.

More specifically, evaluation questions relate to topics such as: who is responsible for ADP planning? is there a method of identifying and assessing the organization-wide risks and value to the aging of the potential payoff of the total ADP investment? does planning cover the entire period during which resources will be spent on each application in the software inventory and the hardware configuration (life cycle projections)? is there a system of objectives and controls to measure and evaluate performance against these objects? is there a reporting requirement?

67. Wagner, Charles R. *The CPA and Computer Fraud*. Lexington, MA: D.C. Heath and Company, 1979, 156 pp.

The author, a professor of accounting, observes that "the CPA has a greater degree of responsibility for the prevention and detection of computer fraud than the auditing profession currently accepts in its expression of auditing standards relating to the subject of fraud."

Chapters, most of them quite brief, treat the vulnerability of computer systems to fraud, information and research about computer fraud, the auditing approaches to computers, roles of internal auditor and CPA, recognizing computer fraud, and the search for the CPA responsibility.

68. Wong, Kenneth K. "Management Audit Of the EDP Systems' Users." ***EDPACS*****, September 1979, pp. 9-11. (DPD)**

In the future, increasing demand for information about management performance not met by audited financial statements will come from investment analysts, shareholders, and government regulatory agencies. "Management audit" (defined here as an audit which results in a statement of opinion about the performance of management) may not evaluate accurately the work of the EDP manager, as EDP problems can often distract management from the consideration of an important success variable for EDP: the management practices of the users of the system.

The user department must bear its fair share of system responsibilities, and its management practices should be audited along with those of the EDP manager. The article includes a user management audit checklist.

A management audit of the users of EDP systems would be greatly facilitated by a formal system development life cycle (SDLC) approach. This forces user participation in many phases of the development and frequent signoffs by appropriate user management. The SDLC becomes a standard against which one can audit. Sources for more information about SDLC are given.

69. Elliott, Robert K. and John J. Willingham. ***Management Fraud: Detection and Deterrence*****. Princeton, NJ: Petrocelli Books, Inc., 1980, 300 pp.**

This book contains a research report by the public accounting firm of Peat, Marwick, Mitchell & Co., and papers presented at a symposium on management fraud sponsored by PMM&Co. In Part I (pp. 1-84), the authors explore the subject and identify research problems. One chapter treats "The Computer and Management Fraud."

Part II (pp. 89-261) presents several papers on "Applying Various Disciplines to Management Fraud," including a chapter on "Computer-Related Management Misdeeds," by Donn Parker.

70. Jancura, Elise G. and Robert V. Boos. *Establishing Controls and Auditing the Computerized Accounting System*. NY: Van Nostrand Reinhold, 1980, 304 pp.

A practical guide to the internal controls and audit procedures relevant to computerized accounting systems. The authors describe how to document reviews and evaluations of internal controls in a range of computerized accounting systems. They also present computer-assisted auditing techniques and the preparation of documentation that supports findings and conclusions. Flow charts, diagrams, tables and audit programs clarify the text.

Among topics covered: EDP controls; controls in systems design and development; auditing in a computerized environment; computer-assisted audit techniques; service bureaus and other data processing services and organizations; the audit and control of distributed, interactive and integrated systems.

71. Sardinas, Joseph L., Jr., John G. Burch Jr. and Richard J. Asebrook. *EDP Auditing: A Primer*. NY: John Wiley & Sons, Inc., 1981, 209 pp.

This book is intended for the beginner in EDP auditing and draws much of its material from the authors' *Computer Control and Audit: A Total Systems Approach* (John Wiley & Sons, Inc., 1978), *q.v.* Major emphasis is on computer controls with chapters on introduction to controls, administrative controls, operational controls, documentation controls and security controls.

This book is prepared for teaching, with questions at the end of each chapter and an extensive appendix consisting of case studies, examination questions and glossary. Text material is very sparce, supplemented with charts and questionnaires. For example, the chapter on security controls consists of two pages of text and an eight-page questionnaire.

The authors believe auditors "should view themselves as the mirror image of the systems analyst."

72. United States General Accounting Office. *Evaluating Internal Controls in Computer-Based Systems: Audit Guide*, Washington, DC: U.S. Government Printing Office, June 1981, 279 pp.

As indicated in the Foreword the purpose of the guide is to help auditors make a detailed review and evaluation of internal controls in computer-based systems. The guide is intended to be a comprehensive document that incorporates techniques learned over the past several years. The procedures presented in the guide cover four phases—data collection, internal control, detailed analysis and testing, and reporting.

The guide includes check lists, questionnaires, and internal control matrices. One of the important features is the discussion of processing test data. Two approaches are discussed—parallel processing and integrated test facility (ITF). Another important feature of the guide is the discussion of risk assessment provided in Appendix II. The general format is that for each control characteristic a determination is made as to whether or not the control is in place and whether or not it is effective. Based upon the answers to these two questions the level of potential risk can be determined—i.e., low, medium, or high. A low risk means that it is unlikely that more audit tests are required. A medium level of risk means that it is likely that more audit tests are required and a higher level of risk means that more audit tests are definitely required.

Evaluating internal controls in computer-based systems involves gathering data on top management controls, general controls, and application centers. In addition analyses are performed on data flow, user satisfaction, test data, computer programs, data retrieval, and job accounting.

SECTION D. ADDITIONAL REFERENCES

73. House, Robert. "A Path Goal Theory of Leader Effectiveness." *Administrative Science Quarterly*, September 1971, pp. 321-338.

74. Samson, T.F. "Computer Auditing." *The Arthur Young Journal*, Autumn/Winter 1972-73 special edition, pp. 26-34.

75. American Management Association. *EDP Auditing: Concepts and Techniques*. NY: American Management Association, 1973.

76. Canadian Institute of Chartered Accountants. *Computer Control Guidelines*, 3rd printing, Toronto, Ontario, Canada: Canadian Institute of Chartered Accountants, 1973.

77. Davis, Gordon B. *Auditing and EDP*. New York, NY: American Institute of Certified Public Accountants, 1973.

78. American Institute of Certified Public Accountants. *Audits of Service-Center Produced Records*, especially Chapter 2, "Evaluating Controls at Service Centers." NY: American Institute of Certified Public Accountants, 1974.

79. American Institute of Certified Public Accountants. *The Effects of EDP on the Auditor's Study and Evaluation of Internal Control*, Statement of Auditing Standards 3, 1974.

80. House, Robert J. and Terence R. Mitchell. "Path-Goal Theory of Leadership." *Journal of Contemporary Business*, Autumn 1974, p. 86.

81. Institute of Internal Auditors, Inc. *Auditing Fast Response Systems*. Modern Concepts of Internal Auditing Series. Altamonte Springs, FL: Institute of Internal Auditors, Inc., 1974.

82. Institute of Internal Auditors, Inc. *Auditing Computer Centers*. Modern Concepts of Internal Auditing Series. Altamonte Springs, FL: Institute of Internal Auditors, Inc., 1974.

83. Burns, D.C. and J.K. Loebbecke. "Internal Control Evaluation: How the Computer Can Help." *Journal of Accountancy*, August 1975, pp. 60-70.

84. California Society of CPAs. *The Auditor's Preliminary Review of EDP Accounting Controls*. Palo Alto, CA: California Society of CPAs, 1975.

85. Canadian Institute of Chartered Accountants. *Computer Control Guidelines*, 3rd printing. Toronto, Ontario, Canada: Canadian Institute of Chartered Accountants, 1973.

86. Jancura, Elise G. *Audit and Control of Computer Systems*. NY: Van Nos Reinhold Co., 1975.

87. Kinney, William R., Jr. "Decision Theory Aspects of Internal Control System Design/Compliance and Substantive Tests." *Journal of Accounting Research*, Supplement 1975, pp. 14-37.

88. Jancura, Elise. *Audit & Control of Computer Systems*. NY: Petrocelli Books, 1976.

89. Jancura, E.G., and J.A. Drefs. "EDP Auditing Tips for Neophytes." *Internal Auditor,* April 1976, pp. 67-73.

90. Kuong, Javier F. *Audit and Control of Computerized Systems*. Wellesley Hills, MA: Management Advisory Publications, 1976.

91. London, Keith R. *The People Side of Systems: The Human Aspects of Computer Systems*. NY: McGraw-Hill Book Co., 1976.

92. Touche Ross & Company. (William C. Mair, Donald R. Wood and Keagle W. Davis.) *Computer Control and Audit*. Altamonte Springs, FL: The Institute of Internal Auditors, Inc., 1976.

93. U.S. General Accounting Office. *Guide for Reliability Assessment of Controls in Computerized Systems: Financial Statement Audits*. Exposure Draft. Washington, DC: U.S. General Accounting Office, 1976.

94. American Institute of Certified Public Accountants. *The Auditor's Study and Evaluation of Internal Control in EDP Systems*. NY: American Institute of Certified Public Accountants, 1977.

95. Cash, J.I., Jr., A.D. Bailey Jr. and A.B. Whinston. "A Survey of Techniques for Auditing EDP-Based Accounting Information Systems." *Accounting Review*, October 1977, pp. 813-832.

96. Dale, C. "The Systems Life-Cycle Approach to EDP Auditing." *The Internal Auditor*, April 1977, pp. 59-63.

97. Jancura, E.G., and F.L. Lilly. "SAS No. 3 and the Evaluation of Internal Control." *Journal of Accountancy*, March 1977, pp. 69-74.

98. Perry, William E. and W. Thomas Porter. *EDP Controls and Auditing*. 2nd ed. Belmont, CA: Wadsworth Publishing Co., Inc., 1977.

99. Reneau, J. Hall. "Auditing in a Data Base Environment." *Journal of Accountancy*, December 1977, pp. 59-65.

100. Rittenberg, L.E. and G.B. Davis. "The Roles of Internal and External Auditors in Auditing EDP Systems." *Journal of Accountancy*, December 1977, pp. 51-58.

101. Stanford Research Institute. *Systems Auditability and Control Study*. Volume 1, Altamonte Springs, FL: Institute of Internal Auditors, Inc., 1977.

102. Stanford Research Institute. *Systems Auditability and Control Study: Data Processing Control Practices*. Volume 2, Altamonte Springs, FL: The Institute of Internal Auditors, Inc., 1977.

103. Thierauf, Robert J., Robert C. Klekamp and Daniel W. Geeding. *Management Principles and Practices: A Contingency and Questionnaire Approach*. Santa Barbara, CA: Wiley/Hamilton, 1977.

104. Arthur Andersen & Company. *A Guide For Studying and Evaluating Internal Controls*. Chicago: Arthur Anderson & Co., January 1978.

105. Mair, W.C., D.R. Wood and K.W. Davis. *Computer Control & Audit*. Altamonte Springs, FL: The Institute of Internal Auditors, Inc., 1976, 1978.

106. Burch, John and Joseph Sardinas. *Computer Control and Audit: A Total Systems Approach*. NY: Wiley and Hamilton, 1979.

107. Hubbert, James F. "Audit Criticality Measurement for EDP Applications." *EDPACS*, July 1979, pp. 1-6.

108. Lott, Richard W. *Auditing the Data Processing Function*. NY: American Management Association, 1979.

SECTION E
EDP AUDITING TOOLS AND TECHNIQUES

ANNOTATED BIBLIOGRAPHY

1. **Adams, Donald L. and John F. Mullarkey. "A Survey of Audit Software."** ***The Journal of Accountancy*****, September 1972, pp. 39-66. (ABI-72-02916)**

This broad view of audit software provides guidelines for selecting a generalized audit package that will meet the specific requirements of both the auditor and the audit. The authors, who are strong advocates of computer auditing illustrate their discussion with appendices outlining how each of the 17 audit programs surveyed fulfill the basic criteria required by the auditor and listing the names and addresses of the study participants. The study was designed to accomplish the following objectives. Discuss the use of computers as an audit aid. Present an overview of the capabilities of audit packages and the various approaches taken in developing them. Provide an outline of the information a CPA must provide to the computer system. Review package implementation. Outline steps to be used in selecting the best package.

2. **Welke, William R. and Karl G. King. "Using the Computer as an Audit Tool."** ***CPA Journal*****, November 1972, pp. 930-932. (ABI-72-03744)**

The new EDP systems environment now includes sophisticated hardware and software, consolidated records, unfamiliar audit trails, and control frameworks in which manual and machine controls are highly independent. The auditor needs to acquire additional training in EDP technology and the utilization of computer-oriented audit techniques. This article discusses the advantages of using the computer as an audit tool and the techniques for implementing its use in the conduct of the audit.

3. **Clark, Gary F. "Software to Audit Computer Records."** ***Journal of Systems Management*****, December 1974, pp. 26-30. (ABI-75-00098)**

Audit retrieval packages are an effective means of auditing computer records, and usually consist of a series of prewritten computer programs that can be easily linked together and readily adapted by the auditor to the requirements of a specific audit situation. Some of the uses of audit retrieval packages include search and retrieval of items that have audit significance, selection of samples either by random sampling techniques or to satisfy desired statistical confidence levels, mathematical computations, file comparison, merges, and sorts, summarizing and reporting, and printing and punching. Since most packages were developed primarily for in-house use by national CPA firms, they are generally both conceptually and technically diverse. Packages should be evaluated in terms of availability, user experience with it, installation support needed, maintenance agreements, and cost.

4. **Adams, Donald. "Alternative to Computer Audit Software."** ***The Journal of Accountancy*****, November 1975, pp. 54-57. (ABI-75-12212)**

Computer audit software enables the auditor to manipulate the contents of a data-processing file. IBM has 15 such packages that can be used by auditors in the areas of testing aids, report generators, control aids, and data management aids. Some examples include the following. The data base/data communication drive system allows the simulation of an operation by using communications facilities to access the database system. The test data generator will create a file of test data, with the user describing the characteristics of the fields to be generated. The interactive query and report processor is used to obtain information out of a file and generate a report. The SMF-Graphical Analysis Program is used to collect accounting information about processing activities that take place within a system. Finally, the 3660 Exception Log Processing Subsystem is used to analyze a system's log.

5. **Appert, Richard H. "Computer Audit Software."** ***Retail Control*****, August 1975, pp. 38-50. (ABI-75-10218)**

Audit software presents an effective approach to handling the large amounts of data created by automated and centralized business transactions. It can be invaluable in controlling store operations if a versatile package is chosen, if auditors are trained in its use and data processing managers support the system. Audit software can be used in the following audit and management information tasks. Summaries of amounts in the aging category of a customer's master record may be made on a balance forward system. These are compared with customer totals and exceptions along with grand totals in the aging category and printed in a report. Finance charges can be recomputed based on the past month's balance. Calculated charges may be compared to actual charges and an exception report with grand totals printed. A summary of inter-store transfer by departments may be made to identify stockage and coordination problems.

6. **Dorricott, Keith O. "Appraising Computer Assisted Audit Techniques."** ***Canadian Chartered Accountant*****, August 1975, pp. 24-29. (ABI-75-08988)**

Three major categories of computer assisted audit techniques are—first, data testing programs, which are computer programs which the auditor supplies and uses on the client's data. This technique is particularly applicable to the auditing function of substantive testing. A second category is system testing techniques which are intended to form a conclusion on the performance of the client's system per se, and is used for testing accounting processes. The third category is problem solving programs which are separate from the regular processing system and are used for independent calculations. These techniques force the auditor to become directly involved with the computer and give him a firsthand understanding of the client's internal control procedures. Table. References.

7. **Dorricot, Keith O. "Audit Control Over Computer-Assisted Audit Techniques."** ***EDPACS*****, September 1975, pp. 9-11. (ABI-75-11192)**

Because of the complex and invisible nature of EDP processing, audit control deficiencies are harder to detect and to overcome than they would be in a manual system. The client should ideally not be involved at all in the audit work. This, however, is not always practical or desirable, and other audit control techniques may have to be employed. Seven such techniques are available: (1) physical custody; (2) physical presence and observation of the processing; (3) testing; (4) certain processes can be checked by means of balancing and comparison procedures; (5) details of the audit application should be kept as confidential as possible—critical parameters on one or more control cards could be inserted at the last minute; (6) build into programs a number of precautions; (7) also reduce the opportunity for error or manipulation. None of these techniques is foolproof, but when used together, they reduce the risk of problems.

8. **Jancura, Elise G. "The Auditor's Responsibilities in Examining Computer Processed Reports."** ***International Journal of Government Auditing*****, July 1975, pp. 13-17. (ABI-75-08439)**

Auditing of financial statements requires the auditor to evaluate internal control, test transactions, test balances, form an opinion about the reliability of the financial statements, and properly report that opinion. The auditor needs to choose those techniques that test the system and the data records, using where appropriate either the computer or manual skills. The use of the computer provides two benefits to the auditor. It minimizes the time spent on the routine aspects of auditing, and it allows the auditor to extend the scope of his examination by substituting the computer's speed of information retrieval and calculation abilities for the more expensive time of audit personnel. However, extensive use of computers means that the auditor must be adequately trained and sufficiently familiar with electronic data processing techniques to adapt to new approaches. Chart.

9. **Grihalva, Richard A. "A Computer Operations Audit Package."** ***Internal Auditor*****, October 1976, pp. 70-78. (ABI-76-11575)**

Auditing electronic data processing operations is difficult because of a lack of reviewable matter. Yet, the use of IBM's system management facility (SMF) can help if coupled with limited access to computers through use of remote job entry (RJE or RES) and online applications. The SMF monitors the computer system's accounting, data set activity, volume information, system use information, and subsystem use information. Its reports separate development and production work, check production execution, note improperly logged programs, and check security. With security reports made in batch mode, updates of documentation online, and online inquiry, the SMF can help users determine their job progress, improve scheduling, and determine if jobs are ready to run. Through these various aids, it can improve security in terms of access and use.

10. **Hall, Robert S. "A Canadian Government View of Computer Assisted Audit."** ***Tax Executive*****, July 1976, pp. 341-351. (ABI-76-09387)**

Canada has been training EDP audit specialists for some years, with the objective of making it feasible to use the speed and computational powers of computers to improve audit efficiency wherever possible. A major element of the computer-assisted audit program is the use of generalized computer audit packages which enable the auditor to complete a few specification cards rather than write and test a specific audit program for each situation. Another essential requirement is that the appropriate accounting information must have been retained in a machine sensible format. In preparation for publishing guidelines for the retention of data by taxpayers, record retention evaluations comprise much of the EDP auditor workload. By ensuring that EDP auditors have a very high degree of competency and the appropriate software tools and training, it will be possible to minimize costs related to an EDP audit. The reaction to the program so far has been encouraging.

11. Jenkins, A. Milton and Robert Weber. "Using DBMS Software as an Audit Tool—The Issue of Independence." ***The Journal of Accountancy*****, April 1976, pp. 67-69. (ABI-76-04778)**

One objection to using data base management system software as an audit tool is that it compromises the auditor's independence. However, independence is only one issue to consider when DBMS software is used as an audit tool. There are various strategies for determining the integrity of the operating system and DBMS software. The approach of using a generalized audit software package within a DBMS environment also involves some compromise of independence. Since software integrity is always subject to question, the auditor must consider how critical software integrity is within the internal control framework and assess the relative cost/benefit tradeoff in determining the existence of such integrity. It is argued that integrity of the software affects the quality of the evidence obtained only, it cannot affect the auditor's independence. The basic problem is that the auditor must ascertain the integrity of the software.

12. Knowlton, Roger A. "Audit Software Package Evaluation." ***EDPACS*****, August 1976, pp. 1-3. (ABI-76-09967)**

Selecting the right audit software package requires the following work plan: (1) define basic objectives; (2) arrange these objectives in order of importance; (3) assign a weighted value reflecting the importance of the particular objective in light of the overall goals; (4) survey by questionnaire the available software packages, and then rate each package in terms of how well it meets the objectives; (5) multiply each objective's weighted value times the rating assigned to get the weighted score for each objective; (6) by totaling each package's weighted scores to obtain a total evaluation, an estimate is derived that gives the overall strength of each software package as measured by its ability to meet the requirements of a particular installation. Another consideration should be to insure that the software can operate under several different operating systems on various vendor's hardware. Thus, the package could still be used if equipment is changed in the future.

13. Perry, William E. "Using SMF as an Audit Tool–Security." *EDPACS*, January 1976, pp. 108. (ABI-76-02060)

The use of system management facilities (SMF) data in the review of security within an installation is described. SMF is available under both IBM's OS and VS operating systems. The variety of audits that might be based upon SMF information is virtually unlimited. A major SMF security audit verifies that all users of data sets are properly authorized. Systems that are password protected can have an SMF record produced for each invalid password used in an attempt to access the system. In the data set library audit, the data set library should have records for all active files in the organization. A representative sample of data sets can be selected from SMF records and checked against the library records. The run frequency audit can check the possible security problem in the excessive execution of a particular system. SMF offers the auditor access to an abundance of computer operations data. Utilizing this data in a security review provides the auditor with a new audit perspective.

14. Adams, Donald L. "Audit Applications of Flowcharting Software." *EDPACS*, May 1977, pp. 1-18. (ABI-77-11033)

It would be difficult to justify spending a lot of money on a flowcharting package that would be used solely for audit purposes. Acquisition of a package should be a joint effort of systems and EDP audit. If it is possible to justify a large expenditure, two choices emerge. When an understanding of logic flow is most important, "logicchain" should get the nod. The most suitable option for auditors is Quick Draw. Quick Draw requires improvement of its check on modifications, but it is an interesting capability from the auditor's point of view. Flowcharting software should be of interest to auditors. An auditor attempting to review program code will find the output of a flowcharting package to be extremely useful. Very few auditors have utilized these software packages. More auditors should take the time to evaluate and test their potential as an audit aid.

15. Neuman, Albrecht J. *Computer Science and Technology: Features of Seven Audit Software Packages–Principles and Capabilities.* Washington, DC: U.S. Department of Commerce, July 1977.

This report is based on a study of features of available audit software packages which was prepared during the summer of 1976 under the sponsorship of the Internal Revenue Service. The seven audit software packages are: (1) Auditape (Haskins & Sells); (2) DYL260 (DYLAKOR Software Systems, Inc.); (3) Easy Trieve (Pan Sophic Systems, Inc.); (4) EDP-Auditor (Cullinone Corporation); (5) HEWCAS (U.S. Department of Health, Education and Welfare); (6) Mark IV/Auditor (Informatics, Inc. System Products); and (7) SCORE (Informatics, Inc.).

The report includes address of the software manufacturers and a price list (1976). Some of the basic functions of the programs are:

1. *Copying*. Reproducing a file (including some changes in format if desired).
2. *Sorting*. Arranging records in a desired sequence.
3. *Multiple File Input*. Inputs of several files for purposes of comparison, merging or matching in a desired sequence.
4. *Merging*. Combining of two or more files into a single file.
5. *File Validation*. Checking of data for corrections or compliance with applicable rules, standards, convention (e.g., a money file cannot be negative).
6. *File Matching*. Comparison of two or more files to identify duplications.
7. *Arithmetic*. Addition, subtraction, multiplication, division, counting, percentages, and standard deviation, totaling, averages.
8. *Relational Operations*. Compare data of equal (=) to, less than (<), or greater than (>).
9. *Logical*. Logical capabilities including and, or and-not operations, or conditional, i.e., if, then.

10. *Stratification*. Separation of records into sets of classes, e.g., all accounts receivable $5,000 or less (count and total amounts) and all A/R $5,000 and above.

11. *Aging*. Placing of records in ranges based on time (three months, six months).

12. *Selection*. Selection of certain records from a file based upon certain attributed-account number, location, ranges, or count, such as every fifth record.

13. *Summarization*. Summing of numerical totals, or subtotals for items with common attributes.

14. *Diagnostic and Control*. Procedures to identify errors, invalid addresses or illegal addresses, code errors, invalid data records, etc.

15. *Report Preparation*. Formats for printing out data in required formats including columnar headings, spacing, totalling, totals, etc. For example, auditors confirmation notices.

The report discusses further the types of hardware and software on which the software can be used, modes of use, i.e., specification forms, and other sources for providing instructions (specification) to the program, and the amount of core required, bytes (generally 8 bits) (binary digit 0 or 1) that represents one alphanumeric character or two decimal digits.

16. Warder, Benton B. "The Use of Computers in a Local Government Financial Audit." *Internal Auditor*, February 1977, pp. 74-77. (ABI-77-01979)

This is a case study detailing the use of computer audit testing procedures in governmental auditing. A large general purpose computer and a computerized record keeping system was used in the annual financial audit of a major northeastern county. Since payrolls and social services accounted for the major portion of the annual budget, the decision was made to use computerized techniques to audit those costs. The success of this procedure was due to careful planning and evaluation of audit objectives and scope, and to a team effort by the audit staff and the firm's data processing specialists. As a consequence, significant savings of time and effort were realized.

17. Will, Hart J., Henk Brussel, et al. "An Invitation to Help Develop New Audit Software." ***Canadian Chartered Accountant*****, May 1977, pp. 35-39. (ABI-77-13219)**

Audit command language (ACL), the first interactive audit language, is a prototype that can be used to perform currently identified interrogative audit tasks. Its innovative design provides auditors with the means to construct and maintain an individualized computer audit package of professional expertise. At the same time, ACL provides a basis for analyzing audit behavior, thus further contributing to audit software development. Prototype research indicates that most auditors prefer the dual feature of ACL, i.e., the fact that they can switch modes. The batch mode seems to be preferred in the initial phase of an audit when all audit planning is packed onto one large program designed to provide both a comprehensive overview and a breakdown of the whole audit into smaller phases. These smaller phases are then performed interactively on the extracted subfiles, often in several iterations at different levels of detail. Chart.

18. Boritz, J. Efrim. "The Use of Computer-Assisted Audit Techniques." ***Canadian Chartered Accountant*****, January 1978, pp. 74-76. (ABI-78-03663)**

Increasingly, managers are making use of computer assisted audit techniques (CAAT) to make audits faster, more accurate, and more economical. They are using generalized computer software and generalized computer audit packages to increase the effectiveness of internal audits. CAATS can help in substantive verification, compliance verification, compensating audit procedures, etc. In order for the advantages to be realized, certain requirements must be met: (1) there must be plenty of advanced planning so that there is enough development lead time; (2) CAATS can be integrated into the audit; (3) the audit staff understands the processing procedures, etc. CAATS are being used in a variety of specific applications such as substantive testing, accounts receivable, inventory, and fixed assets. Standardized approaches are being developed for particular industries, also. CAATS also have a promising future in compliance testing and in compensating audit procedures, such as matching and balancing. Tables.

19. Burger, Albert D. "EDP Audit: Don't Forget the User." *Internal Auditor*, February 1978, pp. 20-26. (ABI-78-02484)

The primary objective of an electronic data processing (EDP) operational audit is to assess the overall performance of the data processing department. Since most corporate data processing departments view themselves as service organizations dedicated to filling the information processing needs of various user departments, it seems logical that the EDP auditor would be interested in seeing if this goal is met. One successful communication technique is the user evaluation survey sheet. The survey questionnaire, accompanied by a cover letter explaining the auditor's request, is sent to all users of DP services. The user evaluation survey sheet allows the auditor to quantify user satisfaction. By determining where the user thinks a problem exists, the survey alerts the EDP auditor to potential communication problems or functional shortcomings. With additional investigation, the auditor can pinpoint the problem and solve it. Charts.

20. Carlson, Arthur. "Changing Role of the Auditor." *Journal of Systems Management*, November 1978, pp. 30-35. (EDPACS)

The article examines an approach to auditing in an electronic environment which the author refers to as auditing "with" the computer. The author maintains that his is a broader concept than auditing "through" the computer. It involves tests of the operation of built-in internal controls. Further, audit software packages may be used to carry out additional audit functions. The auditor reviews various control devices and techniques such as file security devices, hardware controls, controls over data transformation and software, and separation of duties and functions.

Several audit software techniques are discussed, e.g., the use of test decks, parallel simulation and generalized audit software packages (GASP).

Some common functions of generalized audit software packages include: diagnostic—a check on the instructions written by the auditor to determine they are logical and in the proper format; create—provides for the conversion of desired data from the client's file(s) into a format which can be processed by the GASP; update or merge—the ability to combine two client files into one file that can be processed by the GASP; summarize—the process of combining data to produce summary records while the audit trail may be destroyed, the summary data will reduce processing requirements; sort—the ability to arrange data in a sequence that will facilitate audit processing. For example, a random selection of transactions may be sequenced to facilitate additional audit verification; calculate–allows the auditor to duplicate logical and mathematical processing performed by client programs. For audit purposes, exception reports can be produced and special computations can be done; output modes–the auditor can generate printed reports including confirmation requests, in almost any format.

21. Perry, William E. "Selecting Computer Audit Practices." *EDPACS*, March 1978, pp. 1-11. (DPD)

Auditors need to consider six criteria when selecting a computer audit practice:

1. Computer audit practices must satisfy an audit objective or need in a given situation;

2. The auditor should possess the necessary skill level;

3. Auditors must have the resources to perform the practice;

4. The practice can be operational when it is needed;

5. It can be performed within budgetary limits;

6. The computer audit practice should be cost-effective.

The golden rule of auditing should be "select your audit objectives prior to commencing an audit." Auditors have not agreed upon a standard classification of audit objectives. The following represent EDP audit objectives often used in current practice: (1) select areas for audit; (2) compliance test procedural rules; (3) compliance test how the data were processed; (4) analyze rules that govern exception processing; (5) analyze data exception handling; (6) extended monitoring of how data was processed; (7) evaluate system of internal control; (8) perform substantive tests; (9) test the efficiency and economy of procedures; (10) assure proper audit supervision; (11) review control development. An EDP Audit Practice Usage Matrix cross-references EDP audit practices with the eleven audit objectives. Auditors can use this chart to help them select practices to meet specific objectives.

Practicing internal auditors usually do not document the cost and time required to develop and utilize computer audit techniques. There are no algorithms internal auditors can use to cost out techniques. A chart lists development considerations and cost experiences of some organizations that have used the computer audit practices identified in the Institute of Internal Auditors' Systems Auditability and Control (SAC) project. Evaluating this chart, one can draw several conclusions about the cost and development considerations for specific computer audit practices:

1. Manual techniques require a minimal audit effort;

2. Techniques that utilize the computer may demand considerably more time than is available on the traditional three-to-four week audit;

3. A large percentage of the computer audit practices appear applicable only to large organizations.

An attempt was made to evaluate not only the effectiveness of the computer audit practice, but also the potential for continued and/or expanded usage. . . .It was felt that control guidelines for use during systems development will be the most fruitful computer audit practice in the near future. The category of practices with limited future potential includes the two computer audit practices that involve analysis of program code. Since this is a technically complex undertaking, it is easy to understand why it would have a poor cost/benefit rating. In the third group, techniques with very limited future potential, most of the practices included are those that demand an extensive knowledge of programming. This seems to support the belief that the future internal auditor will expend his effort at the systems rather than at the program level.

22. Perry, William E. and Donald L. Adams. "Use of Computer Audit Practices." *EDPACS*, November 1978, pp. 1-18. (ABI-79-01412)

Stanford Research Institute (SRI) conducted a systems auditability and control research study. Twenty eight EDP audit practices which are used in audits of application systems, computer service center operations, and in reviews of the internal controls of systems being developed were identified by SRI. A questionnaire designed to determine who used the techniques, the frequency of use, and an evaluation of each approach was distributed at the eighth conference on computer audit, control and security. Generalized audit software was found to be the most used technique, and 90 percent of its users considered it to be effective. The post-installation audit was the second most used technique, and 85 percent of the respondents considered it to be effective. Other widely used practices include special-purpose audit programs, the test data method, control flowcharting, and audit area selection. Among the least used audit practices are competency center, base case system evaluation, extended records, scoring, and integrated test facility. Tables.

23. Scott, George M. "Auditing the Data Base: Down the Tortuous Transaction Path." ***CA Magazine*****, October 1978, pp. 52-59. (DPD)**

Data bases are a cornerstone of management information systems (MIS). A data base systematically organizes and manages all of the available data related to the broad categories of operations around which the data base is organized. It also provides rapid access to and correlation of this data according to the criteria specified in the applications programs. Managers can now receive routine reports from the data base on an on-call basis, and special reports can be prepared with much less programming effort and delay.

Most data base systems have the following general components: (1) the data base itself; (2) the data base management system (DBMS); (3) a host language interface system, which communicates between the DBMS and the applications programs; (4) the applications programs; (5) a natural language interface system, or query language, which permits online update and inquiry; (6) online access and update terminals; (7) the output system, or report generator, which provides job results and special reports; and (8) the computer's operating system also interacts extensively with the data base system.

Data base auditing refers to the review, testing, and evaluation of the data base system controls, processing and surrounding environment by an auditor independent from the data processing. In a given data base audit the objective may be one or more of the following: attestation, preventive, detective, corrective, or utilization.

Auditors must work with data base personnel to understand the intricacies of the system while they conduct their audits. Auditors must also work closely with the various user groups, since data base systems affect many different parts of the organization.

CA firms are primarily concerned about the attest objective. The CA's attestation verifies that there are no material misstatements in the company's financial statements.

In the past, CAs have largely fulfilled their financial audit responsibilities by doing most of their auditing outside the computer area, or by using audit software packages. Large data bases may be so all encompassing that there will not be enough processing outside the computer area to permit the auditor to carry out a proper audit this way. Unfortunately, most audit software packages cannot interface with data bases and alternative data base audit techniques are not yet fully developed.

Internal auditors and company management must also be concerned about data base auditing.

Several general characteristics of the data base environment cause particularly serious problems for data base auditors: (1) data bases are complex; (2) data bases are integrated; (3) data bases are comprehensive; (4) data bases have "insulated data"; and (5) the data base state of the art.

There are now two broad types of audit software packages: specialized packages designed specifically for particular audit tasks; and "generalized audit software packages" (GASP). Every major public accounting firm has developed a proprietary GASP, as have several independent software vendors, so that approximately 25 are now in existence. Most GASPs are designed for use by auditors who have relatively little EDP knowledge. GASPs are designed for conventional file systems, but so far most have not been able to interface with most data base systems. Several approaches are possible for accessing the data base for audit purposes: (1) revise GASPs to interface with the DBMS; (2) revise GASPs to directly access the data base, bypassing the DBMS; (3) dump the data base, then audit the data; (4) build audit functions into the DBMS; and (5) ad hoc methods.

As auditors begin to appreciate the significance of the data base administration functions, we can expect to see the following two effects: (1) pressure to develop a data base administration function; and (2) better and more efficient audits. Auditors' attention must be focused on three activities in this second area: (1) defining in an audit context precisely what a data base administrator should do; (2) determining how to evaluate in specific instances whether or not the data base administrator does what he or she should do, and if so, how well; and (3) establishing guidelines indicating the consequences to auditing of the data base administration activities.

24. American Institute of Certified Public Accountants. *Computer-Assisted Audit Techniques*, New York, NY: American Institute of Certified Public Accountants, 1979, 102 pp.

The objective of the guide is to provide guidance to the auditor who elects to use the computer as an audit tool. The guide points out that the auditor's objectives do not change when a client uses a computer for accounting applications; however, different audit techniques are available to accomplish these objectives. These objectives include review of the system of internal accounting control, test of compliance, tests of details of transactions and balances and analytical reviews (p. 2, exhibit 1-1). The guide distinguishes between generalized audit software and other computer-assisted audit techniques.

Generalized audit software package is a computer program or series of programs designed to perform certain data processing functions where the data is maintained on computer files and where the auditor needs to access, reformat, and consolidate the data and to present it in a more meaningful and convenient manner.

Other computer-assisted audit techniques (Chapter 3) include:

- Test data, including Integrated Test Facility (ITF) and Program Tracing
- Review of Program Logic
- Program Comparisons
- Utility Programs (e.g., SORTS, MERGE, COPY, EDIT routines)
- Specialized Audit Programs
- Time Sharing Programs (e.g., Sampling, Analysis)
- Additional techniques (e.g., Modeling, Embedded Modules).

Each of these is discussed in terms of description, examples or illustrations, and evaluation of the particular technique.

The Appendices include: (1) a list of potential audit software applications; (2) a case study to demonstrate how generalized audit software can be used to accomplish a typical audit objective (including flow charts, coding and report outputs); (3) a list of tasks that the auditor may wish to consider in using generalized audit software; and (4) a list of programmed procedures as they relate to the types of errors or irregularities they are designed to prevent or detect.

25. **Hinde, Stephen. "Approaching the First-Time Computer Audit."** ***Accountancy*, May 1979, pp. 77-81. (ABI-79-11475)**

Computer auditing or auditing around the computer is not completely satisfactory. What is needed is an anditor who can take computerized accounting systems in his stride. The approach to the audit can continue along traditional lines. Authorizations are still checked for existence and adequacy, input documents are still validated, and then posted to ledger accounts. Control totals are still checked. Two forms have been designed by the author to identify control total trails and to prove them. The inputs, processes and outputs are recorded by use of flowcharting symbols. Control totals are identified by letters to facilitate ease of reference on the control total flowcharts. The control total approach is easy to master and does not require training in computer auditing. Flowcharts.

SECTION E. ADDITIONAL REFERENCES

26. **Porter, W. Thomas. "Generalized Computer-Audit Programs."** ***Journal of Accountancy*, January 1969, pp. 54-62.**

27. **Leishman, R.O. "The Computer as an Audit Tool."** ***The Internal Auditor*, January/February 1971.**

28. **Reid, G.F., and J.A. Demiak. "EDP Implementation with General Purpose Software."** ***Journal of Accountancy*, July 1971, pp. 35-46.**

29. **Mair, W.C. "New Techniques in Computer Program Verification."** ***Tempo*, Touche Ross & Company, Winter 1971-72, pp. 10-19.**

30. **California Society of CPAs.** ***The Computer as an Audit Tool*, Palo Alto, CA: California Society of CPAs, 1974.**

31. **Weber, R. "The Demise of Generalized Audit Software Packages."** ***Journal of Accountancy*, November 1974, pp. 46-48.**

SECTION F
TRAINING AND DEVELOPING EDP AUDIT COMPETENCE

ANNOTATED BIBLIOGRAPHY

1. Cutting, Richard W., Richard J. Guiltinan and Fred L. Lilly Jr. "Technical Proficiency for Auditing Computer Processed Accounting Records." ***The Journal of Accountancy*****, October 1971, pp. 74-82.**

The authors point out that the use of computers to process financial data has a significant effect on the skills required to meet generally accepted auditing standards. The experience and skills required to perform an audit in the EDP environment should be resident within the audit team assigned to the engagement. The authors point out that while it is impractical to train and continually update each staff member to a very high level of expertise in computer auditing, three different proficiency levels for persons assigned to the audit are appropriate: (1) the general audit staff member; (2) computer audit specialist; and (3) the data processing professional. The authors point out that while all three generally require knowledge about the same functional areas, it is obviously a matter of degree. These areas are: understanding basic computer concepts, understanding and being able to analyze the concentration of control in an EDP environment, understanding flowcharts, familiarity with program language, use of computer auditing software, concepts of file processing, and when to need a specialist. At the end of the spectrum of the general audit staff member, his knowledge and skill need only to be elementary whereas the other end of the spectrum, the data processing specialist, knowledge and skills should be advanced and highly developed. Of course, the data processing professional may not understand the audit requirements and the standard of field work so that the accountant in charge must assume full responsibility for seeing that these requirements and standards are met even though the work is being done in an area outside his own professional technical competence. He may call upon the services of a computer audit specialist to assist him in understanding the audit problems and procedures in such highly technical situations.

For the computer audit specialist to play an increasingly important audit role as indicated in the article necessitates the development of such computer audit specialists by training audit staff members who should be selected from the best available personnel.

2. **Messbaum, Martin. *Opportunities in Electronic Data Processing*, NY: Universal Publishing and Distributing Corporation, 1972, 160 pp.**

The emphasis of the book is on education and on the schools, societies, organization and information sources for those concerned with the management and operation of EDP as well as for persons seeking career information.

The book provides job descriptions and qualifications for several occupations involved in EDP, including the EDP manager, EDP systems engineers, business systems analyst. Under each classification there is a description of duties, education, training, and experience requirements, aptitudes, interests, temperaments, physical activities and working conditions, and salaries. The author provides an annotated history of certain technical and professional societies and organizations, national trade publications, community and junior colleges, colleges and universities offering courses and degrees in EDP, and home study courses. The information is dated (1972) but does provide some starting point for obtaining information on EDP opportunities.

3. **Lord, Kenniston W., Jr. "Certification for Data Processing Practitioners." *The Office*, January 1974, pp. 70-71.**

Mr. Lord projects the future 1980s when certification will be needed to prevent law suits and to protect the data processors from consumers. He suggests for the practitioner there should be a body of knowledge by a competent authority, certification of competence, a code of ethics for good performance, a judicial licensing authority who can recall the practitioner, periodic updating of skills, and periodic recertification. The practice of the above protects the practitioner as well as the employeer.

4. **Morris, Martin A., Jr. "Certification of Professional Data Processors." *Datamation*, August 1974, pp. 149-151.**

This article is designed to reacquaint the reader with the value of certification of Professional Data Processors.

The author presents his ideas related to what the CDP examination should cover and its frequency. Since it would be almost impossible to establish an exam meeting standards for all phases of the data processing industries, it would have to be general in nature and the data processor professionals will have to try to enhance what is already existing.

5. **Smith, Leighton F. "The Internal Computer Auditor."** ***The Arthur Andersen Chronicle*****, Janaury 1974, pp. 8-14. (ABI-74-04603)**

The auditing of computers requires an in-depth technical knowledge and ability in two separate areas—accounting and auditing, and electronic data processing. The internal computer auditor must have thorough knowledge of the organization and functioning of the business enterprise and must be well versed in industry practices. Many companies get started by creating two man teams consisting of an experienced auditor and a computer technician, as very few people within the corporate organization possess the required in-depth competency in both areas. The basic complement is augmented by adding people having competency in other areas such as industrial engineering, operations research or industrial relations. A definite pattern of evolution is apparent in the development of this organization. They are the compliance audit and the audit of computer systems. Newer computer based tools are being applied with some degree of success, e.g., probes, evaluators, screens, standards and minicomputers.

6. **Morrison, James W.** ***CDP: Certificate in Data Processing Examination*****. NY: ARCO Publishing Company, Inc., 1976, 640 pp.**

The book was written to help the candidate interested in passing the Certificate in Data Processing (CDP) examination given by the Institute for Certification of Computer Professionals (ICCP). The book contains 900 CDP Examination questions and answers for practice.

The text includes eight topics: (1) Data Processing Equipment; (2) Computer Programming and Software; (3) Principles of Management; (4) Data Processing Management; (5) Accounting; (6) Mathematics; (7) Statistics and (8) Systems Analysis and Design.

Although somewhat dated, the author presents a survey of job opportunities in the federal government for computer specialists.

Management concepts and techniques are also included, for example: line vs. staff, project management, breakeven analysis and financial statements and interpretation, among many other items. The author discusses briefly two auditing EDP approaches, auditing "around" the computer and auditing "through" the computer. One feature of the book is the selected bibliography for each of the eight topics.

Although written to prepare the candidate for the CDP examination, it is an excellent source of information on EDP systems.

7. "Professionalism: Coming or Not?" ***EDP Analyzer*****, March 1976, pp. 1-11.**

This paper is a comparative overview on the subject of professionalism in the computer field beginning as early as 1968. The Institute for Certification of Computer Professionals (ICCP) has formed the Informatics Institute of Canada (IIC), which is one of the charter members of the ICCP. The United Kingdom, Scandinavia, and the Netherlands are other countries mentioned in the article as moving toward establishing standards and credentials for individuals in the computer field.

Professionalism is defined as a body of knowledge of high intellectual content, defined standards of competence, examinations, code of ethics, and disciplinary capability.

The article addresses two other forms of regulation or constraints on employers, namely system certification and the unionization of programmers and analysts. It concludes by stating that true professionalism may be more than five years off for systems analysts and programmers; however, substantial progress will be made in areas of defining the jobs of analyst and programmer. Need is for job-related examinations, well-developed curricula by the education community related to the job definition. "Only then can we have system certification and an enforcement mechanism for a code of ethical behavior and then professionalism."

8. Byrne, Dan R., Jr. and George M. Scott. "Closing the Computer Audit Gap." ***Internal Auditor*****, April 1977, pp. 27-32. (ABI-77-09211)**

The advent of advanced EDP systems increases the risk of significant control failures. Until the computer auditing ability gap is substantially narrowed, internal auditors will not be able to guarantee that the risk level of computer related losses is acceptable. How quickly the audit gap can be closed depends on the degree of specialization required of the EDP auditors, the numbers, quality, and EDP experience of personnel in the EDP audit group, the cooperation and assistance from EDP personnel, and the external assistance available from computer auditor specialists. Internal auditors should be able to provide reasonable assurance that system program controls are strong. The auditor who is also a hardware specialist will be responsible for understanding the physical characteristics of the computer hardware and their control implications. Communications systems must also be addressed, and concentration on sensitive applications and historic study is advised. Chart.

9. Perry, William E. "Skills Needed to Utilize EDP Audit Practices." *EDPACS*, November 1977, pp. 1-13. (ABI-78-01841)

The minimum qualifications for a general staff EDP auditor are that he: (1) understand basic computer concepts; (2) understand and be able to analyze the concentration of controls in a data processing environment; (3) understand flowcharts; (4) have general familiarity with at least one computer programming language; (5) understand the use of computer audit software; (6) understand concepts of file processing; and (7) know when to call for assistance. Knowledge areas for internal auditors include: (1) data processing principles and concepts; (2) computer application systems structure; (3) computer application system controls and procedures; (4) data management; (5) computer service center controls; (6) application system development controls; and (7) computer application programming. Auditors trying to decide what type of training they need to improve their EDP auditing capabilities can gain some insight by analyzing the required skills. Improving these skills advances employment opportunities. Tables.

10. Dorricott, Keith O. "Organizing a Computer Audit Specialty." *Canadian Chartered Accountant*, May 1979, pp. 66, 68, 70. (ABI-79-10109)

Many chartered accountant (CA) firms have already set up an effective computer audit specialty within their practice, and there has been a remarkable diversity in the way it has been handled. They do have one thing in common; they serve as a technical resource for processing applications of computer-assisted audit techniques (software packages). Whether electronic data processing (EDP) professionals or auditors, most CA firms have found that the auditing background is preferred because computer auditing is perhaps 80 percent auditing and 20 per-percent computers. If there is more than one practice office, it is preferable to have a core of highly trained and experienced specialists who can benefit from each other's experience and knowledge and who can be sent out to meet the needs of local situations. Using specialists on a full-time basis provides advantages in terms of better control over their work, time utilization, and reduction of scheduling conflicts. Part-time specialists can use their ability when required and, also, retain their general auditing skills. Chart.

11. Jancura, Elise G. "Developing Concepts of Technical Proficiency in EDP Auditing." ***Ohio CPA*****, Spring 1979, pp. 55-59. (ABI-79-08652)**

If computers are not properly controlled, the risk of incurring losses from processing errors is high. The increasing use of computers creates a question of determining what level of electronic data processing (EDP) competence the auditor must have in order to meet the professional responsibilities outlined in Statement on Auditing Standards No. 3. Auditors should know and understand the principles of processing, operations, computer programming, software, systems analysis and design, EDP management, computer control, and computer auditing. Audit firms should consider developing audit teams to approach the task of computer auditing. Currently, no optimum solution regarding EDP knowledge or audit staff organization has emerged. The audit team concept, though, seems to be a good approach to developing technical proficiency in EDP audits based on individuals' physical capacity and the diverse audit environments. Exhibits. References.

12. Mathieson, Robert. "Computer Auditing–Some Basic Considerations." ***The Accountant's Magazine*****, January 1979, pp. 13-15. (EDPACS)**

The article defines a computer auditor as "an auditor who has received sufficient technical training in and obtained suitable experience of computers and computer systems to allow him/her to advise the general audit partner or staff on matters pertaining to their clients who possess or make use of a computer."

A program to train EDP auditors should cover the following points: (1) basic computer concepts such as hardware, software, input and output media, and binary arithmetic; (2) organization of the data processing department; (3) an overview of programming languages and utilities; (4) data representation and data set organization; (5) concepts of hardware channels and buffers; (6) an overview of operating system functions; and (7) teleprocessing monitors.

In addition, EDP auditors must be able to read and understand system descriptions, systems review, use of computer assisted audit techniques, and must be able to communicate with the client's staff and with their own audit teams.

SECTION F. ADDITIONAL REFERENCES

13. Campfield, William L. "An Inquiry Into the Nature of Judgment Formation and its Implications to the Public Accounting Profession." Doctoral Dissertation. Urbana, IL: University of Illinois, 1951.

14. Campfield, William L. "Trends in Auditing Management Plans and Operations." *The Journal of Accountancy*, July 1967.

15. Roy, Robert H., and James H. MacNeill. *Horizons for a Profession: The Common Body of Knowledge for Certified Public Accountants,* 1967.

16. Campfield, William L. "Insights and Guidelines for Increasing the Proficiency of Accountants. *Singapore Accountant*, Vol. 3, Fall 1968.

17. Knowles, Malcolm S. *The Modern Practice of Adult Education*. NY: Association Press, 1970.

18. Kuhn, Thomas S. *The Structure of Scientific Revolutions*, 2nd ed. Chicago: University of Chicago Press, 1970.

19. Jancura, Elise. "Technical Proficiency for Auditing Computer Processed Accounting Records." *Journal of Accountancy*, October 1975.

20. Knowles, Malcom S. *Self-Directed Learning: A Guide for Learners and Teachers*. NY: Association Press, 1975.

21. Schultz, Joseph J., Jr. "A View of the Educational Methods at the University of Illinois at Urbana-Champaign." *The EDP Auditor*, December 1977, p. 7.

22. Campfield, William L. "Programming to Training Goals: A Format for the Small Scale Practitioner." *The National Public Accountant*, December 1979.

23. Edwards, James B., James R. Davis and Al L. Hartgraves. "Toward Professionalism of Accounting Education: An Alternative Approach." *Collegiate News and Views*, Fall 1979.

24. Hubbert, James F. "Profile of a Computer Audit Specialist." *EDPACS*, May 1979, pp. 11-14.

APPENDIX
EDP-AUDIT CHECKLIST

On the following pages is the complete SAS No. 3 Audit Guide developed and used by Fox & Company, certified public accountants for field audits of computerized accounting systems. Reproduced by permission.

CLIENT______________________ AUDIT DATE______________________

INSTRUCTIONS

This checklist should be completed for all clients who use a computer[1] to process significant accounting applications.[2]

ALL COMPANIES	N/A	YES	NO	REMARKS
1. Has the EDP 100 work plan been completed?				
2. Have all significant accounting applications using EDP been considered?				
3. EDP-100, when properly utilized, generally satisfies the requirements of SAS No. 3 for a preliminary review and an assessment of the significance of EDP controls within the accounting applications (represented on the flow chart on the following page as Steps 1 and 2).				
If EDP accounting controls are to be relied upon, have EDP reviews been completed, and have tests of compliance been performed on the controls which are to provide the basis of reliance (represented on the flow chart as Steps 3 through 7)?				

[1]A "computer" is defined as an electronic data processing machine, consisting of a central processing unit and input and output devices, which performs a series of operations in accordance with internally stored instructions.

[2]"Significant accounting applications" are those that relate to accounting information that can materially affect the financial statements the auditor is examining.

STUDY AND EVALUATION OF EDP-BASED SYSTEMS

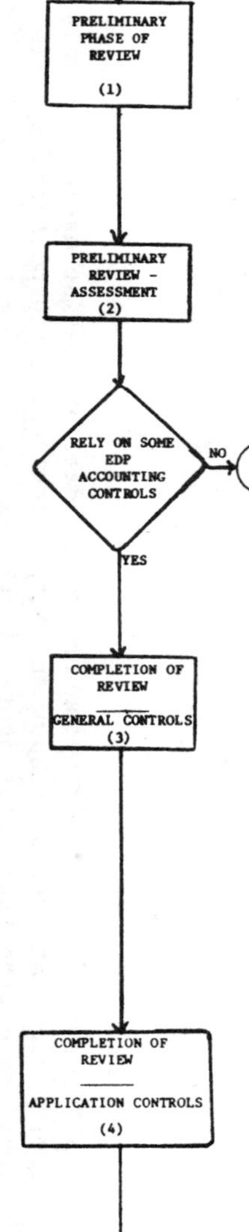

(1) - PRELIMINARY PHASE OF REVIEW

PURPOSE

UNDERSTAND:

ACCOUNTING SYSTEM INCLUDING BOTH EDP AND NON-EDP SEGMENTS:

. FLOW OF TRANSACTIONS AND SIGNIFICANCE OF OUTPUT

. EXTENT TO WHICH EDP IS USED IN SIGNIFICANT ACCOUNTING APPLICATIONS

. BASIC STRUCTURE OF ACCOUNTING CONTROL, INCLUDING BOTH EDP AND USER CONTROLS

METHODS

INQUIRY AND DISCUSSION - OBSERVATION - REVIEW OF DOCUMENTATION - TRACING OF TRANSACTIONS - CONTROL QUESTIONNAIRES AND CHECKLISTS

(2) - THE PRELIMINARY REVIEW - ASSESSMENT

PURPOSE

. ASSESS SIGNIFICANCE OF EDP AND NON-EDP ACCOUNTING CONTROLS

. DETERMINE EXTENT OF ADDITIONAL REVIEW WITHIN EDP

METHOD

JUDGEMENT

(3) - COMPLETION OF REVIEW GENERAL CONTROLS

PURPOSE

. IDENTIFY GENERAL CONTROLS ON WHICH RELIANCE IS PLANNED AND DETERMINE HOW THEY OPERATE

. DETERMINE THE EFFECT OF STRENGTHS AND WEAKNESSES ON APPLICATION CONTROLS

. CONSIDER TESTS OF COMPLIANCE THAT MAY BE PERFORMED

METHODS

DETAILED EXAMINATION OF DOCUMENTATION - INTERVIEW INTERNAL AUDITORS, EDP AND USER DEPARTMENT PERSONNEL - OBSERVE OPERATION OF GENERAL CONTROLS

(4) - COMPLETION OF REVIEW - APPLICATION CONTROLS

PURPOSE

. IDENTIFY APPLICATIONS AND RELATED CONTROLS ON WHICH RELIANCE IS PLANNED, AND DETERMINE HOW THE CONTROLS OPERATE

. CONSIDER TESTS OF COMPLIANCE THAT MAY BE PERFORMED

. CONSIDER THE POTENTIAL EFFECT OF IDENTIFIED STRENGTHS AND WEAKNESSES ON TESTS OF COMPLIANCE

METHODS

DETAILED EXAMINATION OF DOCUMENTATION - INTERVIEWING INTERNAL AUDITORS, EDP & USER DEPARTMENT PERSONNEL - OBSERVING OPERATIONS OF APPLICATION CONTROLS

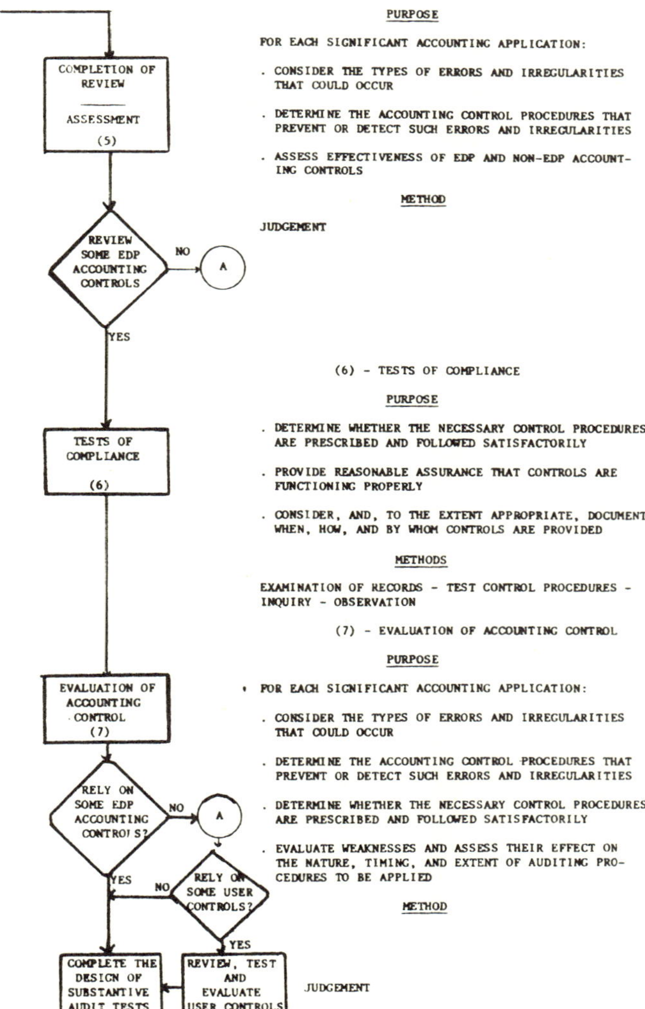

(5) - COMPLETION OF REVIEW - ASSESSMENT

PURPOSE

FOR EACH SIGNIFICANT ACCOUNTING APPLICATION:

. CONSIDER THE TYPES OF ERRORS AND IRREGULARITIES THAT COULD OCCUR

. DETERMINE THE ACCOUNTING CONTROL PROCEDURES THAT PREVENT OR DETECT SUCH ERRORS AND IRREGULARITIES

. ASSESS EFFECTIVENESS OF EDP AND NON-EDP ACCOUNTING CONTROLS

METHOD

JUDGEMENT

(6) - TESTS OF COMPLIANCE

PURPOSE

. DETERMINE WHETHER THE NECESSARY CONTROL PROCEDURES ARE PRESCRIBED AND FOLLOWED SATISFACTORILY

. PROVIDE REASONABLE ASSURANCE THAT CONTROLS ARE FUNCTIONING PROPERLY

. CONSIDER, AND, TO THE EXTENT APPROPRIATE, DOCUMENT WHEN, HOW, AND BY WHOM CONTROLS ARE PROVIDED

METHODS

EXAMINATION OF RECORDS - TEST CONTROL PROCEDURES - INQUIRY - OBSERVATION

(7) - EVALUATION OF ACCOUNTING CONTROL

PURPOSE

FOR EACH SIGNIFICANT ACCOUNTING APPLICATION:

. CONSIDER THE TYPES OF ERRORS AND IRREGULARITIES THAT COULD OCCUR

. DETERMINE THE ACCOUNTING CONTROL PROCEDURES THAT PREVENT OR DETECT SUCH ERRORS AND IRREGULARITIES

. DETERMINE WHETHER THE NECESSARY CONTROL PROCEDURES ARE PRESCRIBED AND FOLLOWED SATISFACTORILY

. EVALUATE WEAKNESSES AND ASSESS THEIR EFFECT ON THE NATURE, TIMING, AND EXTENT OF AUDITING PROCEDURES TO BE APPLIED

METHOD

JUDGEMENT

	N/A	YES	NO	REMARKS
4. Has STRATA, or other software been utilized for compliance and/or substantive testing? If so, has the EDP Audit Application Questionnaire (EDP-60) been utilized as an aid?				
5. Was the assistance of a computer audit specialist utilized?				
6. Have suggested improvements in EDP controls or processing been included in the management letter or in a separate report?				
COMPANIES USING A SERVICE CENTER (In addition to above procedures)				
1. Has the company's data processing service center and related contract been reviewed with regard to the matters discussed in Appendix D of the Audit Guide "Audits of Service Center Produced Records"?				
2. Have the other items discussed in the Service Center Audit Guide been given proper consideration? (SAS No. 3 and its related audit guide are the more authoritative documents in this area and the Service Center Audit Guide should not be used as a substitute for SAS No. 3 or its Audit Guide.)				

Other Comments:

____

____

____

____

____

____

Completed by ______________________________ Date______________
(Supervisor or Manager)

Reviewed by______________________________ Date______________
(Partner)

PRELIMINARY REVIEW OF EDP ACCOUNTING CONTROLS

CLIENT NAME ______________________ AUDIT DATE ____________

SCOPE

A preliminary review of EDP Accounting Controls must be completed in audits where EDP is used in accounting applications which may materially affect the financial statements under examination. Such review should be performed without regard to the complexity of the EDP system, its applications, or the relationship between the client and the data processing facility (in-house, time sharing, or other type of service bureau). This plan has been designed to be completed by audit personnel knowledgeable of the client's entire accounting system, and EDP accounting controls.

The scope of the plan, however, is limited to that which is required for the auditor's completion of the preliminary phase of an SAS No. 3 review. Review completion, compliance testing and substantive testing of EDP accounting control is highly dependent on the EDP system and its relative complexities. A special audit plan will be required for review completion and compliance testing which may require the expertise of an EDP specialist in addition to regular audit engagement personnel.

To facilitate use, the plan is presented in four sections as follows:

I. - Basic understanding of accounting systems

II. - General controls

III. - Application controls

IV. - Preliminary review appraisal

BASIC UNDERSTANDING OF ACCOUNTING SYSTEMS

Prior to the initiation of the EDP preliminary review, it is necessary that all accounting systems which utilize EDP and may <u>materially affect the financial statements under examination</u> be identified and documented with respect to their basic operation. This has traditionally been accomplished through the use of descriptive memoranda and/or flowcharts of the client's systems.

1. Complete the following with respect to accounting systems utilizing EDP which may materially affect the financial statements under examination.

System Application	Date Audit Documentation Initially Prepared	Date of Last Update	By Whom	Workpaper Reference

PRELIMINARY REVIEW OF EDP ACCOUNTING CONTROLS

W/P Reference

2. With respect to each of the above identified systems, document its flow with respect to EDP by use of descriptive memo or flowcharts obtained from the client or prepared by the auditor. Make reference to the following to the extent necessary to document EDP and non-EDP system flow in general. Audit file information on existing clients should contain similar information. __________
   - A. Activities and related source documents that start the flow of transactions (these should be identified in the basic documentation previously accumulated in audit files).
   - B. EDP processing applied to the source doucments (this should likewise have been previously identified).
   - C. Conversion of data into machine-sensible form (this may have been identified in the basic documentation previously accumulated).
   - D. Flow of machine-sensible transactions through significant accounting applications.
   - E. Procedures for the correction of errors.
   - F. Output reports produced for significant accounting applications.

G. Non-EDP processing of output reports (this step may have also been documented in the system documentation previously accumulated).

3. To augment the understanding and extent of EDP utilization in each significant accounting application subjected to the above procedures, consider obtaining the following information as well as any other indicators which might be appropriate:

   A. Number and type of transactions processed.

   B. Total dollar value of each type of transaction.

   C. The extent and nature of the processing accomplished within EDP, including the extent to which transactions are automatically created within the EDP system, the relative sophistication of such applications, etc.

   D. Division of flow of transactions between EDP and non-EDP activities.

PRELIMINARY REVIEW OF EDP ACCOUNTING CONTROLS

CLIENT NAME________________________ AUDIT DATE________________________

GENERAL CONTROLS

INTRODUCTION TO GENERAL CONTROLS

This section of the workplan presents a methodology for performing a preliminary review of EDP General Controls. General Controls are those disciplines and controls which are common to the processing of all application systems. Areas of concern in examining General Controls include:

- Organizational controls
  - Separation of duties
  - Employment practices
  - Vacation policy
  - Activities of the Internal Audit Department
- Control over systems and programming functions
  - Documentation standards and compliance therewith
  - Control over development of new systems, including appropriate user approval and participation in the development of new systems
  - Control over system and program changes including evidence of proper approval and a record of changes made

  - Control over the implementation of new or altered programs
  - Control over the conversion of data files
  - Testing standards and procedures

- Hardware and operating system controls
  - Preventative maintenance practices
  - Modifications to standard vendor operating system

- Control over computer operations
  - Access to EDP equipment
  - Adequacy of operations documentation
  - Supervision and rotation of operations personnel
  - Data control activities

- Control over data files and negotiable instrument forms
  - Retention policies
  - Access to data files
  - Control over documents used in printing negotiable instruments

PRELIMINARY REVIEW OF EDP ACCOUNTING CONTROLS

- Catastrophe prevention and recovery capabilities

  - Physical security of computer area
  - Fire detection and suppression equipment
  - Procedures regarding the periodic off-site rotation of data and system files and documentation
  - Identification of alternative hardware facilities
  - Existence of a comprehensive and systematic recovery plan, and location of the plan at a remote site
  - Insurance coverage

In reviewing General Controls, it is important to bear in mind that strong General Controls ensure the consistent application of controls found in individual processing systems.

The following procedures are for the preliminary phase of the review and will enable the auditor to gain and record the client's representation of controls. At the end of the preliminary review, the auditor should be able to assess the significance of EDP controls as well as the feasibility and cost benefit of relying on these controls in limiting substantive testing. Reliance must <u>not</u> be placed on any of these controls, without completing the EDP control review and performing related tests of compliance on the controls which are to be the basis of reliance.

This workplan is designed for small to medium-sized batch oriented data processing installations; it does not address the special control considerations arising from client utilization of data communication, real time systems, or Data Base Management Systems.

PRELIMINARY REVIEW OF EDP ACCOUNTING CONTROLS

W/P Reference

PROCEDURES FOR PRELIMINARY REVIEW OF GENERAL CONTROLS

1. Secure a copy of the EDP department organization chart for the workpapers. If an organization chart does not exist, prepare one. Individual boxes and specific identification for personnel without supervisory responsibilities are not necessary; merely indicate the number and type of personnel in one box. For supervisory personnel, annotate the organization chart with the number of years of EDP experience and the number of years with the client. ________

2. Describe employment screening practices. ________

   Consider:

   Are references checked? If so, what type and how many? Previous employment? Credit? Personal?

   Is there a trial or probationary employment period?

   If other employees of the client are normally bonded, are EDP department employees bonded?

3. Describe vacation policy. ________

Consider:

How much vacation is earned for different categories of longevity ? When must it be taken?

Is there any penalty for not taking vacation during or immediately following the year in which it was earned?

Can additional compensation be elected in lieu of vacation?

Do members of the operations staff normally take vacation every year?

Are there any specific members of the operations staff who have not taken a vacation in the past year?

4. Describe instances of inappropriate segregation of duties within the EDP department.

Consider:

Do programmers routinely substitute for operators during lunch periods, illness, etc.?

Do programmers routinely have "hands-on" computer time for testing?

Do operators perform data control functions?

Is there a separate data control function?

PRELIMINARY REVIEW OF EDP ACCOUNTING CONTROLS

W/P Reference

Is there a separate librarian function?

Do any operators have programming skills? Have any production programs been programmed by members of the operations staff? Which programs? By whom?

5. Describe instances of inappropriate segregation of duties between the EDP department and user departments.

Consider:

Is the EDP department physically segregated from other departments?

Are any personnel shared between the EDP department and other departments?

Do user department personnel ever have occasion to operate EDP equipment? Or program?

Do EDP department personnel ever originate or authorize accounting transactions or changes to accounting master files? (This question is not intended to refer to the authorization for payment of

EDP related invoices or other accounting data which are subsequently processed through the Accounting Department prior to introduction into a computer-assisted system.)

Are the only copies of certain key user reports filed in the EDP department?

6. Describe participation of the Internal Audit Department in monitoring EDP activities.

Consider:

Does the Internal Audit Department have EDP audit specialists?

Does the Internal Audit Department routinely conduct operational audits of EDP department practices? If so, secure a copy of their latest report.

Does the Internal Audit Department receive copies of program change requests?

What is the participation of the Internal Audit Department in monitoring the development of new systems?

Does the Internal Audit Department test specific systems to ensure compliance with management directives and that output is consistent with processing objectives?

PRELIMINARY REVIEW OF EDP ACCOUNTING CONTROLS

	W/P Reference
7. Review documentation standards and note in workpapers elements of documentation required by the standards.	______

Consider:

Do standards require the following elements of documentation:

- System narrative
- System flowchart
- Record layouts
- Program narratives
- Legends of codes used
- Record of program changes
- Key entry instructions
- Operations documentation, including
  - Systems flowchart
  - Operating instructions
  - Restart procedures

    - Responses to console inquiries
    - Job control specifications
- Data control and balancing procedures
- Sample system input and output documents
- User documentation

8. Review available documentation of two selected systems for compliance with standards. Note results of review in workpapers.

   Consider:

   If the installation has no standards, what elements of documentation are present? Absent?

   Does documentation appear to be current?

   Are current program listings available?

9. Note in workpapers how program listings and systems and programming documentation are physically secured as well as who has access.

   Consider:

   Are these materials kept under lock and key?

PRELIMINARY REVIEW OF EDP ACCOUNTING CONTROLS

W/P Reference

Are these materials only available to authorized members of the programming staff?

Can members of the computer operations staff gain access to such materials?

Are program source statements (either on card or other media) adequately secured?

10. Describe participation of user departments and other parties in developing new systems.

Consider:

Are new systems reviewed and evaluated by the Internal Audit Department or other independent party (i.e., EDP Steering Committee, etc.) at critical stages during development?

Do user departments actively participate in defining system requirements?

Do user departments review written systems specifications prior to the initiation of other developmental work?

Is their approval of such specifications evidenced in writing?

Are user departments given the opportunity to review and approve test results?

How are deviations from original design specifications approved?

11. Describe procedures used in approving the implementation of new systems.
Consider:

Is final approval of the user department and appropriate management personnel required?

What management personnel are involved in this decision?

Is their approval evidenced in writing?

Is documentation reviewed for acceptance prior to installation? By whom?

Who reviews final test results?

Are implementation procedures documented? Are they reviewed for approval? By whom?

Are the specifics of data file conversion procedures documented? Are data indicating control over such conversion reviewed and approved by user department and management personnel?

PRELIMINARY REVIEW OF EDP ACCOUNTING CONTROLS

W/P Reference

12. Describe techniques utilized to control and record changes to existing systems and programs.

    Consider:

    Some changes will result from correcting operating failures within the EDP department. Others will result from altered processing objectives; are these changes initiated by user request?
    If not, are such changes approved by the user prior to the start of work?

    Is a written description of the change prepared prior to starting the work?

    Is there evidence of user approval of such changes?

    Are test results reviewed by appropriate management and user department personnel?

    Do programmers have access to "live" data files for testing purposes?

    Are records of changes filed with system documentation?

Is system documentation updated to reflect changes.

Are changes to the operating system and other systems software subject to review and approval by data processing management?

Are records of changes to the operating system and system software maintained?

13. Describe in workpapers EDP equipment on site. Indicate whether equipment is owned, leased, or rented.

    Consider:

    Manufacturer, model number, and core capacity of CPU.

    Quantity, manufacturer, number of tracks, and recording density of tape drives.

    Quantity, manufacturer, model number, and storage capacity of disk drives.

    Quantity, manufacturer, model number, and rated speeds of various unit record I/O equipment.

    Quantity, manufacturer, and model number of key transcription devices.

    Characteristics of other equipment.

PRELIMINARY REVIEW OF EDP ACCOUNTING CONTROLS

W/P Reference

14. Describe in workpapers nature of equipment service arrangements. ________

    Consider:

    Does the service agreement provide for regularly scheduled preventative maintenance?

    If the equipment is rented, does the manufacturer assume responsibility for full maintenance?

    If maintenance is provided under a separate contract, what service is provided?

15. Describe the operating system used. ________

    Consider:

    Vendor and operating system name.

    Is the version of the operating system used the most current available from the vendor?

Does the operating system support multi-programming? How many partitions or regions can be supported?

Is the operating system tailored to specific installation requirements through a system generation procedure? Or is it a canned package provided by the vendor without local tailoring?

Has the operating system been modified with code not provided by the system vendor? If so, why?

16. Describe controls over access to computer hardware.

Consider:

Do members of the programming staff have routine access to the computer room? Or are they allowed access only under controlled circumstances?

Do user department personnel have routine access to the computer room?

Are visitors to the computer room escorted?

Is the computer room secured by lock and key when no one is present? Who has keys, combination codes, etc.? Are keys maintained in any particular places i.e., an unlocked desk drawer? Are the locations of certain keys commonly known? When are keys, combination codes, etc. changed?

PRELIMINARY REVIEW OF EDP ACCOUNTING CONTROLS

W/P Reference

17. Describe shift rotation practices for operations staff. __________

    Consider:

    In a multi-shift shop, operators should periodically be rotated to insure that one operator doesn't consistently operate the same application. Supervisors may not be rotated.

    Indicate in workpapers shifts worked by computer operations - i.e., two shifts per day, five days per week.

18. Describe controls over data files. __________

    Consider:

    Is there a separate librarian function?

    Are data files secured in a manner ensuring that they are not available except when required for processing?

Are data files secured under lock and key? Who has keys? Are keys maintained in any particular places i.e., an unlocked desk drawer? Are locations of certain keys commonly known?

Do members of the programming staff, or user departments, or any other unauthorized personnel have access to data files?

Does the installation have a library control software system?

Is retention sufficient to provide a capability to recover from operating failures and other mishaps (i.e., grandfather-father-son concept)?

19. Describe techniques used to control documents used in printing negotiable instruments: checks, stock certificates, etc.

Consider:

Are supplies of these documents kept in the computer department or user department when not being used?

Are the documents stored in a locked area?

Are these documents pre-numbered?

Do user departments maintain records of control numbers of documents used?

What is the disposition of printer voids?

PRELIMINARY REVIEW OF EDP ACCOUNTING CONTROLS

W/P Reference

20. Describe data control functions in effect within the data processing department. ________

    Consider:

    Is there an independent data control function?

    Does the data processing department perform report review and balancing procedures?

    Does the data processing department verify correctness of file control totals of data processed?

    Is a record of data received from users maintained?

    Are there controls in effect within the EDP department to track data as it flows from one functional area to another?

    Does the data processing department maintain records to ensure that all detected errors are resolved and resubmitted by user departments?

    Does the data processing department maintain controls to assure distribution of output reports to appropriate personnel?

21. Describe controls in effect to assure capability to recover from catastrophic incidents.

Consider:

What fire detection and suppression equipment is present in the areas where computer equipment, data files, and system documentation is maintained?

Is physical security adequate to prevent malicious tampering?

Is equipment location appropriate considering risk of flood waters, including possible damage from overhead plumbing?

Is there a provision for the periodic rotation of machine sensible data backup (including source programs and job control statements) to a remote location?

Are copies of significant systems documentation stored off-site? Are they periodically updated?

What controls exist to guard against excessive atmospheric conditions (i.e., temperature, humidity, etc.)?

Has a comprehensive disaster recovery plan been prepared? Is it stored off-site?

PRELIMINARY REVIEW OF EDP ACCOUNTING CONTROLS

W/P Reference

Have specific backup hardware facilities been identified? Have the two parties drawn up a reciprocity agreement? Has the backup site been tested?

Does the client's insurance cover such losses and is the coverage adequate? Does it include coverage of:

- Loss of EDP equipment
- Loss of other building contents
- Loss of data media and cost to reconstruct such data
- Business interruption
- Additional cost incurred
- Other special data processing risks?

22. Review findings documented in workpapers and assess significance of EDP General Controls. Describe strengths and weaknesses noted.

23. Prepare management letter comments.

PREPARED BY:____________________ DATE:________________

REVIEWED BY:____________________ DATE:________________

PRELIMINARY REVIEW OF EDP ACCOUNTING CONTROLS

CLIENT NAME ______________________ AUDIT DATE ______________________

APPLICATION CONTROLS

For each application identified as significant in the "Basic Understanding of Accounting Systems" section, complete a copy of this document. Note application name in upper right-hand corner of each page.

INTRODUCTION

This section of the workplan presents a methodology for performing a preliminary review of EDP Application Controls. Application Controls are those controls and disciplines which may be unique to individual processing systems. Areas of concern in examining Application Controls include:

- Input controls
  - Controls to verify the authorization, accuracy, and completeness of records processed
  - Controls related to the rejection, resolution, and resubmission of erroneous data
  - Controls over the receipt of data to be processed
  - Controls to ensure utilization of current generation of master or history files

- Output controls
  - Control and report balancing procedures performed
  - Control over output distribution
  - Run-to-run controls and audit trail
- Processing controls
  - Controls that have been programmed to perform elements of input and output control functions

In reviewing Application Controls, it is important to consider the effects that weak or absent General Controls may have on the Application Controls.

The following procedures are for the preliminary phase of the review and will enable the auditor to gain and record the client's representation of controls. At the end of the preliminary review, the auditor should be able to assess the significance of EDP accounting controls and the feasibility of relying on these controls in limiting substantive testing. Reliance must <u>not</u> be placed on any of these controls without completing the EDP control review and performing related tests of compliance on controls which are to be the basis of reliance.

This section of the workplan is designed for a batch oriented data processing system; it does not address the special control considerations arising from client utilization of data communication, on-line systems, or Data Base Management Systems.

PRELIMINARY REVIEW OF EDP ACCOUNTING CONTROLS

PROCEDURES FOR PRELIMINARY REVIEW OF APPLICATION CONTROLS	W/P Reference
1. Review system data obtained and documented in the "Basic Understanding" section of the workplan.	________
2. Secure a copy of the application system flowchart.	________
3. Review system flow, by reference to the flowchart, to assure understanding of document and data flow.	________
4. Note all system internally generated transactions, by type and purpose.	________
5. Evaluate system flowchart in conjunction with (1) above to assure that EDP/non-EDP interfaces are consistently represented. Obtain clarification and document resolution to any apparent differences between "Basic Understanding" data and that of the system flowchart.	________

6. Briefly describe control techniques used in transmitting data from the generating department to the data processing department.

Consider:

Is such data submitted under control of a batch transmittal?

Does the transmittal indicate the following information:

- Batch identification designation?
- Inclusive numbers of pre-numbered documents?
- Indication of type of data being submitted and by whom?
- Number of documents submitted?
- Significant monetary or hash totals of control fields?
- Batch authorization in lieu of individual document authorization?
- Date and time of submission?

PRELIMINARY REVIEW OF EDP ACCOUNTING CONTROLS

W/P Reference

Is a copy or record of the batch transmittal retained by the user?

If user authorization is not specifically indicated at the time of data submission, does the user department review appropriate transaction registers to ascertain that only authorized transactions were processed?

7. Briefly describe control techniques used in controlling receipt of data within the data processing department. ________

   Consider:

   Does data processing maintain a record of data received?

   Is data reviewed for appropriate authorization?

8. Briefly describe control techniques applied to the key transcription process to ensure accuracy and completeness of processing. ________

   Consider:

   Are all transactions key-verified?

   Does data control maintain records to ensure that all activity submitted for transcription is processed and returned?

9. Briefly describe techniques by which movement of data within the EDP department is controlled.

Consider:

Does the batch transmittal accompany data being processed?

Is the batch transmittal annotated as each major processing step is completed?

Can the EDP department account for and locate all documents submitted for processing?

(Note - A data control log may be being used in lieu of a batch transmittal.)

10. Briefly describe computer controls to validate the accuracy of data being processed.

Consider:

Is data edited by a program which tests the characteristics of data being processed? Typical tests include:

- Comparison against another file
- Specific code testing
- Range tests

PRELIMINARY REVIEW OF EDP ACCOUNTING CONTROLS

W/P Reference

- Exclusivity tests
- Combination tests
- Numeric tests
- Non-blank tests
- Check digits
- Limit testing
- Sign testing

Is a listing produced which itemizes transactions processed and annotates rejected items with the reason for rejection?

Are all significant codes validated by the system?

11. Briefly describe computer controls to validate the completeness and authorization of transactions being processed.

Consider:

Does computer validation include tests to assure completeness and authorization of data processed? Typical tests include:

- Accumulation of hash or significant monetary totals and comparison to user provided batch totals

- Sequence checking of serially numbered documents

- Self balancing of documents requiring multiple entries

- Record counts

Are trailer records present which contain totals of the preceding details? Do programs verify that accumulated totals of details processed correspond to totals in trailer records?

Are there any system controls to assure the subsequent reintroduction of rejected items?
Are standard file labels used in the system?
Are there any application system controls to ensure that the correct generations of data input as well as history or master files are used? Header records? Date checking? Storage of file identification on other media? (This question is not intended to address controls in the operating system or an independent library control system.)

Is the disposition of each detail transaction indicated on system reports?
Does the system produce totals which can be reconciled to independent control figures of input data?

PRELIMINARY REVIEW OF EDP ACCOUNTING CONTROLS

W/P Reference

12. Briefly describe controls in effect in the EDP or user departments to ensure that detected errors are resolved and resubmitted. __________

    Consider:

    Are error corrections resubmitted as a separate batch?

    When items are resubmitted is the original error notification annotated to indicate resubmission? By whom?

    Are controls in effect to ensure that error lists are eventually "cleared" of all unresolved errors?

13. Briefly describe controls to ensure reports have been correctly generated. __________

    Consider:

    Are reports reviewed for reasonableness and control totals balanced prior to report distribution?

Are key run-to-run controls verified to each other?

Are output control totals reconciled to input and processing totals?

If control totals are not used, is output tested by comparison to source documents?

14. Briefly describe controls to ensure that systems output is distributed only to authorized users.

Consider:

Has the EDP department prepared a list of output reports and recipients?

Are reports with sensitive information delivered directly to the authorized user? If not, are they picked up by the authorized user?

PRELIMINARY REVIEW OF EDP ACCOUNTING CONTROLS

	W/P Reference
15. Review findings documented in workpapers and assess significance of EDP Application Controls. Describe strengths and weaknesses noted.	

16. Prepare management letter comments.

PREPARED BY:____________________ DATE:______________

REVIEWED BY:____________________ DATE:______________

PRELIMINARY REVIEW OF EDP ACCOUNTING CONTROLS

CLIENT NAME____________________ AUDIT DATE____________________

ASSESSMENT OF PRELIMINARY REVIEW

SAS No. 3, paragraph 26, states:

> After completing the preliminary phase of his review as described in paragraph 25, for each significant accounting application the auditor should be in a position to assess the significance of accounting control within EDP in relation to the entire system of accounting control and therefore to determine the extent of his review of EDP accounting control.
>
> a. The auditor may conclude that accounting control procedures within the EDP portions of the application or applications appear to provide a basis for reliance thereon and for restricting the extent of his substantive tests. In that event, unless the auditor chose to follow the procedures described in paragraph 26c, he would complete his review of the EDP accounting control procedures, perform related tests of compliance, and evaluate the control procedures to determine the extent of his reliance thereon and the extent to which substantive tests may be restricted.

b. The auditor may conclude that there are weaknesses in accounting control procedures in the EDP portions of the application or applications sufficient to preclude his reliance on such procedures. In that event, he would discontinue his review of those EDP accounting control procedures and forgo performing compliance tests related to those procedures; *he would not be able to rely* on those EDP accounting control procedures. The auditor would assess the potential impact on the financial statements he is examining of such weaknesses as have come to his attention, and would accomplish his audit objectives by other means.

c. The auditor may decide not to extend his preliminary review and not to perform tests of compliance related to accounting control procedures (either in general or as to certain procedures) within the EDP portions of the application or applications even though he concludes that the controls appear adequate. In that event, *he would not be able to rely* on those EDP accounting control procedures. Situations of this type could be those in which –

(1) The auditor concludes that the audit effort required to complete his review and test compliance would exceed the reduction in effort that could be achieved by reliance upon the EDP accounting controls.

(2) The auditor concludes that certain EDP accounting control procedures are redundant because other accounting control procedures are in existence.

PRELIMINARY REVIEW OF EDP ACCOUNTING CONTROLS

W/P Reference

1. With respect to the entire EDP system and each specific application reviewed specifically state which option, A, B, C-1, or C-2, is being selected for purposes of this audit.

2. Describe how the standard audit plan has been adapted, to support the conclusions expressed above.

PREPARED BY:________________ DATE:________

REVIEWED BY:________________ DATE:________

INDEX OF NAMES

SUBJECT INDEX*

*Italicized page numbers refer to Part II, Annotated Bibliography and Additional References.